MW00647881

To the members of the Stone-Campbell Dialogue
and to all who work for Christian unity

INTRODUCTION

"O the quiet holy joy of the silent hour, when the soul is alone with God! Have you learned to love it, dear reader? If not, you have yet to attain to one of the purest and sweetest pleasures possible to the Christian in this life" (J.H. Garrison, *Alone with God*, 21).

If this quotation has appeal to you, you are not alone. Many of us long to spend time alone with God. But an hour? In our busy lives?

Perhaps, like me, you have desired and intended for years to have a regular quiet time with God, but did not know how to begin. If so, then this volume provides a starting point, a daily five-minute devotional that can begin your time with God. Or perhaps, like me, you have recently by God's grace developed a habit of setting time aside each day for prayer, reflection, and meditation. If so, this book can be used as a helpful way to structure that time.

There is no deeper joy and greater privilege than to be alone with the God who made us, who loves us, and who calls himself our Father. There is no greater friendship than the one we have with our brother, Jesus, who for our sake became one of us. There is no more intimate relationship than the one we enjoy with the Holy Spirit, God himself living in us.

This marvelous life with God is a free gift. But as with all relationships, we must make time to cultivate that fellowship with God. Jesus himself felt the need to make time to be alone with God. So must we. Of course, a few minutes each day are not enough to spend alone with God. But they are a start. God will bless such efforts by meeting us in that quiet time.

HOW TO USE THIS DEVOTIONAL GUIDE

This devotional guide is based on two firm convictions. First, that God is at work within us and among us. Secondly, that we are not the first God has worked within and among. Each daily devotional here begins with a theme, a direction for the day, a signpost of how God is working in us. It continues with an invitation to hear God's voice from a biblical Psalm. Each of the 150 psalms is used throughout the year. For thousands of years, God's people have used these precious words to express their joy, frustration, and trust in God. For a few moments each day, we can make these deeply honest words to God our own.

Each devotional also has a scripture reading on the day's theme. Every book in the Bible is represented during the year. This allows us to hear God's voice in his word, the Bible, and to let him shape our day and our lives. The psalm and scripture are meant to be read slowly, meditated upon, and taken as our "to be" and "to do" list for the day. A brief prayer thought ends each devotional. These are prayer starters that should lead you into a longer and deeper period of prayer.

MEDITATING WITH THE STONE-CAMPBELL MOVEMENT

What is unique about this daily devotional is the opportunity it presents to interact with a particular group of Christians who have gone before us. Each day provides a spiritual quotation from a leader in what historians call the Stone-Campbell Movement, a movement that gave birth to the Christian Church (Disciples of Christ), the Churches of Christ, and the Christian Churches and Churches of Christ. Today there are over 4 million members of these churches in the United States, and millions in other parts of the world.

Why listen to the voices of these Christian leaders of an earlier time? Perhaps because you are a member of one of these churches and want to discover your spiritual heritage. More importantly, because they were faithful to God in their age. Even if you have no direct ties to these churches, it is helpful to pray with those who have seen God at work in their time. It can help open our eyes and hearts to what he is doing among us now.

In selecting these quotations, I have concentrated on a few writers in the period before the division of the Stone-Campbell Movement into three major groups. In that time they were both unified and a movement for unity among all Christians. In making these spiritual thoughts available to a new audience, I have modernized some spelling and vocabulary (although one can still experience the nineteenth century flavor of the language). I have also modified the male-oriented language of the quotations, but have retained traditional language for God.

THE AUTHORS OF THE QUOTATIONS

These brief descriptions will introduce you to the eight writers most often quoted in the daily devotional guides. If you want to read more about them, consult their biographical articles in *The Encyclopedia of the Stone-Campbell Movement* (Eerdmans, 2004).

Barton W. Stone (1772-1844) was a preacher and editor widely known for the saintliness of his character. Even his theological opponents had to admit the genuineness of his walk with God. Stone often wrote on the importance of life in the Spirit in his monthly paper, the *Christian Messenger*.

As a preacher, debater, educator, and editor, **Alexander Campbell** (1788-1866) was the most influential early leader of the movement. Although Campbell's mind was trained for rational thought, he had a warm piety, evident in the quotations here from his books and religious journals.

Closely associated with Campbell was **Robert Richardson** (1806-1876), who worked to guard the movement from reliance on a strict rationalism. Instead, he emphasized the influence of God on the heart, writing the first devotional classic of the movement, *Communings in the Sanctuary*.

Walter Scott (1796-1861), was the great evangelist of the early movement, along with being an educator and writer. He penned some of the earliest theological works of the movement, including *The Gospel Restored* and *The Messiahship*. Scott's devotion was centered on Jesus as the promised Messiah.

Named for his famous great-uncle, **Benjamin Franklin** (1812-1878) edited the most popular religious paper of his time, the *American Christian Review*. His influence as a preacher was extended by printed volumes of his sermons, many of which are rich in emotional exhortations to holiness and obedience.

Robert Milligan (1814-1875) was a noted educator and scholar. His book, *Scheme of Redemption*, was an influential theology for the movement and is still used in some schools today. After his death, one of his students founded Milligan College in Johnson City, Tennessee in his honor.

Johnson Bible College in Kimberlin Heights, Tennessee, (near Knoxville) was begun by **Ashley S. Johnson** (1857-1925) in 1893 as the School of the Evangelists. In addition to being an educator, he was a popular writer.

J.H. Garrison (1842-1931) was a tireless advocate for Christian unity in his preaching and publishing. He wrote extensively on the devotional life and the experience of the Holy Spirit in the life of believers.

A Word of Encouragement

There are no shortcuts in the life of the Spirit. Five to ten minutes a day alone with God will not automatically make one spiritual. However, it is a start. God will honor our intentions and work in ways beyond our imaginations if we make the time daily to be with him.

If you do not make that time now, I encourage you to begin. I believe your experience will be the same as mine in compiling this book. At first, it was a thrill and a joy to reflect on the Bible and to hear the voices of Christians now with God. However, after a while it became so daily. But it is in sticking to our pledge to be alone with God each day, particularly when we are busy or we don't feel like it, that we receive a greater blessing.

God calls us his beloved children. He wants to spend time with us. My prayer is that this book can be a tool to help you enjoy quiet, holy moments with Him.

January 1

SEEING GOD

PSALM

One thing I asked of the Lord, that will I seek after:
to live in the house of the Lord all the days of my life,
to behold the beauty of the Lord,
and to inquire in his temple.

PSALM 27:4

MEDITATION

The Christian religion, in short, proposes nothing less than an entire reformation of the human character....The pure in heart are related to each other because they are alike, and they are related to God and will be admitted to his presence because they resemble him.

ROBERT RICHARDSON, *Communings in the Sanctuary*, 106

SCRIPTURE

When I saw him, I fell at his feet as though dead. But he placed his right hand on me, saying, "Do not be afraid; I am the first and the last, and the living one. I was dead, and see, I am alive forever and ever; and I have the keys of Death and of Hades."

REVELATION 1:17-18

PRAYER

Father, by your grace and mercy, admit me into your holy presence. Holy God, through the power of your Spirit, transform me into the image of your Son, Jesus. Lord Jesus, give me life through your resurrection.

January 2

THE SACRIFICE OF JESUS

PSALM

"Be still, and know that I am God!
I am exalted among the nations, I am exalted in the earth."
The Lord of hosts is with us; the God of Jacob is our refuge.

PSALM 46:10-11

MEDITATION

Christ himself had to suffer in order to meet the just and necessary demands of the Divine government, or otherwise the whole human race must perish forever. He saw it! He understood it! He felt it! He no longer hesitated. He accepted the dread alternative. He was borne to the cross as an innocent lamb is borne to the altar, and his blood was poured out for the sins of the world!

ROBERT MILLIGAN, *Scheme of Redemption*, 236

SCRIPTURE

So we are ambassadors for Christ, since God is making his appeal through us; we entreat you on behalf of Christ, be reconciled to God. For our sake he made him to be sin who knew no sin, so that in him we might become the righteousness of God.

2 CORINTHIANS 5:20-21

PRAYER

O God, you have always been the refuge of your people. Thank you for reconciling me through the death of Jesus. Make me your ambassador of reconciliation this day.

January 3

THE COMPASSION OF GOD

PSALM

For as the heavens are high above the earth,
so great is his steadfast love toward those who fear him;
as far as the east is from the west,
so far he removes our transgressions from us.
As a father has compassion for his children,
so the Lord has compassion for those who fear him.

PSALM 103:11-13

MEDITATION

Hear me: All the voices of God in creation, providence, and redemption proclaim from the throne of light, love and mercy in the heavens and in every land and on every sea that there is one God and only one, and that he is our Father, in the highest, deepest and broadest sense of the word. Our earthly fathers love us; our heavenly Father is love (1 John 4:16)!

ASHLEY S. JOHNSON, *The Life of Trust*, 31

SCRIPTURE

On that day you will ask nothing of me. Very truly, I tell you, if you ask anything of the Father in my name, he will give it to you. Until now you have not asked for anything in my name. Ask and you will receive, so that your joy may be complete.

JOHN 16:23-24

PRAYER

Compassionate Father, open my heart to the line of communication you give me in prayer. Hear me when I call.

January 4

TRUST

PSALM

Will you not revive us again, so that your people may rejoice in you?
Show us your steadfast love, O Lord, and grant us your salvation.
Let me hear what God the Lord will speak,
for he will speak peace to his people, to his faithful,
to those who turn to him in their hearts.

PSALM 85:6-8

MEDITATION

There is a critical point in the life of trust which is difficult to pass. On this side of the line are doubts, hesitation, and uncertainty; on the other, trust, unselfish labor and peace.

ASHLEY S. JOHNSON, *The Life of Trust*, 11

SCRIPTURE

All of these died in faith without having received the promises, but from a distance they saw and greeted them. They confessed that they were strangers and foreigners on the earth, for people who speak in this way make it clear that they are seeking a homeland. If they had been thinking of the land that they had left behind, they would have had opportunity to return.

HEBREWS 11:13-15

PRAYER

Lord, I believe, help my unbelief! Give me the trust that Abraham, Moses, and Rahab had in you. Turn my heart to you this day and make me your faithful servant.

January 5

JUDGMENT AND MERCY

PSALM

Let the floods clap their hands;
let the hills sing together for joy at the presence of the Lord,
for he is coming to judge the earth.

PSALM 98:8-9

MEDITATION

Though the love of God has been despised, the agonies of the Savior in the garden of Gethsemane have been condemned, the sufferings of Jesus on the cross have been unheeded by millions of our ungrateful and wayward race, his streaming blood to cleanse us from sin has been set at naught for many long centuries, the wonderful forbearance of God is still extended, and the nations are still invited to the Lamb of God who takes away the sins of the world!

BENJAMIN FRANKLIN, *The Gospel Preacher*, VOL. 1, 454

SCRIPTURE

From new moon to new moon, and from sabbath to sabbath, all flesh shall come to worship before me, says the Lord.

ISAIAH 66:23

PRAYER

Father, I thank you for your astounding patience with the world and with me. I praise you for your justice and your mercy. May the day come quickly when all will acknowledge you as Lord.

January 6

THE CITY OF GOD

PSALM

There is a river whose streams make glad the city of God,
the holy habitation of the Most High.
God is in the midst of the city; it shall not be moved;
God will help it when the morning dawns.

PSALM 46:4-5

MEDITATION

Hence it is, that with love's memories of the past, we can blend the joyful hopes of the future, and thus continue to celebrate the death of Christ until he comes. For he it is, that lives and was dead; and behold he is alive forevermore, and hath the keys of death and hades.

ROBERT RICHARDSON, *Communings in the Sanctuary*, 86

SCRIPTURE

I saw no temple in the city, for its temple is the Lord God the Almighty and the Lamb.
And the city has no need of sun or moon to shine on it, for the glory of God is its light,
and its lamp is the Lamb.

REVELATION 21:22-23

PRAYER

Dear God, I thank you that through Jesus you invite me into your city, the new Jerusalem. May you reign in the temple of my body until that day I see you face to face as eternal light.

DEPENDENCE ON GOD

PSALM

Bless the Lord, all his hosts,
his ministers that do his will.
Bless the Lord, all his works,
in all places of his dominion.
Bless the Lord, O my soul.

PSALM 103:21-22

MEDITATION

Prayer is the offering up of our desires to God for things agreeable to his will.
The habitual performance of this duty produces that habitual sense of the
presence and inspection of God, and of our entire dependence upon him,
which is the foundation of a holy life.

BARTON W. STONE, *Christian Messenger* (1826), 235

SCRIPTURE

Everything that the Father gives me will come to me, and anyone who comes to me I will
never drive away; for I have come down from heaven, not to do my own will, but the will of
him who sent me. And this is the will of him who sent me, that I should lose nothing of all
that he has given me, but raise it up on the last day. This is indeed the will of my Father,
that all who see the Son and believe in him may have eternal life;
and I will raise them up on the last day.

JOHN 6:37-40

PRAYER

Lord Jesus, feed me with the living bread of your presence. Father, give me
this day my daily bread. I praise you for your steadfast love.

January 8

ADORATION OF CHRIST

PSALM

Open to me the gates of righteousness,
that I may enter through them
and give thanks to the Lord.
This is the gate of the Lord;
the righteous shall enter through it.
I thank you that you have answered
me and have become my salvation.

PSALM 118:19-21

MEDITATION

Hence the apostles adored Christ, and offered prayers to him both before and after his glorification; and established the Messianic worship in the first church—the Jerusalem church which Christ himself founded—the mother indeed of all other churches—which, says the apostle, "is the mother of us all."

WALTER SCOTT, *The Messiahship*, 217

SCRIPTURE

For in him all the fullness of God was pleased to dwell, and through him God was pleased
to reconcile to himself all things, whether on earth or in heaven,
by making peace through the blood of his cross.

COLOSSIANS 1:19-20

PRAYER

Lord Jesus, I praise you as the fullness of God. This day may that praise be not only in word but also in deed. Thank you, Father God, for saving me from death and reconciling me to yourself.

SEEING GOD

PSALM

I lift up my eyes to the hills—
from where will my help come?
My help comes from the Lord,
who made heaven and earth.
He will not let your foot be moved;
he who keeps you will not slumber.
He who keeps Israel
will neither slumber nor sleep.

PSALM 121:1-4

MEDITATION

O, the wondrous favors of God; O, the inexhaustibleness of his love; O, the intensity of his care for us in the things that pertain to our pilgrimage here! May God have mercy upon you, and enlarge your heart to know him and open your eyes to see him as he really is in his relations to you!

ASHLEY S. JOHNSON, *The Life of Trust*, 184

SCRIPTURE

Again Jesus spoke to them, saying, "I am the light of the world. Whoever follows me will never walk in darkness but will have the light of life."

JOHN 8:12

PRAYER

Father, open my eyes to see your love and help for me today. Lord Jesus, be the light that shines on my path. May I always live by the light of your love.

January 10

ETERNAL REST

PSALM

Though I walk in the midst of trouble,
you preserve me against the wrath of my enemies;
you stretch out your hand,
and your right hand delivers me.
The Lord will fulfill his purpose for me;
your steadfast love, O Lord, endures forever.
Do not forsake the work of your hands.

PSALM 138:7-8

MEDITATION

Let us then, dear brothers and sisters, never forget our birthright. Let us pray always; but let us also labor to enter into that rest which remains for the people of God.

ROBERT MILLIGAN, *A Brief Treatise on Prayer*, 67

SCRIPTURE

If you conquer, you will be clothed like them in white robes, and I will not blot your name out of the book of life; I will confess your name before my Father and before his angels. Let anyone who has an ear listen to what the Spirit is saying to the churches.

REVELATION 3:5-6

PRAYER

Father, as I labor for you today, do not forsake me as the work of your hands. Through the power of the resurrected Christ, may I conquer and reign with him forever.

January 11

UNDERSTANDING GOD

PSALM

It is good to give thanks to the Lord,
to sing praises to your name, O Most High;
to declare your steadfast love in the morning,
and your faithfulness by night.

PSALM 92:1-2

MEDITATION

The moral soundness of vision consists in having the eyes of the understanding fixed solely on God himself, his approbation and complacent affection for us.

ALEXANDER CAMPBELL, *The Christian System*, 17

SCRIPTURE

So if you have been raised with Christ, seek the things that are above, where Christ is, seated at the right hand of God. Set your minds on things that are above, not on things that are on earth, for you have died, and your life is hidden with Christ in God. When Christ who is your life is revealed, then you also will be revealed with him in glory.

COLOSSIANS 3:1-4

PRAYER

Lord Most High, set my mind on things above, where you live with Christ. Fix my sight solely on you and your steadfast love. Hide my life today with Christ and bring me into your glory.

January 12

FRIENDSHIP WITH GOD

PSALM

Make a joyful noise to the Lord, all the earth.
Worship the Lord with gladness;
come into his presence with singing.
Know that the Lord is God.
It is he that made us, and we are his;
we are his people, and the sheep of his pasture.

PSALM 100:1-3

MEDITATION

Enough! Enough! What shall we render to the Lord for all these gracious benefits? Eternity, eternity will be too short for us to pay the debt of love and praise so justly due.

BARTON W. STONE, *Christian Messenger* (1843), 114

SCRIPTURE

This is my commandment, that you love one another as I have loved you. No one has greater love than this, to lay down one's life for one's friends. You are my friends if you do what I command you. I do not call you servants any longer, because the servant does not know what the master is doing; but I have called you friends, because I have made known to you everything that I have heard from my Father.

JOHN 15:12-15

PRAYER

Father, I am yours. Jesus, you call me friend. I worship, I sing, I praise your name.

January 13

THE INCARNATION

PSALM

Praise the Lord!
Praise, O servants of the Lord;
praise the name of the Lord.
Blessed be the name of the Lord
from this time on and forevermore.
From the rising of the sun to its setting
the name of the Lord is to be praised.

PSALM 113:1-3

MEDITATION

"God was manifested in the flesh!" In Christianity itself or out of it, there is nothing equal to this. The greatness of the manifestation of God in the flesh, the divine in the human, the infinite in the finite, the eternal in the temporal will never be questioned.

WALTER SCOTT, *The Messiahship*, 220

SCRIPTURE

Long ago God spoke to our ancestors in many and various ways by the prophets, but in these last days he has spoken to us by a Son, whom he appointed heir of all things, through whom he also created the worlds. He is the reflection of God's glory and the exact imprint of God's very being, and he sustains all things by his powerful word.

HEBREWS 1:1-2

PRAYER

Lord God, make me constantly aware of the great mystery of the incarnation. You became like me so I might be like you. Christ, live in me today.

January 14

Adoration of God

Psalm

But you, O Lord, are a shield around me,
my glory, and the one who lifts up my head.
I cry aloud to the Lord, and he answers me from his holy hill.

Psalm 3:3-4

Meditation

In prayer, under the deep and solemn conviction that we are on holy ground, and that the eye of God is upon us, we are almost compelled to be humble, to repent of our sins, to forgive our enemies, to sympathize with the afflicted, to adore our Creator, love our Redeemer, and exercise all the powers of our souls in harmony with the will of God.

Robert Milligan, *Scheme of Redemption*, 370

Scripture

It is he who sits above the circle of the earth, and its inhabitants are like grasshoppers;
who stretches out the heavens like a curtain, and spreads them like a tent to live in; who
brings princes to naught, and makes the rulers of the earth as nothing.

Isaiah 40:22-23

Prayer

I adore you, my God, for you are just, you are love, you are my glory. May I praise you with every breath today.

PRAYER

PSALM

Give ear to my words, O Lord;
give heed to my sighing.
Listen to the sound of my cry,
my King and my God,
for to you I pray.
O Lord, in the morning you hear my voice;
in the morning I plead my case to you, and watch.

PSALM 5:1-3

MEDITATION

We have good reasons for believing in the direct and immediate operation of God upon the mind in answer to the prayer of faith and desire.

BARTON W. STONE, *Christian Messenger* (1826), 235

SCRIPTURE

As it is, we do not yet see everything in subjection to them, but we do see Jesus, who for a little while was made lower than the angels, now crowned with glory and honor because of the suffering of death, so that by the grace of God he might taste death for everyone. It was fitting that God, for whom and through whom all things exist, in bringing many children to glory, should make the pioneer of their salvation perfect through sufferings.

HEBREWS 2:8b-10

PRAYER

Lord, hear my cry. My King and my God, give me your glory this day through Jesus Christ, who suffered for me.

January 16

THE WORD OF GOD

PSALM

With my whole heart I seek you;
do not let me stray from your commandments.
I treasure your word in my heart,
so that I may not sin against you.

PSALM 119:10-11

MEDITATION

Where the visible ministries of the church are so largely devoted to the expenditure of spiritual vitality there must be some means of nourishment and recuperation. This is provided in the reading and study of the Word of God, and the atmosphere of prayer in which these privileges should be enjoyed.

J.W. McGARVEY, *A Guide to Bible Study*, 5-6

SCRIPTURE

In the beginning was the Word, and the Word was with God, and the Word was God. He was in the beginning with God. And the Word became flesh and lived among us, and we have seen his glory, the glory as of a father's only son, full of grace and truth.

JOHN 1:1-2, 14

PRAYER

God of love, refresh my spirit today through the power of the Word made flesh. Revitalize me through the power of your Spirit in the words of Scripture. May I treasure your words in my heart to keep me from sin. Let that powerful word go forth in my life this day.

January 17

RECONCILIATION

PSALM

He reached down from on high, he took me;
he drew me out of mighty waters.
He delivered me from my strong enemy,
and from those who hated me;
for they were too mighty for me.

PSALM 18:16-17

MEDITATION

Satan's influence over the world has been greatly curtailed, and a vast multitude of happy spirits redeemed by the blood of the Cross out of every kindred, and tongue, and people, and nation now fill the heavens with their shouts of triumph and their songs of victory.

ROBERT MILLIGAN, *Scheme of Redemption*, 251-252

SCRIPTURE

But now in Christ Jesus you who once were far off have been brought near by the blood of Christ. For he is our peace; in his flesh he has made both groups into one and has broken down the dividing wall, that is, the hostility between us.

EPHESIANS 2:13-14

PRAYER

God of peace, give me victory this day over every enemy that would keep me from you. Be my refuge in times of trouble. Break down every wall—personal, racial, and national—that separates me from others.

January 18

SELF-EXAMINATION

PSALM

I bless the Lord who gives me counsel;
in the night also my heart instructs me.
I keep the Lord always before me;
because he is at my right hand, I shall not be moved.

PSALM 16:7-8

MEDITATION

Live and walk in the Spirit daily at home and abroad. In order to do this be often found on your knees in prayer, and often exercise yourselves in meditation and self-examination.

BARTON W. STONE, *Christian Messenger* (1843), 241

SCRIPTURE

Take care, brothers and sisters, that none of you may have an evil, unbelieving heart that turns away from the living God. But exhort one another every day, as long as it is called "today," so that none of you may be hardened by the deceitfulness of sin. For we have become partners of Christ, if only we hold our first confidence firm to the end.

HEBREWS 3:12-14

PRAYER

O Father who sees all, examine my heart and keep it pure. Protect me from self-deception, fear, and unbelief. May I encourage my brothers and sisters and be encouraged by their faith. Give me a confidence in you that cannot be shaken.

January 19

BLESSINGS

PSALM

*May he grant you your heart's desire,
and fulfill all your plans.
May we shout for joy over your victory,
and in the name of our God set up our banners.
May the Lord fulfill all your petitions.*

PSALM 20:4-5

MEDITATION

And when through faith, repentance, and baptism, we have assumed him as our rightful Sovereign, by his Holy Spirit, in answer to our prayers, he works in us, and by us, and for us, all that is needful for our present, spiritual, and eternal salvation.

ALEXANDER CAMPBELL, *The Christian System*, 67

SCRIPTURE

I pray that, according to the riches of his glory, he may grant that you may be strengthened in your inner being with power through his Spirit, and that Christ may dwell in your hearts through faith, as you are being rooted and grounded in love.

EPHESIANS 3:16-17

PRAYER

Great Giver, I thank you for all the blessings you have lavished upon me. Give me Christ, my heart's desire, and all that comes with life in him. May I praise your Name forever, because of your unfailing love toward me.

January 20

PRAISE

PSALM

Praise the Lord!
Praise God in his sanctuary;
praise him in his mighty firmament!
Praise him for his mighty deeds;
praise him according to his surpassing greatness!

PSALM 150:1-2

MEDITATION

The fact that the whole visible universe with all its impressions and sentiments of beauty, order, variety, sublimity, immensity, stability, and perpetuity, issued without type, from the divine storehouse of the uncreated mind, fills us with the highest admiration of the glorious power, wisdom, and goodness of Almighty God.

WALTER SCOTT, *The Gospel Restored*, 67

SCRIPTURE

"God is spirit, and those who worship him must worship in spirit and truth." The woman said to him, "I know that Messiah is coming" (who is called Christ). "When he comes, he will proclaim all things to us." Jesus said to her, "I am he, the one who is speaking to you."

JOHN 4:24-26

PRAYER

I praise you, My God, for your glorious deeds of creation and redemption. With all my being I glorify you, Christ, as Savior of the world. I thank you, Father, for hearing my cries and prayers. How great you are, O Lord!

January 21

APPROACHING GOD

PSALM

Make me to know your ways, O Lord;
teach me your paths.
Lead me in your truth, and teach me,
for you are the God of my salvation;
for you I wait all day long.

PSALM 25:4-5

MEDITATION

If, then, we would be good and do good, and glorify our Father who is in heaven, let us not forget the duties and privileges of secret prayer; let us often retire to our closets, and when we have shut the door, let us pray to our Father who is in secret, and our Father who seeth in secret will surely reward us openly.

ROBERT MILLIGAN, A *Brief Treatise on Prayer*, 26-27

SCRIPTURE

For we do not have a high priest who is unable to sympathize with our weaknesses, but we have one who in every respect has been tested as we are, yet without sin. Let us therefore approach the throne of grace with boldness, so that we may receive mercy and find grace to help in time of need.

HEBREWS 4:15-16

PRAYER

Father, I come to you boldly through the great High Priest, Jesus Christ. Forgive my sins. Teach me your truth. Guide me in right ways. Teach me to wait for your mercy and grace.

January 22

The Character of God

Psalm

The Lord is the strength of his people;
he is the saving refuge of his anointed.
O save your people, and bless your heritage;
be their shepherd, and carry them forever.

Psalm 28:8-9

Meditation

Creation reveals the power, the wisdom, and the goodness of God;
providence proclaims also his justice, truth, and holiness. Redemption develops
his mercy, compassion, and love; and all these are again characterized by
infinity, eternity, and immutability.

Alexander Campbell, *The Christian System*, 20

Scripture

Do not fear, or be afraid;
have I not told you from of old and declared it?
You are my witnesses!
Is there any god besides me?
There is no other rock; I know not one.

Isaiah 44:8

Prayer

O God, there is no god besides you. I praise you with all my being for your
power, holiness, and love. I praise you for saving me, keeping me from fear, and
carrying me in your arms as my Shepherd.

January 23

PERSEVERANCE

PSALM

Teach me, O Lord, the way of your statutes,
and I will observe it to the end.
Give me understanding, that I may keep your law
and observe it with my whole heart.

PSALM 119:33-34

MEDITATION

Let us reform and be living, humble, holy Christians; then will our aspect be glorious and exemplary. Others seeing our good works will glorify our Heavenly Father.

BARTON W. STONE, *Christian Messenger* (1843), 242

SCRIPTURE

And we want each one of you to show the same diligence so as to realize the full assurance of hope to the very end, so that you may not become sluggish, but imitators of those who through faith and patience inherit the promises.

HEBREWS 6:11-12

PRAYER

Gracious Father, grant me diligence, humility, and understanding. May I boldly hold to my hope and assurance so I will observe your teachings with my whole heart. Let me not be sluggish in my work today, but be an example to others so they will give you glory.

January 24

Trust in God

Psalm

Trust in the Lord, and do good;
so you will live in the land, and enjoy security.
Take delight in the Lord,
and he will give you the desires of your heart.
Commit your way to the Lord;
trust in him, and he will act.

Psalm 37:3-5

Meditation

Let us trust our little selves with the Lord; and rest not, till by faith in the promised Holy Spirit and by incessant prayer we receive and be filled with it, like they were of old, in the ancient order of things.

Barton W. Stone, *Christian Messenger* (1843), 271

Scripture

Be careful then how you live, not as unwise people but as wise, making the most of the time, because the days are evil. So do not be foolish, but understand what the will of the Lord is. Do not get drunk with wine, for that is debauchery; but be filled with the Spirit.

Ephesians 5:15-18

Prayer

Lord, let me trust not in myself, but in you. Act in my life today. Give me your Holy Spirit so I may understand and do your will.

January 25

THE FAITH OF ABRAHAM

PSALM

In you, O Lord, I seek refuge;
do not let me ever be put to shame;
in your righteousness deliver me.
Incline your ear to me;
rescue me speedily.
Be a rock of refuge for me,
a strong fortress to save me.

PSALM 31:1-2

MEDITATION

Abraham is another example. God commanded him to turn his back on home and kindred, and go to a land which he would show him. He had never, as far as we can discover, heard that voice before, but he obeyed. The journey was long and doubtless perilous, but he persevered.

ASHLEY S. JOHNSON, *The Life of Trust*, 111

SCRIPTURE

Now the Lord said to Abram, "Go from your country and your kindred and your father's house to the land that I will show you. I will make of you a great nation, and I will bless you, and make your name great, so that you will be a blessing. I will bless those who bless you, and the one who curses you I will curse; and in you all the families of the earth shall be blessed." So Abram went, as the Lord had told him.

GENESIS 12:1-4

PRAYER

My Father, like Abraham, may I hear your voice and obey. Trusting your faithful love, may I wait for you today, and receive your blessings.

January 26

FORGIVENESS OF SINS

PSALM

Happy are those whose transgression is forgiven,
whose sin is covered.
Happy are those to whom the Lord imputes no iniquity,
and in whose spirit there is no deceit.

PSALM 32:1-2

MEDITATION

He is the propitiation for our sins; and not for our sins only, but also for the sins of the whole world. He now makes his last appeal to our affections. Can we not, and will we not love him, who first loved us? Shall we be found so hardened and abandoned that we cannot love him who withheld not his own Son, but freely gave him up freely for us all?

BENJAMIN FRANKLIN, *The Gospel Preacher*, VOL. 1, 405

SCRIPTURE

And many more believed because of his word. They said to the woman, "It is no longer because of what you said that we believe, for we have heard for ourselves, and we know that this is truly the Savior of the world."

JOHN 4:41-42

PRAYER

Praise be to God for saving me through Jesus! My sins are forgiven! My happiness overflows! I love you, my Lord, with all my heart.

January 27

THIRST FOR GOD

PSALM

O God, you are my God, I seek you,
my soul thirsts for you;
my flesh faints for you,
as in a dry and weary land where there is no water.

PSALM 63:1

MEDITATION

Thirst is, perhaps, the most intense desire the human body may know. Its pangs to the thirsty traveler in the parched desert are almost insufferable. What thirst is to the body, this desire is to the human soul. O that we could realize that it is only in Christ that the soul's needs are fully met.

J.H. GARRISON, *Alone With God*, 28

SCRIPTURE

Therefore, my friends, since we have confidence to enter the sanctuary by the blood of Jesus, by the new and living way that he opened for us through the curtain (that is, through his flesh), and since we have a great priest over the house of God, let us approach with a true heart in full assurance of faith, with our hearts sprinkled clean from an evil conscience and our bodies washed with pure water.

·   HEBREWS 10:19-22

PRAYER

Father, may I thirst for you, and you alone. Let me draw near you with confidence and with a true heart. Lead me away from everything that promises to fulfill my desires and turn to you, the One who can keep those promises.

January 28

GOD REVEALS HIMSELF

PSALM

But I am like a green olive tree
in the house of God.
I trust in the steadfast love of God
forever and ever.
I will thank you forever,
because of what you have done.
In the presence of the faithful
I will proclaim your name, for it is good.

PSALM 52:8-9

MEDITATION

If the light of the glorious gospel has shone upon us; if its heavenly influences have revived us; if we have arisen from the dust of error's death, and our hearts have been opened to receive the holy impressions of divine truth, then shall we be drawn by irresistible attractions, and strengthened more and more by added grace to ascend above the world and to approach the bright light of being and blessedness.

ROBERT RICHARDSON, *Communings in the Sanctuary*, 61

SCRIPTURE

For I want you to know, brothers and sisters, that the gospel that was proclaimed by me is not of human origin; for I did not receive it from a human source, nor was I taught it, but I received it through a revelation of Jesus Christ.

GALATIANS 1:11-12

PRAYER

Holy Father, reveal yourself to me this day, so I can praise your name and thank you forever.

January 29

PSALMS OF PRAISE

PSALM

Great is the Lord and greatly to be praised
in the city of our God.
His holy mountain, beautiful in elevation,
is the joy of all the earth,
Mount Zion, in the far north,
the city of the great King.

PSALM 48:1-2

MEDITATION

The sentiments expressed in the Psalms came from the hearts of the authors, and they show the best effects of the law of Moses, and the experience of Israel on the souls of the devout. One who is familiar with them can readily turn to such as will comfort in any sorrow, cheer in any despondency, and furnish expression to the deepest gratitude and most fervid thanksgiving.

J.W. McGarvey, *A Guide to Bible Study*, 44

SCRIPTURE

Thus says the Lord, your Redeemer, the Holy One of Israel:
I am the Lord your God,
who teaches you for your own good,
who leads you in the way you should go.

ISAIAH 48:17

PRAYER

Lord, teach me your ways so I may rejoice and be glad. Accept the pains, fears, joys, and praise of my heart.

January 30

FORGIVENESS OF SINS

PSALM

They have all fallen away, they are all alike perverse;
there is no one who does good,
no, not one.
Have they no knowledge, those evildoers,
who eat up my people as they eat bread,
and do not call upon God?

PSALM 53:3-4

MEDITATION

Here, then, dear reader, is a new and living way opened for us into the presence of the great God. Through the rent veil of your Redeemer's flesh you may find forgiveness and an entrance into the holiest of all. We beseech you, therefore, not to risk your soul's salvation by offering contempt to the blood of the covenant.

WALTER SCOTT, *The Gospel Restored*, 516

SCRIPTURE

But as it is, he has appeared once for all at the end of the age to remove sin by the sacrifice of himself. And just as it is appointed for mortals to die once, and after that the judgment, so Christ, having been offered once to bear the sins of many, will appear a second time, not to deal with sin, but to save those who are eagerly waiting for him.

HEBREWS 9:26b-28

PRAYER

Father, I confess my sin. I am perverse and do not do the good. Have mercy. Forgive me through the sacrifice of Jesus. Lord Jesus, come quickly and save me forever!

January 31

REFUGE AND COMFORT

PSALM

*It is better to take refuge in the Lord
than to put confidence in mortals.
It is better to take refuge in the Lord
than to put confidence in princes.*

PSALM 118:8-9

MEDITATION

Happiness and heaven are not all in the dim and unexplored hereafter; if we serve Him as He demands, heaven will be in us and around us in the field, in the shop—wherever duty calls; but if duty calls we must answer.

ASHLEY S. JOHNSON, *The Life of Trust*, 189

SCRIPTURE

*Sing for joy, O heavens, and exult, O earth;
break forth, O mountains, into singing!
For the Lord has comforted his people,
and will have compassion on his suffering ones.*

ISAIAH 49:13

PRAYER

O God of love, bring heaven into me and around me this day. May I find refuge and comfort in you, not in human leaders. When duty calls, by the power of your Holy Spirit, move me to answer.

February 1

A Broken Heart

Psalm

For you have no delight in sacrifice;
if I were to give a burnt offering, you would not be pleased.
The sacrifice acceptable to God is a broken spirit;
a broken and contrite heart, O God, you will not despise.

Psalm 51:16-17

Meditation

What an unspeakable satisfaction it is to every human being to know that, however neglected by others, cast off and forsaken; however downtrodden, oppressed, and despised, each one is loved by the Creator and Benefactor of all!

Benjamin Franklin, *The Gospel Preacher*, vol. 1, 383-384

Scripture

But when Christ had offered for all time a single sacrifice for sins, "he sat down at the right hand of God," and since then has been waiting "until his enemies would be made a footstool for his feet." For by a single offering he has perfected for all time those who are sanctified.

Hebrews 10:12-14

Prayer

Lord God, accept my broken and contrite heart. I glory in your love for me, love that cost you a Son. Lord Jesus, continue through your great sacrifice to perfect me for your honor and glory.

February 2

CALMING FEARS

PSALM

My heart is in anguish within me,
the terrors of death have fallen upon me.
Fear and trembling come upon me,
and horror overwhelms me.

PSALM 55:4-5

MEDITATION

When the heart is beset with anxieties, and burdened with care, it cannot well wait for relief until the regular hour for prayer arrives, but goes at once to God for his strength and guidance. Here they find refuge in the midst of the storm, and a haven in which they may anchor and find rest and peace.

J. H. GARRISON, *Alone with God*, 92-93

SCRIPTURE

When they had rowed about three or four miles, they saw Jesus walking on the sea and coming near the boat, and they were terrified. But he said to them, "It is I; do not be afraid." Then they wanted to take him into the boat, and immediately the boat reached the land toward which they were going.

JOHN 6:19-21

PRAYER

Lord Jesus, storms of fear surround me. I live in anxiety and terror. Calm my fears this day by your presence; quiet my heart with your assurance; increase my faith by your power.

RESURRECTION

PSALM

*Nevertheless he regarded their distress
when he heard their cry.
For their sake he remembered his covenant,
and showed compassion according to the abundance of his steadfast love.*

PSALM 106:44-45

MEDITATION

How blissful the assurance that, in becoming partakers of Christ, we share that divine nature in which life is inherent! How wonderful the thought that we who are but, as it were, the creatures of yesterday, may lay hold of the very attribute of the Deity, and be invested with imperishable life and joy!

ROBERT RICHARDSON, *Communings in the Sanctuary*, 20

SCRIPTURE

Jesus said to her, "I am the resurrection and the life. Those who believe in me, even though they die, will live, and everyone who lives and believes in me will never die. Do you believe this?" She said to him, "Yes, Lord, I believe that you are the Messiah, the Son of God, the one coming into the world."

JOHN 11:25-27

PRAYER

Lord Jesus, you are the resurrection and the life. Live in me today! Holy Father, I thank you for receiving me into the Divine life through Jesus. Holy Spirit of life, pour out the love of God into my heart today.

February 4

DELIVERANCE FROM ENEMIES

PSALM

You have kept count of my tossings;
put my tears in your bottle.
Are they not in your record?
Then my enemies will retreat
in the day when I call.
This I know, that God is for me.
In God, whose word I praise,
in the Lord, whose word I praise,
in God I trust; I am not afraid.
What can a mere mortal do to me?

PSALM 56:8-11

MEDITATION

These comforting thoughts, I would commend to the afflicted, the burdened,
the persecuted, the tempted and tried ones. Rest assured that your loving Father
in heaven knows your special trial, means it for your eternal good, and will not
allow you to be tempted above that you are able to bear in his name and strength.

J.H. GARRISON, *Alone with God*, 110

SCRIPTURE

So it was that, when God destroyed the cities of the Plain,
God remembered Abraham, and sent Lot out of the midst of the overthrow,
when he overthrew the cities in which Lot had settled.

GENESIS 19:29

PRAYER

God of power, deliver me this day from evil—from enemies, temptations,
and despair. For the sake of Jesus, remember me and save me from the evil of
my city and this world.

SILENCE

PSALM

For God alone my soul waits in silence;
from him comes my salvation.
He alone is my rock and my salvation, my fortress;
I shall never be shaken.

PSALM 62:1

MEDITATION

In the deep stillness of the heart let every anxious care be hushed, and cheerful hope diffuse her grateful balm. Let the sorrows of the mind be banished from this place, for the being in whose presence we appear is the God of consolation and of hope.

ROBERT RICHARDSON, *Communings in the Sanctuary*, 2

SCRIPTURE

Then they said to him, "What must we do to perform the works of God?" Jesus answered them, "This is the work of God, that you believe in him whom he has sent."

JOHN 6:28-29

PRAYER

Loving God, my heart waits for you in silence and stillness. Feed me with the living bread of Jesus.

COVENANT

PSALM

Have regard for your covenant,
for the dark places of the land are full of the haunts of violence.
Do not let the downtrodden be put to shame;
let the poor and needy praise your name.

PSALM 74:20-21

MEDITATION

This covenant is the last will and testament—the last, the final effort, so to speak—of our most gracious and merciful God, to reclaim and bring back an apostate and sinful race. It contains the infinite goodness and love.

BENJAMIN FRANKLIN, *The Gospel Preacher*, VOL. 1, 225

SCRIPTURE

For the mountains may depart and the hills be removed,
but my steadfast love shall not depart from you,
and my covenant of peace shall not be removed,
says the Lord, who has compassion on you.

ISAIAH 54:10

PRAYER

Loving God, faithful Father, I praise you for your steadfast love. Remember your covenant with me, this day, and with all who are needy and downtrodden. May I live out your covenant in service to others.

February 7

Discipleship

Psalm

In you, O Lord, I take refuge;
let me never be put to shame.
In your righteousness deliver me and rescue me;
incline your ear to me and save me.

Psalm 71:1-2

Meditation

It is feared that many who profess Christianity have not experimentally learned it. This is the cause of so much worldly mindedness, so much death and barrenness, so much division, and so little piety and love.

Barton W. Stone, *Christian Messenger* (1843), 17

Scripture

He called the crowd with his disciples, and said to them, "If any want to become my followers, let them deny themselves and take up their cross and follow me. For those who want to save their life will lose it, and those who lose their life for my sake, and for the sake of the gospel, will save it."

Mark 8:34-35

Prayer

Lord Jesus, who rescued me through your cross, give me grace to take up my own and follow. May I be a disciple not only in word, but in experience. Give me true piety and genuine love for my brothers and sisters.

The Holy Spirit

Psalm

But for me it is good to be near God;
I have made the Lord God my refuge, to tell of all your works.

Psalm 73:28

Meditation

We have been too long engaged with defending ourselves, rather than the truth as it is in Jesus. Let us trust our little selves with the Lord; and rest not, till by faith in the promised Spirit and by incessant prayer we receive and be filled with it, like they were of old in the ancient order of things.

Barton W. Stone, *Christian Messenger* (1843), 271

Scripture

By contrast, the fruit of the Spirit is love, joy, peace, patience, kindness, generosity, faithfulness, gentleness, and self-control. There is no law against such things. And those who belong to Christ Jesus have crucified the flesh with its passions and desires. If we live by the Spirit, let us also be guided by the Spirit.

Galatians 5:22-25

Prayer

Lord God, who keeps his promises, give me more faith in the promise of your Holy Spirit. Forgive me for defending myself instead of trusting in the power of your Spirit. Holy Spirit of God, produce your fruit in me today.

February 9

The Teachings of the Lord

Psalm

Teach me your way, O Lord,
and lead me on a level path
because of my enemies.
Do not give me up to the will of my adversaries,
for false witnesses have risen against me,
and they are breathing out violence.

Psalm 27:11-12

Meditation

Now we may properly say, that as it respects God, there is an understanding distance. All beyond that distance cannot understand God; all within it can easily understand him in all matters of piety and morality. God himself is the center of that circle, and humility is its circumference.

Alexander Campbell, *The Christian System*, 17

Scripture

Then Jesus answered them, "My teaching is not mine but his who sent me. Anyone who resolves to do the will of God will know whether the teaching is from God or whether I am speaking on my own. Those who speak on their own seek their own glory; but the one who seeks the glory of him who sent him is true, and there is nothing false in him."

John 7:16-18

Prayer

Father, humble my heart this day that I might hear and understand your teachings. May I burn with a desire to know your will. Keep me from seeking my own glory. Protect me from all enemies within and without.

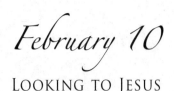

February 10

LOOKING TO JESUS

PSALM

I sought the Lord, and he answered me,
and delivered me from all my fears.

PSALM 34:4

MEDITATION

It is here, amidst the sublime visions beheld by the eye of faith, that God addresses himself to mortals. It is here that his wondrous works are interpreted by precious words. It is here that he appears in his true character as the great Lord and creator of the universe, material and spiritual.

ROBERT RICHARDSON, *Communings in the Sanctuary*, 44

SCRIPTURE

Therefore, since we are surrounded by so great a cloud of witnesses, let us also lay aside every weight and the sin that clings so closely, and let us run with perseverance the race that is set before us, looking to Jesus the pioneer and perfecter of our faith, who for the sake of the joy that was set before him endured the cross, disregarding its shame, and has taken his seat at the right hand of the throne of God.

HEBREWS 12:1-2

PRAYER

Lord Jesus, fix my eyes on you today. Grant me patience to run the race before me. Lord God, may I by faith see your works and character. Fill me with the radiance of your power, holiness, and love.

ACTS OF MERCY

PSALM
Restore us, O Lord God of hosts;
let your face shine, that we may be saved.

PSALM 80:19

MEDITATION

We may boast of raptures, ecstasies, transports, and angelic feelings—but pure and undefiled religion consists in acts of mercy, as visiting the widow and fatherless, and relieving their distresses, and those of suffering humanity, and even of brute creation.

BARTON W. STONE, *Christian Messenger* (1843), 231

SCRIPTURE
Is not this the fast that I choose:
to loose the bonds of injustice, to undo the thongs of the yoke,
to let the oppressed go free, and to break every yoke?
Is it not to share your bread with the hungry,
and bring the homeless poor into your house;
when you see the naked, to cover them, and not to hide yourself from your own kin?

ISAIAH 58:6-7

PRAYER

Father, may I not only feel compassion for those in need, but actively feed, clothe, and house. Give me your passion for justice.

February 12

THE GIFT OF THE SPIRIT

PSALM

Then he led out his people like sheep,
and guided them in the wilderness like a flock.
He led them in safety, so that they were not afraid;
but the sea overwhelmed their enemies.

PSALM 78:52-53

MEDITATION

The denial of the direct operation of the Spirit cuts the very nerves of prayer. We have known some, who were once warmly engaged in the duty of prayer, lose the very spirit and practice of it, by speculating and philosophizing on the subject. Such a doctrine stands opposed to the spirit and practice of Jesus, our pattern, to the doctrines and example of the apostles and primitive saints, and to the experience of every living Christian.

BARTON W. STONE, *Christian Messenger* (1826), 236

SCRIPTURE

For this reason I remind you to rekindle the gift of God that is within you through the laying on of my hands; for God did not give us a spirit of cowardice, but rather a spirit of power and of love and of self-discipline.

2 TIMOTHY 1:6-7

PRAYER

Father, thank you for the gift of your Spirit. May I rekindle that gift so I may be bold with your power, love, and discipline. May I spread the news of your grace to the next generation.

February 13

THE WILL OF GOD

PSALM

Your decrees are my heritage forever;
they are the joy of my heart.
I incline my heart to perform your statutes
forever, to the end.
I hate the double-minded,
but I love your law.
You are my hiding place and my shield;
I hope in your word.

PSALM 119:111-114

MEDITATION

Prayer, when properly offered, must always have a soothing effect on the affections. Its tendency is to allay the passions, to promote the virtues, and to harmonize all the powers and faculties of the soul. It subdues the human will, and makes the will of God the supreme law of the universe.

ROBERT MILLIGAN, *A Brief Treatise on Prayer*, 19-20

SCRIPTURE

I appeal to you therefore, brothers and sisters, by the mercies of God, to present your bodies as a living sacrifice, holy and acceptable to God, which is your spiritual worship. Do not be conformed to this world, but be transformed by the renewing of your minds, so that you may discern what is the will of God—what is good and acceptable and perfect.

ROMANS 12:1-2

PRAYER

Father, may I discern your will today and make it my own. Accept the worship of my body as a holy sacrifice to you. May your instruction be the joy of my heart.

February 14

WHOLE-HEARTED GENEROSITY

PSALM

Teach me your way, O Lord,
that I may walk in your truth;
give me an undivided heart to revere your name.
I give thanks to you, O Lord my God, with my whole heart,
and I will glorify your name forever.

PSALM 86:11-12

MEDITATION

As the Master himself turned away from tempting offers of the world's
power and wealth and honor to walk the lowly path of self-denial, that he
might the better serve humanity, so his disciples must needs often refuse the
prizes which Satan offers in order to walk with their Master in the path of
unselfish service to the race.

J.H. GARRISON, *Alone with God*, 66

SCRIPTURE

Jesus, looking at him, loved him and said, "You lack one thing; go, sell what you own, and
give the money to the poor, and you will have treasure in heaven; then come, follow me."
When he heard this, he was shocked and went away grieving, for he had many possessions.

MARK 10:21-22

PRAYER

Father, by your great power save me, rich person that I am. May I resist this
age of greed and generously give to others as you have given to me. Teach me to
follow the steps of the One who gave himself for me.

February 15

GOOD NEWS TO THE POOR

PSALM

Because you have made the Lord your refuge,
the Most High your dwelling place,
no evil shall befall you, no scourge come near your tent.

PSALM 91:9-10

MEDITATION

But it is amid the disappointments of life, in the days of mourning and desolation, in the hours of self-abasement and penitential love, that we meet with Jesus. It is in the home of poverty and in the lowly mansion of the wretched that we have fellowship with Christ.

ROBERT RICHARDSON, *Communings in the Sanctuary*, 77

SCRIPTURE

The spirit of the Lord God is upon me,
because the Lord has anointed me;
he has sent me to bring good news to the oppressed, to bind up the brokenhearted,
to proclaim liberty to the captives, and release to the prisoners;
to proclaim the year of the Lord's favor, and the day of vengeance of our God;
to comfort all who mourn;

ISAIAH 61:1-2

PRAYER

Lord Jesus, may I this day proclaim good news in the homes of the oppressed, brokenhearted, captive, and poor. May that proclamation be in deed as well as in word, so that by faith I may meet you there.

CHRISTIAN UNITY

PSALM

Satisfy us in the morning with your steadfast love,
so that we may rejoice and be glad all our days.

PSALM 90:14

MEDITATION

Among many subjects of prayer, the union of the children of God has been one constant subject. The cry has been ascending to heaven from the pure in heart, the true and the holy, "O that the time may come when we shall all see eye to eye, and walk hand in hand." Will this supplication be answered? It will be answered as sure as the Lord lives.

BENJAMIN FRANKLIN, *The Gospel Preacher*, VOL. 1, 306

SCRIPTURE

Why do you pass judgment on your brother or sister? Or you, why do you despise your brother or sister? For we will all stand before the judgment seat of God.

. ROMANS 14:10

PRAYER

Father, forgive my judgmental attitude toward my brothers and sisters. May I judge them as I wish to be judged—with mercy and forgiveness. Jesus, bring unity to your spiritual body, so that your prayer might be answered, that all disciples may be one so the world will know the Father who sent you.

OBEDIENCE

PSALM

*If I had cherished iniquity in my heart,
the Lord would not have listened.*

PSALM 66:18

MEDITATION

To hunger and thirst after righteousness, is the very breath of the new creature—the creature created anew in Christ Jesus. Nothing is so desirable to the new creature who therefore takes up the cross daily, and follows Jesus to be holy.

BARTON W. STONE, *Christian Messenger* (1843), 209

SCRIPTURE

Now by this we may be sure that we know him, if we obey his commandments. Whoever says, "I have come to know him," but does not obey his commandments, is a liar, and in such a person the truth does not exist; but whoever obeys his word, truly in this person the love of God has reached perfection. By this we may be sure that we are in him: whoever says, "I abide in him," ought to walk just as he walked.

1 JOHN 2:3-6

PRAYER

Father, I thank you for your steadfast love to me, a sinner. Let me hunger and thirst after righteousness. Give me the desire to obey your commands. Grant me the courage this day to take up my cross and walk as Jesus walked.

February 18

FORGIVENESS

PSALM

I will sing of your steadfast love, O Lord, forever;
with my mouth I will proclaim your faithfulness to all generations.
I declare that your steadfast love is established forever;
your faithfulness is as firm as the heavens.

PSALM 89:1-2

MEDITATION

Remission of sins, then, past sins, all sins, the spirit of God the Holy Spirit,
and life eternal, or life with God in heaven are the distinguishing points of the
true Gospel of Jesus Christ.

WALTER SCOTT, *The Gospel Restored*, 88

SCRIPTURE

*The saying is sure and worthy of full acceptance, that Christ Jesus came into the world to
save sinners—of whom I am the foremost. But for that very reason I received mercy, so
that in me, as the foremost, Jesus Christ might display the utmost patience, making me an
example to those who would come to believe in him for eternal life. To the King of the ages,
immortal, invisible, the only God, be honor and glory forever and ever. Amen.*

1 TIMOTHY 1:15-17

PRAYER

God of love, with my whole being I praise you for completely forgiving my
sins and saving me—sinner that I am. Lord Jesus, thank you for your infinite
patience with me. Holy Spirit, fill my heart and life this day. May I proclaim this
good news to others.

February 19

GOD AS FATHER OF ALL

PSALM

The Lord is king; let the peoples tremble!
He sits enthroned upon the cherubim; let the earth quake!
The Lord is great in Zion;
he is exalted over all the peoples.

PSALM 99:1-2

MEDITATION

The very atheists are often heard to utter exclamations which indicate the wants of their souls, the weakness of their natures, their longing after something which they have never been able to realize, and their dependence on that God whom they have proudly, practically, and theoretically discarded.

ROBERT MILLIGAN, *A Brief Treatise on Prayer*, 9

SCRIPTURE

He was teaching and saying, "Is it not written,
'My house shall be called a house of prayer for all the nations'?
But you have made it a den of robbers."

MARK 11:17

PRAYER

Father of all, hear my prayer and the prayers of all who call upon your Name. May all acknowledge you as King of the universe. May I so live as to be your holy temple, open to everyone from every nation.

February 20

THE GOOD SHEPHERD

PSALM

Help me, O Lord my God!
Save me according to your steadfast love.
Let them know that this is your hand;
you, O Lord, have done it.

PSALM 109:26-27

MEDITATION

The way was steep, the night was dark, and yet the Good Shepherd never hesitated; and how the mountains rang; and what a song arose to the gates of heaven that night over one poor lost sheep—found! I was that sheep!!!

ASHLEY S. JOHNSON, *The Life of Trust*, 133

SCRIPTURE

I am the good shepherd. I know my own and my own know me, just as the Father knows me and I know the Father. And I lay down my life for the sheep. I have other sheep that do not belong to this fold. I must bring them also, and they will listen to my voice. So there will be one flock, one shepherd.

JOHN 10:14-16

PRAYER

Jesus, Great Shepherd of your sheep, hear the praise of your once-lost lamb. Give me your heart this day for those who are lost. May all those who praise your name be one flock with one Shepherd.

February 21

SEEKING GOD

PSALM

O give thanks to the Lord, call on his name,
make known his deeds among the peoples.
Sing to him, sing praises to him;
tell of all his wonderful works.
Glory in his holy name;
let the hearts of those who seek the Lord rejoice.
Seek the Lord and his strength;
seek his presence continually.

PSALM 105:1-4

MEDITATION

Christ has brought us a fuller revelation of God than David knew, and gives new and stronger reasons why the soul should long for him. He is our Father. He so loved the world as to give his only begotten Son to save it. O the infinite depths and tenderness of his love!

J.H. GARRISON, *Alone with God*, 27

SCRIPTURE

I was ready to be sought out by those who did not ask,
to be found by those who did not seek me.
I said, "Here I am, here I am,"
to a nation that did not call on my name.

ISAIAH 65:1

PRAYER

Father, as you have sought me in your love, may I seek your presence continually this day. Keep me close in your grace so I may glory in your name.

The Love of God

Psalm

Let them thank the Lord for his steadfast love,
for his wonderful works to humankind.
For he satisfies the thirsty,
and the hungry he fills with good things.

Psalm 107:8-9

Meditation

"We love God because he first loved us." God was manifested in the flesh, so that whoever saw Jesus saw the Father in him. As one loves and honors the Son, so one loves and honors the Father.

Benjamin Franklin, *The Gospel Preacher*, vol. 1, 390

Scripture

See what love the Father has given us, that we should be called children of God; and that is what we are. The reason the world does not know us is that it did not know him. Beloved, we are God's children now; what we will be has not yet been revealed. What we do know is this: when he is revealed, we will be like him, for we will see him as he is.

1 John 3:1-2

Prayer

God of love, I your unworthy servant give you praise for making me your child. Lord Jesus, thank you for showing me the face of the Father, a face of love. May that day come quickly, O God, when I see you face to face.

MONEY

PSALM

He raises up the needy out of distress,
and makes their families like flocks.
The upright see it and are glad;
and all wickedness stops its mouth.
Let those who are wise give heed to these things,
and consider the steadfast love of the Lord.

PSALM 107:41-43

MEDITATION

We pray not for stores to be laid up for many years. This is the spirit of avarice and independence, and hateful to our God—our gracious, kind, and wise benefactor. His benevolence provides for all, from the tallest angel in glory to the lowest reptile on earth.

BARTON W. STONE, *Christian Messenger* (1844), 143

SCRIPTURE

But those who want to be rich fall into temptation and are trapped by many senseless and harmful desires that plunge people into ruin and destruction. For the love of money is a root of all kinds of evil, and in their eagerness to be rich some have wandered away from the faith and pierced themselves with many pains.

1 TIMOTHY 6:9-10

PRAYER

Lord, deliver me from the desire to be rich. May I trust your steadfast love instead of trusting in my wealth. May I never seek to be independent from your daily care, but glory in your gifts to the needy.

February 24

New Life

Psalm
The Lord is near to all who call on him,
to all who call on him in truth.

Psalm 145:18

Meditation
The subject of this great change, before the new birth, existed in one state; after it, one exists in another. One stands in a new relation to God, angels, and humans. One is now born of God, and has the privilege of being a child of God, and is consequently pardoned, justified, sanctified, adopted, saved.

Alexander Campbell, *The Christian System*, 266

Scripture
From now on, therefore, we regard no one from a human point of view; even though we once knew Christ from a human point of view, we know him no longer in that way. So if anyone is in Christ, there is a new creation: everything old has passed away; see, everything has become new!

2 Corinthians 5:16-17

Prayer
Father, thank you for making me your child. How glad I am to call you my Father! May I see Christ as he is, and not from a merely human point of view. Keep me from judging others the way the world judges them.

REPENTANCE

PSALM

God is my shield,
who saves the upright in heart.
God is a righteous judge,
and a God who has indignation every day.
If one does not repent, God will whet his sword;
he has bent and strung his bow;
he has prepared his deadly weapons,
making his arrows fiery shafts.

PSALM 7:10-13

MEDITATION

He has revealed himself to humanity in all the loveliness of his true character. The joys and bliss of heaven are set forth in a revelation adapted to his comprehension, and thus the goodness of God leads us to repentance.

T.W. BRENTS, *The Gospel Plan of Salvation*, 247

SCRIPTURE

So the ransomed of the Lord shall return, and come to Zion with singing;
everlasting joy shall be upon their heads; they shall obtain joy and gladness,
and sorrow and sighing shall flee away.

ISAIAH 51:11

PRAYER

Gracious Father, move my heart to repentance this day. Wash me so I can come to you with clean hands and pure heart. May I return to you with joy and singing.

February 26

THE HOLY SPIRIT

PSALM

When the Lord restored the fortunes of Zion,
we were like those who dream.
Then our mouth was filled with laughter,
and our tongue with shouts of joy;
then it was said among the nations,
"The Lord has done great things for them."

PSALM 126:1-2

MEDITATION

We are getting to be very fond of co-operating meetings. Can we not appoint one for the express purpose of praying to the Lord to give us his Holy Spirit? Do you not believe that he will give his Holy Spirit to them that ask him? I know you profess it. Such a meeting as this I should rejoice to attend before I die.

BARTON W. STONE, *Christian Messenger* (1843), 272

SCRIPTURE

For in him every one of God's promises is a "Yes." For this reason it is through him that we say the "Amen," to the glory of God. But it is God who establishes us with you in Christ and has anointed us, by putting his seal on us and giving us his Spirit in our hearts as a first installment.

2 CORINTHIANS 1:20-22

PRAYER

O God, who keeps his promises through Christ, send me your promised Holy Spirit this day. May your Spirit fill my heart as the first installment of all the wonderful promises you have in store for me.

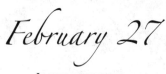

February 27

INFLUENCE

PSALM

Let my cry come before you, O Lord;
give me understanding according to your word.
Let my supplication come before you;
deliver me according to your promise.

PSALM 119:169-170

MEDITATION

But the one whose evil passions have been subdued, and whose love, mercy, and benevolence have been excited and strengthened by the devotions of the closet is a savor of life unto life wherever one goes. Such a person is a living illustration of the power of the gospel on the soul, and must always have an attractive as well as a transforming influence on the minds and hearts of others.

ROBERT MILLIGAN, *A Brief Treatise on Prayer*, 26

SCRIPTURE

But Ruth said, "Do not press me to leave you or to turn back from following you!
Where you go, I will go; where you lodge, I will lodge;
your people shall be my people, and your God my God."

RUTH 1:16

PRAYER

Father, as I spend time alone with you, transform me so that others may see you in me. May I lead those around me to claim my God as their God.

PRAYER

PSALM

Your name, O Lord, endures forever,
your renown, O Lord, throughout all ages.
For the Lord will vindicate his people,
and have compassion on his servants.

PSALM 135:13-14

MEDITATION

A modern theory of prayer, held by some good people, to the effect that its influence is wholly subjective, that it is a sort of spiritual exercise which makes people better, but that it in no way affects God, is doing much, we fear, to sap the foundation of prayer and of personal piety. This is not the scriptural view of prayer. Above all, it is not in harmony with Christ's teaching on the subject of prayer.

J. H. GARRISON, *Alone with God*, 58

SCRIPTURE

And this is the boldness we have in him, that if we ask anything according to his will, he hears us. And if we know that he hears us in whatever we ask, we know that we have obtained the requests made of him.

1 JOHN 5:14-15

PRAYER

Father, I thank you that you hear my prayers, that they touch your very heart. Listen to my cries of pain this day. Have compassion on me. Vindicate me. May I praise your name forever.

WISDOM

PSALM
Teach me to do your will, for you are my God.
Let your good spirit lead me on a level path.

PSALM 143:10

MEDITATION
Be an example in spirit. Always cherish a meek, gentle, and quiet spirit—a humble, loving, heavenly, and praying spirit. Such a spirit will almost silence the tongue of slander, or cause its poisoned darts to fall harmless at the feet.

BARTON W. STONE, *Christian Messenger* (1843), 259

SCRIPTURE
Does not wisdom call, and does not understanding raise her voice?
On the heights, beside the way, at the crossroads she takes her stand;
beside the gates in front of the town, at the entrance of the portals she cries out:
"To you, O people, I call, and my cry is to all that live.
O simple ones, learn prudence; acquire intelligence, you who lack it."

PROVERBS 8:1-5

PRAYER
Father, give me the gentleness and humility I need to receive wisdom. Teach me this day to do your will.

March 1

OBEDIENCE

PSALM

I will sing to the Lord as long as I live;
I will sing praise to my God while I have being.
May my meditation be pleasing to him,
for I rejoice in the Lord.

PSALM 104:33-34

MEDITATION

How noble it is to acquiesce in the divine will; to let our will be swallowed up in the will of God! Then, when the soul is in the "spirit of obedience," and in a condition to inquire in the word of the Lord, for instruction, it is easy to find the right way and walk in it. May we, in humility, love, and submission to our Heavenly King, find and walk in the right way of the Lord, and finally be brought to the enjoyment of his everlasting kingdom!

BENJAMIN FRANKLIN, *The Gospel Preacher* VOL. 2, 217

SCRIPTURE

Those who love their life lose it, and those who hate their life in this world will keep it for eternal life. Whoever serves me must follow me, and where I am, there will my servant be also. Whoever serves me, the Father will honor.

JOHN 12:25-26

PRAYER

Jesus, may I serve and follow you, hating my life so I may keep it. Father, may your will be mine! Give me this day, a spirit of obedience.

CHILDREN

PSALM

Praise the Lord, O Jerusalem!
Praise your God, O Zion!
For he strengthens the bars of your gates;
he blesses your children within you.

PSALM 147:12-13

MEDITATION

Why do we not more frequently retire to our closets, and pray more earnestly for the salvation of immortal souls? How much more parents might do in this way to promote the present and eternal well-being of their children than they can by constantly laboring to secure for them a large supply of the riches, and the honors, and the pleasures of this vain world!

ROBERT MILLIGAN, *A Brief Treatise on Prayer*, 25

SCRIPTURE

But take care and watch yourselves closely, so as neither to forget the things that your eyes have seen nor to let them slip from your mind all the days of your life; make them known to your children and your children's children.

DEUTERONOMY 4:9

PRAYER

Father, grant us courage and wisdom to pass our faith on to our children. Bless them this day with your love and protection. May I receive your kingdom like a little child.

March 3

LIGHT

PSALM

There are many who say, "O that we might see some good!
Let the light of your face shine on us, O Lord!"

PSALM 4:6

MEDITATION

It is thus, in the moral world, that the sun of righteousness shines forth out of Zion upon the darkness of the soul. "God is light, and in him is no darkness at all." And it is from the mount of his holiness, from Zion, the joy of the earth, that he sends forth the light of life.

ROBERT RICHARDSON, *Communings in the Sanctuary*, 90

SCRIPTURE

Jesus said to them, "The light is with you for a little longer. Walk while you have the light,
so that the darkness may not overtake you. If you walk in the darkness, you do not know
where you are going. While you have the light, believe in the light,
so that you may become children of light."

JOHN 12:35-36

PRAYER

Father, shine your light into my heart this day. Lord Jesus, increase my faith in you as the light of the world. May I let my light shine so others will glorify your name.

MONEY

PSALM
For the wicked boast of the desires of their heart,
those greedy for gain curse and renounce the Lord.

PSALM 10:3

MEDITATION

Rich persons are never pre-eminent in religion. The necessary cares of this life
and the deceitfulness of riches choke the word, that they may bring no fruit to
perfection. The mania at this day for acquiring wealth has seized upon the
religious community and almost is religion, pure and undefiled religion, banished
from the earth. This mania has also invaded the ministers of the gospel.

BARTON W. STONE, *Christian Messenger* (1844), 329

SCRIPTURE
"Do not store up for yourselves treasures on earth, where moth and rust consume and
where thieves break in and steal; but store up for yourselves treasures in heaven, where
neither moth nor rust consumes and where thieves do not break in and steal. For where
your treasure is, there your heart will be also."

MATTHEW 6:19-21

PRAYER

O Father, deliver me from times of prosperity! Cure me of the desire for
more money. Let you alone be my treasure, my security, and my honor.

WEAKNESS

PSALM

How long, O Lord? Will you forget me forever?
How long will you hide your face from me?
How long must I bear pain in my soul,
and have sorrow in my heart all day long?
How long shall my enemy be exalted over me?

PSALM 13:1-2

MEDITATION

Prayer must be the sincere expression of the soul's inmost desires. But unless we pause awhile, in the quiet of our own chamber, and introspect our hearts and lives, and examine ourselves in light of God's word, there can be no intelligent appreciation of our needs and no fervency of desire for those spiritual blessings which alone can satisfy the soul.

J.H. GARRISON, *Alone with God*, 88

SCRIPTURE

And, besides other things, I am under daily pressure because of my anxiety for all the churches. Who is weak, and I am not weak? Who is made to stumble, and I am not indignant? If I must boast, I will boast of the things that show my weakness.

2 CORINTHIANS 11:28-30

PRAYER

Father, you know my weakness. Hear me and give me your strength, for I cannot stand of my own power. Take away my pain and sorrow, and satisfy me with yourself.

March 6

PRAYER

PSALM
They confronted me in the day of my calamity;
but the Lord was my support.
He brought me out into a broad place; he delivered me,
because he delighted in me.

PSALM 18:18-19

MEDITATION
It is therefore, a most benevolent and gracious provision of the Scheme of Redemption that God permits, invites, and encourages his children to pray; to pray always, to pray everywhere, and to pray for all things necessary to their present and eternal well-being.

ROBERT MILLIGAN, *Scheme of Redemption*, 367

SCRIPTURE
"Ask, and it will be given you; search, and you will find; knock, and the door will be opened for you. For everyone who asks receives, and everyone who searches finds, and for everyone who knocks, the door will be opened."

MATTHEW 7:7-8

PRAYER
My Father, in my distress I call on you. Hear my call! Open the door. Give me what I ask. May I find in you all I seek. Provide for all my needs this day, and let me trust in you and you alone.

March 7

RESCUE

PSALM

My God, my God, why have you forsaken me?
Why are you so far from helping me,
from the words of my groaning?

PSALM 22:1

MEDITATION

Yes, proofs, numerous and incontestable, that God cares for us, and that nothing that pertains to us can be foreign to him. From this I conclude that God is never forgetful of our temporal wants. He has made abundant provision for our bodily needs, and He must be pleased when we cast ourselves on Him in time of bodily want.

ASHLEY S. JOHNSON, *The Life of Trust*, 12

SCRIPTURE

But the Lord stood by me and gave me strength, so that through me the message might be fully proclaimed and all the Gentiles might hear it. So I was rescued from the lion's mouth. The Lord will rescue me from every evil attack and save me for his heavenly kingdom. To him be the glory forever and ever. Amen.

2 TIMOTHY 4:17-18

PRAYER

Father, rescue me from all attacks this day. Do not forget me. When I cannot see your helping hand, give me eyes of faith to trust your care and give you eternal glory.

FORGIVENESS

PSALM

Gracious is the Lord, and righteous;
our God is merciful.
The Lord protects the simple;
when I was brought low, he saved me.

PSALM 116:5-6

MEDITATION

If we do not forgive those who have trespassed against us, neither will our heavenly Father forgive our trespasses. This is because the unforgiving spirit is an impenitent spirit, and therefore in no condition to receive forgiveness.

J.H. GARRISON, *Alone with God*, 116

SCRIPTURE

If your enemies are hungry, give them bread to eat;
and if they are thirsty, give them water to drink;
for you will heap coals of fire on their heads,
and the Lord will reward you.

PROVERBS 25:21-22

PRAYER

O God, be merciful to me a sinner. May I embrace your forgiveness, but keep my weakness ever before me so that I may show mercy to others. Lord, forgive my unforgiving spirit. Bless my enemies this day.

March 9

REVERENCE

PSALM
Praise the Lord!
Praise God in his sanctuary;
praise him in his mighty firmament!
Praise him for his mighty deeds;
praise him according to his surpassing greatness!

PSALM 150:1-2

MEDITATION

Do we not ofttimes treat God with less respect, carrying into his presence sins unrepented of, hearts ungrateful for his daily mercies, and minds preoccupied with worldly thoughts and cares, having an indistinct idea of the favors we need?

J.H. GARRISON, ALONE WITH GOD, 58

SCRIPTURE

Therefore, since we are receiving a kingdom that cannot be shaken, let us give thanks, by which we offer to God an acceptable worship with reverence and awe; for indeed our God is a consuming fire.

HEBREWS 12:28-29

PRAYER

Holy God, King of the Universe, I bow before you today in reverence and awe. Your love is indeed a consuming fire in my heart. I praise you for your unsurpassed greatness. I thank you for giving me your unshakable kingdom.

JUDGMENT

PSALM

Rise up, O Lord!
Do not let mortals prevail;
let the nations be judged before you.

PSALM 9:19

MEDITATION

The law of God, the highest, the grandest, and most sublime law known to mortals, has not only a penalty, but the most terrible, fearful, and awful penalty ever described by human tongue as its divine sanction. Its salvation, therefore, means something. Its pardon, justification, and deliverance of the soul from sin mean something.

BENJAMIN FRANKLIN, *The Gospel Preacher*, VOL. 1, 479

SCRIPTURE

Do not follow other gods, any of the gods of the peoples who are all around you, because the Lord your God, who is present with you, is a jealous God. The anger of the Lord your God would be kindled against you and he would destroy you from the face of the earth.

DEUTERONOMY 6:14-15

PRAYER

Lord, keep me faithful to you, and you alone. Remove every idol from my heart, so I might not fall under your judgment.

March 11

HEARING

PSALM

Rise up, O God, plead your cause;
remember how the impious scoff at you all day long.

PSALM 74:22

MEDITATION

And it is in the unsearchable riches of Christ; in the infinite magnitude of
the Divine perfections, the depths of his wisdom, the greatness of his power,
the wonders of his redeeming love, that all the facilities of our nature may find
their noblest exercise and most illimitable freedom.

ROBERT RICHARDSON, *Communings in the Sanctuary,* 25

SCRIPTURE

And he said to them, "Pay attention to what you hear; the measure you give will be the
measure you get, and still more will be given you. For to those who have, more will be
given; and from those who have nothing, even what they have will be taken away."

MARK 4:24-25

PRAYER

Father, open my ears and heart today to the reality of your presence. May I
become all you created me to be through the love of your Son Jesus and the
power of your Holy Spirit.

March 12

DOING

PSALM

You have commanded your precepts
to be kept diligently.
O that my ways may be steadfast
in keeping your statutes!
Then I shall not be put to shame,
having my eyes fixed on all your commandments.

PSALM 119:4-6

MEDITATION

Since, therefore, all the other attributes of the Almighty are found in concentrated splendor in his will, and that his word is his will, and his will himself, it follows of necessity, that to believe or receive his word, or adopt his will, is to receive him, and to merge our own individuality in his individuality, and to become in our highest nature, our spiritual nature, essentially one with him.

WALTER SCOTT, *The Messiahship*, 341

SCRIPTURE

For it is not the hearers of the law who are righteous in God's sight,
but the doers of the law who will be justified.

ROMANS 2:13

PRAYER

O God, may I do your word this day and so enter into your life, becoming one with you.

PROCLAMATION

PSALM
We give thanks to you, O God;
we give thanks; your name is near.
People tell of your wondrous deeds.

PSALM 75:1

MEDITATION

Jesus Christ, crucified, buried, risen, and glorified, was the burden of all the apostle's preaching. He is everywhere represented by them as the living, reigning, and Almighty Sovereign of heaven and earth; but at the same time, as being ever ready to receive and save to the uttermost all who will come unto God by Him.

ROBERT MILLIGAN, *The Great Commission*, 111

SCRIPTURE

As he was getting into the boat, the man who had been possessed by demons begged him that he might be with him. But Jesus refused, and said to him, "Go home to your friends, and tell them how much the Lord has done for you, and what mercy he has shown you."

MARK 5:18-19

PRAYER

Father, give me the love and the boldness to proclaim this day what Christ has done for me. May I thank you and praise you by all my actions for your great mercy.

HOLINESS

PSALM
Yet you are holy, enthroned on the praises of Israel.
PSALM 22:3

MEDITATION
And who that has any just conceptions of his new relations, his privileges, and his birthrights as a child of God and an heir of heaven, would not be animated and encouraged to the greatest possible extent by such a call? Who that realizes that the Spirit of the living God dwells and works within would not also labor with all diligence to work out one's own salvation and keep the heart pure?

ROBERT MILLIGAN, *Scheme of Redemption*, 284

SCRIPTURE
Or do you not know that your body is a temple of the Holy Spirit within you, which you have from God, and that you are not your own? For you were bought with a price; therefore glorify God in your body.
1 CORINTHIANS 6:19-20

PRAYER
Father, holy is your name! Work today through your Holy Spirit to make me holy in your sight. Mold me into the image of your holy Son, Jesus. May my holy life this day bring others to your grace.

Repentance

Psalm

Restore us, O God;
let your face shine, that we may be saved.

Psalm 80:3

Meditation

We must return to the government, laws, and ordinances of our rightful king, the Lord Jesus, before we shall be ever gathered together and become worthy subjects of his kingdom.

Barton W. Stone, *Christian Messenger* (1844), 227

Scripture

For if you truly amend your ways and your doings, if you truly act justly one with another, if you do not oppress the alien, the orphan, and the widow, or shed innocent blood in this place, and if you do not go after other gods to your own hurt, then I will dwell with you in this place, in the land that I gave of old to your ancestors forever and ever.

Jeremiah 7:5-7

Prayer

Father, turn my heart to you. Break me of the desire to serve the ways of the world. Give me purity of heart to serve you alone. May I show my devotion to you by acts of justice and service to others.

March 16

FAITH

PSALM

We will not hide them from their children;
we will tell to the coming generation
the glorious deeds of the Lord, and his might,
and the wonders that he has done.

PSALM 78:4

MEDITATION

Now the belief of what Christ says of himself, terminates in trust or confidence in him: and as the Christian religion is a personal thing, both as respects subject and object, that faith in Christ which is essential to salvation is not the belief of any doctrine, testimony, or truth, abstractly, but belief in Christ; trust or confidence in him as a person, not a thing.

ALEXANDER CAMPBELL, *The Christian System*, 53

SCRIPTURE

Now the words, "it was reckoned to him," were written not for his sake alone, but for ours also. It will be reckoned to us who believe in him who raised Jesus our Lord from the dead, who was handed over to death for our trespasses and was raised for our justification.

ROMANS 4:23-25

PRAYER

Lord Jesus, I believe in you! Increase my faith. Father, I trust you as the one who raised Jesus from the dead. May my faith and trust be in you personally, Father, Son, and Spirit. Help me as I proclaim your great deeds.

TRIALS

PSALM

*Uphold me according to your promise, that I may live,
and let me not be put to shame in my hope.
Hold me up, that I may be safe
and have regard for your statutes continually.*

PSALM 119:116-117

MEDITATION

To learn this lesson—that all life's crosses and trials and conflicts, and the performance of our daily tasks, no matter how humble, are the very means which God has ordained for our spiritual discipline, and the stepping-stones by which we are to rise from earth to heaven, from bitter sorrows and lowly duties to celestial joys and heavenly employments—is to know the meaning of life and to master the secret of contentment and happiness in our earthly lot.

J.H. GARRISON, *Alone with God*, 109

SCRIPTURE

*Is there no balm in Gilead? Is there no physician there?
Why then has the health of my poor people not been restored?*

JEREMIAH 8:22

PRAYER

Jesus, Great Physician, heal me from my sickness of soul. Free me from the tyranny of self. Transform my daily tasks into glorious acts of service. Keep me steadfast in times of trial. Let me not be put to shame in my hope.

March 18

HEARING

PSALM

Let me hear what God the Lord will speak,
for he will speak peace to his people,
to his faithful, to those who turn to him in their hearts.
Surely his salvation is at hand for those who fear him,
that his glory may dwell in our land.

PSALM 85:8-9

MEDITATION

In the name then of our Lord Jesus the Christ, our only Savior, let us come to our Father, who always hears us and who is faithful to keep that which is committed to his hands; who will be with us in every trial, in all our sufferings, and in crossing the cold river, where he will receive us to himself to be with him forever and ever.

BENJAMIN FRANKLIN, *The Gospel Preacher*, VOL. 2, 193

SCRIPTURE

As he went ashore, he saw a great crowd; and he had compassion for them, because they were like sheep without a shepherd; and he began to teach them many things.

MARK 6:34

PRAYER

Father, hear my prayer. I thank you that you ever hear me. Lord, open my ears and heart to hear your word to me. Lord Jesus, thank you for teaching me with compassion and gentleness. May I live with you in glory in this land.

March 19

SEEKING THE LOST

PSALM
O come, let us worship and bow down,
let us kneel before the Lord, our Maker!
For he is our God, and we are the people of his pasture,
and the sheep of his hand.
O that today you would listen to his voice!

PSALM 95:6-7

MEDITATION
We try to "attract" the people to the house of God. Jesus went to the people, sought them. In reference to this world his only question would have been: "Is it lost, does it need me?" His only question in reference to the individual, you, is: "Are you lost, are you helpless, do you need me?" He did not make any special effort to find the so-called respectable sinners—all were lost in his sight.

ASHLEY S. JOHNSON, *The Life of Trust*, 132

SCRIPTURE
For though I am free with respect to all, I have made myself a slave to all,
so that I might win more of them.

1 CORINTHIANS 9:19

PRAYER
Loving God, thank you for seeking and finding me when I was lost. Jesus, Savior, continue to look for me! May I be a slave to all I meet today, so that you might win them and find them through me.

RIGHTEOUSNESS

PSALM

It is he who remembered us in our low estate,
for his steadfast love endures forever;
and rescued us from our foes,
for his steadfast love endures forever.

PSALM 136:23-24

MEDITATION

To love God with all our heart, and our neighbor as ourselves, with a correspondent walk, is righteousness.

BARTON W. STONE, *Christian Messenger* (1843), 208

SCRIPTURE

But thanks be to God that you, having once been slaves of sin, have become obedient from the heart to the form of teaching to which you were entrusted, and that you, having been set free from sin, have become slaves of righteousness.

ROMANS 6:17-18

PRAYER

Holy Father, through your Son Jesus you have made me righteous in your sight. Give me hunger and thirst for what truly satisfies, for your righteousness alone. Make me your slave. Give me your cross. Remember me this day.

COMMUNION WITH GOD

PSALM

Happy are the people who know the festal shout,
who walk, O Lord, in the light of your countenance;
they exult in your name all day long,
and extol your righteousness.

PSALM 89:15-16

MEDITATION

It is here that everything should promote that solemn stillness and that reverential awe, which prepare the heart for communion with God and a better appreciation of the deep mysteries of his grace.

ROBERT RICHARDSON, *Communings in the Sanctuary*, 8

SCRIPTURE

The cup of blessing that we bless, is it not a sharing in the blood of Christ? The bread that we break, is it not a sharing in the body of Christ? Because there is one bread, we who are many are one body, for we all partake of the one bread.

1 CORINTHIANS 10:16-17

PRAYER

Father, I approach you on bended knee, with reverence and awe, asking you to share your life with me this day. Lord Jesus, when I drink the cup and eat the bread, may I share in your body and blood. Make your Presence real to me!

RESCUE FROM DEATH

PSALM

Extol the Lord our God;
worship at his footstool.
Holy is he!

PSALM 99:5

MEDITATION

The love of God in the gift of his Son—Christ's own love and infinite condescension, his incarnation, his heavenly but hazardous mission to the Jews, his transfiguration, his sorrows and teachings, his death, burial, resurrection, ascension, and glorification preached, and as it were, dropped into the mind successively, or in other words, addressed to the human heart with all the evidence of truth and the sweetness of love, decompose all sin, and separate it from the mind and spirit, reducing a person thereby to simplicity and childlike docility.

WALTER SCOTT, *The Messiahship*, 42

SCRIPTURE

Wretched man that I am! Who will rescue me from this body of death? Thanks be to God through Jesus Christ our Lord! So then, with my mind I am a slave to the law of God, but with my flesh I am a slave to the law of sin.

ROMANS 7:24-25

PRAYER

Praise be to you, O God, for rescuing me from sin and death! I extol you with every breath.

PROVIDENCE

PSALM

But you, O Lord my Lord,
act on my behalf for your name's sake;
because your steadfast love is good, deliver me.
For I am poor and needy,
and my heart is pierced within me.

PSALM 109:21-22

MEDITATION

All nature is but a case of instruments in the hands of God, by means of
which, through the agency of the Spirit, he not infrequently accomplishes his
benevolent designs in reference to the sanctification of the saints, as well as in
reference to the conversion of sinners.

ROBERT MILLIGAN, *Scheme of Redemption*, 282

SCRIPTURE

But Joseph said to them, "Do not be afraid! Am I in the place of God?
Even though you intended to do harm to me, God intended it for good,
in order to preserve a numerous people, as he is doing today."

GENESIS 50:19-20

PRAYER

Ruler of all, act in my life today. Turn evil into good, as you did for Joseph
long ago. Open my eyes to your work in the world through your Holy Spirit. Use
me to preserve and save those I meet.

LIVING BREAD

PSALM

My flesh and my heart may fail,
but God is the strength of my heart and my portion forever.

PSALM 73:26

MEDITATION

If Jesus had not died we could not have lived; for it is only through him who died for us that we can live to God. It is only by partaking of that bread which came down from heaven and which was given for the life of the world that we can live forever.

ROBERT RICHARDSON, *Communings in the Sanctuary*, 18

SCRIPTURE

"I am the bread of life. Your ancestors ate the manna in the wilderness, and they died. This is the bread that comes down from heaven, so that one may eat of it and not die. I am the living bread that came down from heaven. Whoever eats of this bread will live forever; and the bread that I will give for the life of the world is my flesh."

JOHN 6:48-51

PRAYER

Lord Jesus, I hunger and thirst for you. Feed me with the living bread. Fill me with your presence this day that I might have life. Keep me from wanting to be filled with all the unhealthy things of the world. Increase my faith!

March 25

The Great Shepherd

Psalm
When they are diminished and brought low
through oppression, trouble, and sorrow,
he pours contempt on princes
and makes them wander in trackless wastes;
But he raises up the needy out of distress,
and makes their families like flocks.

Psalm 107:39-41

Meditation
O the precious comfort of knowing that Christ is over us continually with a shepherd's watchful eye, and that he is mighty and able to save!

J.H. Garrison, *Alone with God*, 32

Scripture
Then I myself will gather the remnant of my flock out of all the lands where I have driven them, and I will bring them back to their fold, and they shall be fruitful and multiply. I will raise up shepherds over them who will shepherd them, and they shall not fear any longer, or be dismayed, nor shall any be missing, says the Lord.

Jeremiah 23:3-4

Prayer
Jesus, loving Shepherd, watch over me, your little lamb, this day. Correct me with your rod. Guide me with your staff. Father God, I thank you for giving me shepherds under the Great Shepherd, to lead me in paths of righteousness.

DISCIPLINE

PSALM

On the glorious splendor of your majesty,
and on your wondrous works, I will meditate.

PSALM 145:5

MEDITATION

The habit of secret prayer is no exception to this general law. In no other religious exercise are we brought so near to God; in no other can we be so familiar with the Creator of our bodies and the Father and preserver of our spirits.

ROBERT MILLIGAN, *A Brief Treatise on Prayer,* 17-18

SCRIPTURE

Do you not know that in a race the runners all compete, but only one receives the prize?
Run in such a way that you may win it. Athletes exercise self-control in all things; they do
it to receive a perishable wreath, but we an imperishable one. So I do not run aimlessly,
nor do I box as though beating the air; but I punish my body and enslave it, so that after
proclaiming to others I myself should not be disqualified.

1 CORINTHIANS 9:24-27

PRAYER

Father, grant me self-control and discipline. May I form the habits of prayer and meditation so I may come to know you. Deliver me from self-centeredness and desires for pleasures that do not fulfill. Send your Holy Spirit to make me holy as you are holy.

March 27

HUMILITY

PSALM

Love the Lord, all you his saints.
The Lord preserves the faithful,
but abundantly repays the one who acts haughtily.
Be strong, and let your heart take courage,
all you who wait for the Lord.

PSALM 31:23-24

MEDITATION

How far above the standard of humble Christians have we risen! We must sink down to the standard of Christian perfection, humility, love, kindness, goodness, and meekness. We must be stripped of the love of the world, of the honor that cometh from others, of the love of money, and be filled with the Spirit of our Lord, else the door of heaven will be shut and barred against us forever. Solemn thought!

BARTON W. STONE, *Christian Messenger* (1843), 50

SCRIPTURE

But they were silent, for on the way they had argued with one another who was the greatest. He sat down, called the twelve, and said to them, "Whoever wants to be first must be last of all and servant of all."

MARK 9:34-35

PRAYER

Father, make me a servant. Purge me of the desire to be greatest. Fill me with your Spirit so I may seek to serve rather than to be served. Have mercy on me, a sinner!

FAITH

PSALM

Those who trust in the Lord are like Mount Zion,
which cannot be moved, but abides forever.

PSALM 125:1

MEDITATION

Is God really our Father? I have asked and answered this great question because of its relation to The Life of Trust, or if you choose, believing prayer. If God is our Father, really, truly, always, it follows that he hears us, for our earthly parents hear us, when, in our distress, we cry unto them.

ASHLEY S. JOHNSON, *The Life of Trust*, 32

SCRIPTURE

Jesus heard that they had driven him out, and when he found him, he said, "Do you believe in the Son of Man?" He answered, "And who is he, sir? Tell me, so that I may believe in him." Jesus said to him, "You have seen him, and the one speaking with you is he." He said, "Lord, I believe." And he worshiped him.

JOHN 9:35-38

PRAYER

Lord, I believe, help my unbelief. Increase my trust in you, Father. May my trust not be in money, governments, plans, or programs, but in you and you alone. This day may I truly believe and worship.

March 29

LIGHT

PSALM

But you, O Lord, are a shield around me,
my glory, and the one who lifts up my head.

PSALM 3:3

MEDITATION

To the sacrifice of Christ, we always look for the basis of our pardon; to his blood that cleanses us from all sin, for justification and personal acceptance; and to his Word we look for counsel and instruction in Christian piety and righteousness. We are as dependent on his Word for light, as we are upon his blood for pardon.

ALEXANDER CAMPBELL, *The Christian System*, 50

SCRIPTURE

This is the message we have heard from him and proclaim to you, that God is light and in him there is no darkness at all. If we say that we have fellowship with him while we are walking in darkness, we lie and do not do what is true; but if we walk in the light as he himself is in the light, we have fellowship with one another, and the blood of Jesus his Son cleanses us from all sin.

1 JOHN 1:5-7

PRAYER

God of light, show me the right path today so I may walk in you. Jesus, Light of the world, enlighten me today in your love. Give me fellowship with you, O God, that I may never stray.

March 30

HOLINESS

PSALM

For the Lord is righteous; he loves righteous deeds;
the upright shall behold his face.

PSALM 11:7

MEDITATION

Holiness is not a mere ecstasy of feeling; it is not a glowing desire to be Christlike, though that is a good beginning. It is an actual achievement in overcoming the temptations and trials of life, through faith, and by the indwelling power of the Holy Spirit.

J.H. GARRISON, *The Holy Spirit*, 175

SCRIPTURE

Like obedient children, do not be conformed to the desires that you formerly had in ignorance. Instead, as he who called you is holy, be holy yourselves in all your conduct; for it is written, "You shall be holy, for I am holy."

1 PETER 1:14-16

PRAYER

Father, give me your Spirit today to make me holy. Transform me into the image of your Son. Take from me all rebellion and selfishness, that I may be your obedient child.

March 31

THE CROSS

PSALM

I wait for the Lord, my soul waits,
and in his word I hope;
my soul waits for the Lord
more than those who watch for the morning,
more than those who watch for the morning.

PSALM 130:5-6

MEDITATION

In his flesh and blood on the cross, we see a foundation laid for salvation, redemption, pardon, justification, sanctification, and glorification, to a fallen world. Here then is soul satisfying food, as boundless as our wants, and as lasting as eternity.

BARTON W. STONE, *Christian Messenger* (1843), 113

SCRIPTURE

"For this reason the Father loves me, because I lay down my life in order to take it up again. No one takes it from me, but I lay it down of my own accord. I have power to lay it down, and I have power to take it up again. I have received this command from my Father."

JOHN 10:17-18

PRAYER

God of love, I thank you for the gift of your Son. Lord Jesus, I praise you for your marvelous gift. May I wait on your salvation.

April 1

MONEY

PSALM

O Lord, my heart is not lifted up,
my eyes are not raised too high;
I do not occupy myself with things
too great and too marvelous for me.

PSALM 131:1

MEDITATION

Millions reap the dire results of the mad rush after more than they need who at last die in helpless poverty which indeed they must do even if they succeed. Beware: you can shut out the sun, yea, all heaven from your vision with the smallest coin that ever came from the mint if you hold it close enough to your eye. It is not the amount you secure but the closeness and affection with which you hug the delusion to your heart that works your ruin.

ASHLEY S. JOHNSON, *The Life of Trust*, 178

SCRIPTURE

Then Jesus looked around and said to his disciples, "How hard it will be for those who have wealth to enter the kingdom of God!" And the disciples were perplexed at these words. But Jesus said to them again, "Children, how hard it is to enter the kingdom of God! It is easier for a camel to go through the eye of a needle than for someone who is rich to enter the kingdom of God."

MARK 10:23-25

PRAYER

Lord Jesus, in your compassion free me from the love of money. May possessions not find their way into my heart, but may my treasure be in you alone. May I give generously to those in need as you became poor for my sake.

TURNING THE HEART

PSALM

Do not harden your hearts, as at Meribah,
as on the day at Massah in the wilderness,
when your ancestors tested me,
and put me to the proof, though they had seen my work.
For forty years I loathed that generation
and said, "They are a people whose hearts go astray,
and they do not regard my ways."
Therefore in my anger I swore,
"They shall not enter my rest."

PSALM 95:8-11

MEDITATION

Prayer implies certain conditions that cannot coexist with impenitence, such as faith in God, a proper reverence for his name, consciousness of our spiritual needs, and a hungering and thirsting after righteousness. The impenitent have no taste for prayer. The desire to pray is about the first sign of true penitence.

J.H. GARRISON, *Alone with God*, 81-82.

SCRIPTURE

Note then the kindness and the severity of God: severity toward those who have fallen,
but God's kindness toward you, provided you continue in his kindness;
otherwise you also will be cut off.

ROMANS 11:22

PRAYER

Father, turn my heart toward you. Soften my heart and grant me true repentance that I may turn to you in faith. This day let me proclaim your kindness to all I meet. May I never put you to the test, O Lord, and please deliver me from the time of testing.

New Covenant

Psalm

By the rivers of Babylon—there we sat down and
there we wept when we remembered Zion.
How could we sing the Lord's song in a foreign land?

Psalm 137:1, 4

Meditation

Under the new covenant, the best covenant, founded on better promises, they are not in it by virtue of the first, or natural birth, but being born again; not on the ground of being born of parents in the church, but a spiritual relationship to God; not in the covenant in ignorance to God, so as to have to be taught to know the Lord, but by faith in our Lord Jesus Christ.

Benjamin Franklin, *The Gospel Preacher*, vol. 1, 212

Scripture

But this is the covenant that I will make with the house of Israel after those days, says the Lord: I will put my law within them, and I will write it on their hearts; and I will be their God, and they shall be my people. No longer shall they teach one another, or say to each other, "Know the Lord," for they shall all know me, from the least of them to the greatest, says the Lord; for I will forgive their iniquity, and remember their sin no more.

Jeremiah 31:33-34

Prayer

Father, I thank you for remembering my sins no more. Keep me faithful to your covenant this day. May I claim and embrace your promises and fulfill the vows I have made to you.

April 4

The King of Glory

Psalm

Lift up your heads, O gates!
and be lifted up, O ancient doors!
that the King of glory may come in.
Who is the King of glory?
The Lord, strong and mighty,
the Lord, mighty in battle.

Psalm 24:7-8

Meditation

He is admitted, crowned king—angels, principalities, and powers are made subject to him. The Holy Spirit is dispatched with the joyful tidings from heaven to Jerusalem.

T.W. Brents, *The Gospel Plan of Salvation*, 160

Scripture

Rejoice greatly, O daughter Zion!
Shout aloud, O daughter Jerusalem!
Lo, your king comes to you;
triumphant and victorious is he, humble and riding on a donkey,
on a colt, the foal of a donkey.

Zechariah 9:9

Prayer

Lord Jesus, I crown you king of my life. Reign in my heart today. Come quickly, so that every knee will bow and every tongue confess you as Lord.

COMFORT

PSALM

Create in me a clean heart, O God,
and put a new and right spirit within me.
Do not cast me away from your presence,
and do not take your holy spirit from me.

PSALM 51:10-11

MEDITATION

A heart that is cold and callous, and insensible to the sorrows and woes of the world, and to its own perils, may not feel the need of prayer; but a heart, tender and responsive to others' woes, and realizing the awful peril of sin, and with a sympathy so deep and wide that like the Master it can weep over the sins and sorrows of others, would break but for the solace and strength found in prayer.

J.H. GARRISON, *Alone with God*, 76

SCRIPTURE

Blessed be the God and Father of our Lord Jesus Christ,
the Father of mercies and the God of all consolation, who consoles us in all our affliction,
so that we may be able to console those who are in any affliction with the consolation with
which we ourselves are consoled by God.

2 CORINTHIANS 1:3-4

PRAYER

Father, comfort me with your forgiveness. Give me a new and clean heart. Keep me close to you through your Holy Spirit. Open my eyes to those who need your comforting presence.

SUFFERING

PSALM

Turn, O Lord, save my life;
deliver me for the sake of your steadfast love.
For in death there is no remembrance of you;
in Sheol who can give you praise?

PSALM 6:4-5

MEDITATION

Where are the mourners in Zion? Where are the tears whose fountain is the heart, bursting from streams from the eyes of Christians for the desolations of the world? Where are the sacrifices made for their recovery? Alas! Where?

BARTON W. STONE, *Christian Messenger* (1843), 274

SCRIPTURE

I want to know Christ and the power of his resurrection and
the sharing of his sufferings by becoming like him in his death,
if somehow I may attain the resurrection from the dead.

PHILIPPIANS 3:10-11

PRAYER

Father, let me share in the sufferings of Christ, sufferings for others. Almighty God, bring justice and healing to those who are downtrodden. Give me compassion for others. Empower me to put that compassion into action this day.

April 7
God Hears

Psalm
But I call upon God,
and the Lord will save me.
Evening and morning and at noon
I utter my complaint and moan,
and he will hear my voice.
He will redeem me unharmed
from the battle that I wage,
for many are arrayed against me.

Psalm 55:16-18

Meditation
Come then, in childlike confidence, to our blessed and glorious Father; not as a formality, nor merely as a duty, but because you need his Almighty Arm to protect and shield you in the midst of the evils in the world, and finally to save you.

Benjamin Franklin, *The Gospel Preacher*, vol. 2, 193

Scripture
"Now my soul is troubled. And what should I say—'Father, save me from this hour'? No, it is for this reason that I have come to this hour. Father, glorify your name." Then a voice came from heaven, "I have glorified it, and I will glorify it again."

John 12:27-28

Prayer
Loving Father, as Jesus trusted you in the hour of trial, may I also trust when pain and suffering falls on me. Lord, hear! Lord, save!

April 8

THE LAST SUPPER

PSALM

Let me hear of your steadfast love in the morning,
for in you I put my trust.
Teach me the way I should go,
for to you I lift up my soul.

PSALM 143:8

MEDITATION

To every disciple he says, "For you my body was wounded; for you my life
was taken." In receiving it the disciple says, "Lord, I believe it. My life sprung
from thy suffering; my joy from thy sorrows, and my hope of glory everlasting
from thy humiliation and abasement, even unto death."

ALEXANDER CAMPBELL, *The Christian System*, 310

SCRIPTURE

While they were eating, he took a loaf of bread, and after blessing it he broke it, gave it to
them, and said, "Take; this is my body." Then he took a cup, and after giving thanks he
gave it to them, and all of them drank from it. He said to them, "This is my blood of the
covenant, which is poured out for many. Truly I tell you, I will never again drink of the
fruit of the vine until that day when I drink it new in the kingdom of God."

MARK 14:22-25

PRAYER

Lord Jesus, words fail me in praising the great gift of your love, the gift of
your own life. May I live as part of your body. May your blood constantly cover
me. Lord, may the day come quickly when I drink with you forever.

THE DEATH OF JESUS

PSALM

My God, my God, why have you forsaken me?
Why are you so far from helping me,
from the words of my groaning?
O my God, I cry by day, but you do not answer;
and by night, but find no rest.

PSALM 22:1-2

MEDITATION

Through his death God has brought to light incorruptibility and life, and the greatest crime ever committed by humanity has been made to us the richest blessing.

ROBERT RICHARDSON, *Communings in the Sanctuary*, 32

SCRIPTURE

Concerning this salvation, the prophets who prophesied of the grace that was to be yours
made careful search and inquiry, inquiring about the person or time that the Spirit of
Christ within them indicated when it testified in advance to the sufferings
destined for Christ and the subsequent glory.

1 PETER 1:10-11

PRAYER

Father, thank you for the gift of your Son. Lord Jesus, praise be to you for the blessing of salvation. Holy Spirit of God, fill my life this day that I might live in the glory of God.

April 10

Our High Priest

Psalm

Though an army encamp against me,
my heart shall not fear;
though war rise up against me,
yet I will be confident.

Psalm 27:3

Meditation

So far as we can comprehend this wonderful subject, we are more and more deeply penetrated with the conviction, that nothing inferior to the voluntary sacrifice of the Son of God could put away sin; and make it both just, and merciful, and honorable, and safe, on the part of his God and Father, to forgive and save one of his rebel race.

Alexander Campbell, *The Christian System*, 49

Scripture

Since, then, we have a great high priest who has passed through the heavens, Jesus, the Son of God, let us hold fast to our confession. For we do not have a high priest who is unable to sympathize with our weaknesses, but we have one who in every respect has been tested as we are, yet without sin. Let us therefore approach the throne of grace with boldness, so that we may receive mercy and find grace to help in time of need.

Hebrews 4:14-16

Prayer

Father of grace, I approach your holy throne boldly, asking for mercy in my time of need. Through Jesus, my great High Priest, I ask for forgiveness, strength, and help.

April 11

THE RESURRECTION

PSALM

Out of my distress I called on the Lord;
the Lord answered me and set me in a broad place.
With the Lord on my side I do not fear.
What can mortals do to me?

PSALM 118:5-6

MEDITATION

How ennobling to contend thus against death and thus with Jesus to wage a warfare against the powers of darkness. How noble the enterprise which the Christian shall thus achieve, and how vain the triumphs of earth's proudest conquerors when compared with the victory of life over death—the rescue of the ransomed from the grave.

ROBERT RICHARDSON, *Communings in the Sanctuary*, 37

SCRIPTURE

When it was evening on that day, the first day of the week, and the doors of the house where the disciples had met were locked for fear of the Jews, Jesus came and stood among them and said, "Peace be with you." After he said this, he showed them his hands and his side. Then the disciples rejoiced when they saw the Lord.

JOHN 20:19-20

PRAYER

Christ is risen! Gracious Father, I praise you for raising him from the dead and raising me with him to new life. Risen Christ, live in my heart and life today. May my every breath proclaim that you are risen indeed.

VICTORY

PSALM

O sing to the Lord a new song,
for he has done marvelous things.
His right hand and his holy arm
have gotten him victory.

PSALM 98:1

MEDITATION

And may the fullness of grace and truth wherewith Christ hath blessed us, flow out, in life-giving streams, to the barren wastes of other lives and make them as fruitful gardens of the Lord!

J.H. GARRISON, *Alone with God*, 45

SCRIPTURE

"You that are Israelites, listen to what I have to say: Jesus of Nazareth, a man attested to you by God with deeds of power, wonders, and signs that God did through him among you, as you yourselves know—this man, handed over to you according to the definite plan and foreknowledge of God, you crucified and killed by the hands of those outside the law. But God raised him up, having freed him from death, because it was impossible for him to be held in its power."

ACTS 2:22-24

PRAYER

Loving Father, who won the victory over death through the resurrection of Jesus, triumph over sin and death in my life this day. May your love overflow in my heart to bring streams of healing to those around me. May my trust be in you, not in my own power.

The Holy Spirit

Psalm

The Lord is merciful and gracious,
slow to anger and abounding in steadfast love.
He will not always accuse,
nor will he keep his anger forever.
He does not deal with us according to our sins,
nor repay us according to our iniquities.

Psalm 103:8-10

Meditation

But by the reception of the Spirit, the Scriptures are experimentally known in their power and glory, and the person renewed in knowledge after the image of him who created him. They are no longer led by the flesh but by the Spirit—they follow not after the flesh, but after the Spirit—they are justified and saved from sin, are new creatures, created anew in Christ Jesus unto good works.

Barton W. Stone, *Christian Messenger* (1844), 9

Scripture

And I will ask the Father, and he will give you another Advocate, to be with you forever.
This is the Spirit of truth, whom the world cannot receive, because it neither sees him nor
knows him. You know him, because he abides with you, and he will be in you. I will not
leave you orphaned; I am coming to you.

John 14:16-18

Prayer

Father, thank you for the great gift of your Holy Spirit. Lord Jesus, thank you for not leaving me an orphan, but for your continued presence in me through the Holy Spirit. Continue to give your Spirit to me so I may walk in your ways!

DELIVERANCE

PSALM

O Israel, trust in the Lord!
He is their help and their shield.
O house of Aaron, trust in the Lord!
He is their help and their shield.
You who fear the Lord, trust in the Lord!
He is their help and their shield.

PSALM 115:9-11

MEDITATION

The exit of Israel was designed of God to shadow forth and throw into bolder relief the major fact or feature in the future Messianic order of things—namely, "Redemption." Their civil and religious deliverance from Pharaoh and idolatry, is therefore but a type on the lower level of thought, analogous in its general features, however, to that redemption from death and sin by the Messiah which the Christian religion offers to our faith on the higher scale of spiritual perception.

WALTER SCOTT, *The Messiahship*, 81-82

SCRIPTURE

The time that the Israelites had lived in Egypt was four hundred thirty years.
At the end of four hundred thirty years, on that very day,
all the companies of the Lord went out from the land of Egypt.

EXODUS 12:40-41

PRAYER

God of love, I praise you for delivering me from the slavery of sin through the resurrection of Jesus. You are my help and my shield! This day protect me from temptation and deliver me from evil. May I trust in you.

MAKING DISCIPLES

PSALM

Let them praise the name of the Lord,
for his name alone is exalted;
his glory is above earth and heaven.
He has raised up a horn for his people,
praise for all his faithful,
for the people of Israel who are close to him.

PSALM 148:13-14

MEDITATION

There can be no growth nor progress in the Divine Life without activity. And hence it is that God has most wisely and benevolently permitted us to cooperate with him in the great work of saving ourselves and redeeming the world.

ROBERT MILLIGAN, *Scheme of Redemption*, 475

SCRIPTURE

When they saw him, they worshiped him; but some doubted. And Jesus came and said to them, "All authority in heaven and on earth has been given to me. Go therefore and make disciples of all nations, baptizing them in the name of the Father and of the Son and of the Holy Spirit, and teaching them to obey everything that I have commanded you. And remember, I am with you always, to the end of the age."

MATTHEW 28:17-20

PRAYER

Jesus, my Savior, be with me always as you have promised. Work in me this day that I may go and make others your disciples. Father God, I praise your name for raising up Jesus as my Savior.

Our Resurrection

Psalm

I shall not die, but I shall live,
and recount the deeds of the Lord.

Psalm 118:17

Meditation

Our great Deliverer has cleansed our souls from sin, in his own blood and, by his omnipotent power, raised us from the dead and freed us from the fetters of the grave forever. He has lifted us up and seated us at his own right hand in the holy city, and has given us riches, and glories, and honors, transcending all human description.

Benjamin Franklin, *The Gospel Preacher*, vol. 1, 477

Scripture

When this perishable body puts on imperishability, and this mortal body puts on immortality, then the saying that is written will be fulfilled: "Death has been swallowed up in victory." "Where, O death, is your victory? Where, O death, is your sting?" The sting of death is sin, and the power of sin is the law. But thanks be to God, who gives us the victory through our Lord Jesus Christ. Therefore, my beloved, be steadfast, immovable, always excelling in the work of the Lord, because you know that in the Lord your labor is not in vain.

1 Corinthians 15:54-58

Prayer

Dear God of life, help my unbelief. Increase my trust in the resurrection of your son, Jesus. May I believe what is too wonderful to believe, that I will live again after death, live with you eternally. May I give my life to you in service this day, knowing that my labor is not in vain.

April 17

END OF SORROW

PSALM

The Lord is just in all his ways,
and kind in all his doings.
The Lord is near to all who call on him,
to all who call on him in truth.
He fulfills the desire of all who fear him;
he also hears their cry, and saves them.

PSALM 145:17-19

MEDITATION

As voyagers across the ocean soon forget the storms and billows which filled their souls with fears, and made their passage uncomfortable, when they have reached their destination and are welcomed by kind friends, so we, tempest-tossed passengers on life's stormy sea, when safely anchored in the quiet haven of everlasting peace, shall find our past sorrows and afflictions swallowed up in the supreme delight of the beatific vision.

J. H. GARRISON, *Alone With God*, 110

SCRIPTURE

Then the Lord God will wipe away the tears from all faces, and the disgrace of his people he will take away from all the earth, for the Lord has spoken. It will be said on that day, Lo, this is our God; we have waited for him, so that he might save us. This is the Lord for whom we have waited; let us be glad and rejoice in his salvation.

ISAIAH 25:8-9

PRAYER

Father, show me your face this day so my sorrows and tears will be wiped away. Lord Jesus, come quickly so I may see my God face to face. Lord God, give me patience to wait on your coming.

April 18

Untroubled Hearts

Psalm

They are not afraid of evil tidings;
their hearts are firm, secure in the Lord.
Their hearts are steady, they will not be afraid;
in the end they will look in triumph on their foes.

Psalm 112:7-8

Meditation

It is indeed in the assembly of the saints that gladness and rejoicing should fill the heart. It is here that we are, in an especial manner, permitted to draw near to Him that is the source of every pure and blissful emotion. In his presence there can be no sorrow, for there all tears are wiped away and there are "pleasures forevermore."

Robert Richardson, *Communings in the Sanctuary*, 5

Scripture

"Do not let your hearts be troubled. Believe in God, believe also in me. In my Father's house there are many dwelling places. If it were not so, would I have told you that I go to prepare a place for you? And if I go and prepare a place for you, I will come again and will take you to myself, so that where I am, there you may be also.
And you know the way to the place where I am going."

John 14:1-4

Prayer

God of all comfort, grant me an untroubled heart today. Keep me from all fear. May I know and follow the way to you—Jesus, the Way, Truth, and Life.

New Birth

Psalm

*Ask of me, and I will make the nations your heritage,
and the ends of the earth your possession.*

Psalm 2:8

Meditation

Into the future and ultimate kingdom of glory we enter, soul and body, by being born from the grave. As Christ, the first born from the dead, entered the heavenly kingdom, so must all his brothers and sisters. And as to this kingdom of which we speak, as now existing in this world, Jesus himself taught that into it no person can legally enter who is not born again, or "born of water and the Spirit."

Alexander Campbell, *The Christian System*, 160

Scripture

Blessed be the God and Father of our Lord Jesus Christ! By his great mercy he has given us a new birth into a living hope through the resurrection of Jesus Christ from the dead, and into an inheritance that is imperishable, undefiled, and unfading, kept in heaven for you, who are being protected by the power of God through faith for a salvation ready to be revealed in the last time.

1 Peter 1:3-5

Prayer

Gracious Father, I thank you for giving me new birth into your holy family. May I enjoy the blessings of my inheritance this day, and enjoy them more fully in the age to come. Increase my faith. Confirm my hope. May I know this day I am your beloved so I in turn may love.

PROTECTION

PSALM

But let all who take refuge in you rejoice;
let them ever sing for joy.
Spread your protection over them,
so that those who love your name may exult in you.
For you bless the righteous, O Lord;
you cover them with favor as with a shield.

PSALM 5:11-12

MEDITATION

Are there lessons here for us? Yes. What are they? God provides, and rules for our good, and He is ready to hear our requests if we in faith measure up to his promises.

ASHLEY S. JOHNSON, *The Life of Trust*, 18

SCRIPTURE

I am not asking you to take them out of the world, but I ask you to protect them from the evil one. They do not belong to the world, just as I do not belong to the world.

JOHN 17:15-16

PRAYER

Father, I run to you this day for refuge. Protect me from all harm today, particularly keep me safe from the evil one who would destroy me. Give me an unwavering faith in your promises to care for me.

ABIDING IN GOD

PSALM

But I trusted in your steadfast love;
my heart shall rejoice in your salvation.
I will sing to the Lord,
because he has dealt bountifully with me.

PSALM 13:5-6

MEDITATION

Take heed to yourself, and learn this truth, that without the Holy Spirit you can do nothing. Christ, the great teacher of the world, never preached the gospel until he was full of the Holy Ghost. His apostles were forbidden to leave Jerusalem and preach the gospel until they had received the Holy Spirit of promise—endued with power from on high.

BARTON W. STONE, *Christian Messenger* (1843), 258

SCRIPTURE

Abide in me as I abide in you. Just as the branch cannot bear fruit by itself unless it abides in the vine, neither can you unless you abide in me. I am the vine, you are the branches. Those who abide in me and I in them bear much fruit, because apart from me you can do nothing.

JOHN 15:4-5

PRAYER

Father, may I trust your unfailing love. Jesus, my Savior, may I always abide in you. Holy Spirit, fill me with your power for ministry and service.

Exiles

Psalm

The Lord is my rock, my fortress, and my deliverer,
my God, my rock in whom I take refuge, my shield,
and the horn of my salvation, my stronghold.
I call upon the Lord, who is worthy to be praised,
so I shall be saved from my enemies.

Psalm 18:2-3

Meditation

I have no deep-rooted affections in this earth, and I desire to become daily more and more indifferent to all its fascinations, that my spirit may be purified as the spirit of my master is pure, and that I may be thus transformed into his likeness even while tabernacling in clay.

Walter Scott, *The Gospel Restored*, 218

Scripture

Beloved, I urge you as aliens and exiles to abstain from the desires of the flesh
that wage war against the soul. Conduct yourselves honorably among the Gentiles,
so that, though they malign you as evildoers, they may see your honorable deeds
and glorify God when he comes to judge.

1 Peter 2:11-12

Prayer

Father, make me less at home in this world. Let me feel myself an alien and stranger, knowing that you have brought me into your home. Deliver me from those enemies who would rob me of that home.

IDOLATRY

PSALM

Those who choose another god multiply their sorrows;
their drink offerings of blood I will not pour out
or take their names upon my lips.

PSALM 16:4

MEDITATION

Idolatry is the last and lowest degradation of humanity and required extreme penalties. These people had seen God's hand stretched out to save them. He had borne them out of Egypt from their cruel taskmasters. They had heard his voice from the mount. Was it possible for them to forget him? It was.

ASHLEY S. JOHNSON, *The Life of Trust*, 24

SCRIPTURE

"If our God whom we serve is able to deliver us from the furnace of blazing fire and out of your hand, O king, let him deliver us. But if not, be it known to you, O king, that we will not serve your gods and we will not worship the golden statue that you have set up."

DANIEL 3:17-18

PRAYER

Holy God, lead my heart away from idolatry. May I worship you alone and not the gods of this age. May I be willing to face the fire of ridicule rather than to conform to this world and its gods.

Asking God for Help

Psalm

The Lord answer you in the day of trouble!
The name of the God of Jacob protect you!
May he send you help from the sanctuary,
and give you support from Zion.

Psalm 20:1-2

Meditation

But what a blessed boon it is, that in every emergency of our lives, it is our privilege to ask help from God: in sickness, to ask for health; in danger, to ask for protection; in temptation and trial, to ask for strength; in moments of perplexity and doubt, to ask for wisdom and guidance.

J.H. Garrison, *Alone with God*, 75

Scripture

The Lord said to Moses, "Go on ahead of the people, and take some of the elders of Israel with you; take in your hand the staff with which you struck the Nile, and go. I will be standing there in front of you on the rock at Horeb. Strike the rock, and water will come out of it, so that the people may drink." Moses did so, in the sight of the elders of Israel.

Exodus 17:5-6

Prayer

Gracious God, give me what I need this day—water, bread, healing, protection, and guidance. I praise you and thank you for all your good gifts.

April 25

VICTORY OVER SIN

PSALM
For the Lord takes pleasure in his people;
he adorns the humble with victory.

PSALM 149:4

MEDITATION
The Holy Spirit is, then, the author of all our holiness; and in the struggle after victory over sin and temptation, "it helps our infirmities" and comforts us by seasonably bringing to our remembrance the promises of Christ, and "strengthens us with all might, in the new or inner person."

ALEXANDER CAMPBELL, *The Christian System*, 66

SCRIPTURE
Do not love the world or the things in the world. The love of the Father is not in those who love the world; for all that is in the world—the desire of the flesh, the desire of the eyes, the pride in riches—comes not from the Father but from the world. And the world and its desire are passing away, but those who do the will of God live forever.

1 JOHN 2:15-17

PRAYER
Father, fill me with your Holy Spirit this day, so I may have victory over sin and temptation. Pour your love into my heart through your Spirit so I may love you and not this world.

GOD'S CARE FOR US

PSALM

The Lord is a stronghold for the oppressed,
a stronghold in times of trouble.
And those who know your name put their trust in you,
for you, O Lord, have not forsaken those who seek you.

PSALM 9:9-10

MEDITATION

If God is our Father, really, truly, always, it follows that he hears us, for our earthly parents hear us, when, in our distress, we cry unto them. Our earthly parents not only try to supply the wants of their children, but they anticipate their wants, study their wants, and even suggest them. Is our heavenly Father as good and thoughtful as this? Beyond a single doubt.

ASHLEY S. JOHNSON, *The Life of Trust*, 33

SCRIPTURE

Humble yourselves therefore under the mighty hand of God, so that he may exalt you in due time. Cast all your anxiety on him, because he cares for you.

1 PETER 5:6-7

PRAYER

Thank you, that I can call you Father. I live in your tender care and trust you as my fortress against all trouble.

April 27

LOVE NOT THE WORLD

PSALM

O Lord, I love the house in which you dwell,
and the place where your glory abides.

PSALM 26:8

MEDITATION

No Christians then considered ought they possessed their own, but the Lord's, and cheerfully resigned them to promote his cause on earth. The Christians then loved not the world, nor the things of the world. They were crucified to the world, and the world to them.

BARTON W. STONE, *Christian Messenger* (1844), 144

SCRIPTURE

May you be made strong with all the strength that comes from his glorious power, and may you be prepared to endure everything with patience, while joyfully giving thanks to the Father, who has enabled you to share in the inheritance of the saints in the light. He has rescued us from the power of darkness and transferred us into the kingdom of his beloved Son, in whom we have redemption, the forgiveness of sins.

COLOSSIANS 1:11-14

PRAYER

Holy God, I confess the world is too much with me. Keep me from every idol that would capture my heart. May I live content in your kingdom this day.

April 28

THE SON OF GOD

PSALM

Do not forsake me, O Lord;
O my God, do not be far from me;
make haste to help me,
O Lord, my salvation.

PSALM 38:21-22

MEDITATION

The Divine Spirit, by the many predictions found in the Ancient Scriptures, had assumed the attitude of a voucher for the Messiah; that in his person and ministry certain great deeds should be accomplished by him.

WALTER SCOTT, *The Gospel Restored*, 136

SCRIPTURE

And when Jesus had been baptized, just as he came up from the water, suddenly the heavens were opened to him and he saw the Spirit of God descending like a dove and alighting on him. And a voice from heaven said, "This is my Son, the Beloved, with whom I am well pleased."

MATTHEW 3:16-17

PRAYER

Holy Father, I thank you that I am your child. Holy Spirit, fall on me as you did on Jesus. Son of God, Messiah, cleanse me from sin by the power of your obedience. May I know this day that I am beloved by God.

MATURE IN CHRIST

PSALM

Take delight in the Lord,
and he will give you the desires of your heart.
Commit your way to the Lord;
trust in him, and he will act.

PSALM 37:4-5

MEDITATION

That is to say, every disciple of Christ, in his measure, is to be a divine incarnation—an embodiment of the grace and virtues, and of that quality of life and character which belong to God.

J. H. GARRISON, *Alone with God*, 41

SCRIPTURE

To them God chose to make known how great among the Gentiles are the riches
of the glory of this mystery, which is Christ in you, the hope of glory. It is he whom we
proclaim, warning everyone and teaching everyone in all wisdom, so that we may present
everyone mature in Christ. For this I toil and struggle with all the energy
that he powerfully inspires within me.

COLOSSIANS 1:27-29

PRAYER

Father, thank you for placing Christ in me through your Holy Spirit. Lord Jesus, live in my heart and my life. Give me hope, wisdom, and energy to be mature in Christ.

April 30

THE FACE OF GOD

PSALM

Hear a just cause, O Lord; attend to my cry;
give ear to my prayer from lips free of deceit.
From you let my vindication come;
let your eyes see the right.
If you try my heart, if you visit me by night,
if you test me, you will find no wickedness in me;
my mouth does not transgress.
As for me, I shall behold your face in righteousness;
when I awake I shall be satisfied, beholding your likeness.

PSALM 17:1-3, 15

MEDITATION

Happy are they who are permitted thus to approach to behold the glory of God in the face of Jesus Christ as he appears in his holy temple, and to dwell in the house of the Lord forever. Who can behold without loving him? Who can love him without joy? We set our affections on things above when we place them upon Jesus.

ROBERT RICHARDSON, *Communings in the Sanctuary*, 62

SCRIPTURE

But now, dear lady, I ask you, not as though I were writing you a new commandment,
but one we have had from the beginning, let us love one another.

2 JOHN 1:5

PRAYER

God of love, may I seek your presence this day by placing all my desires on Jesus.

FOLLOWING CHRIST

PSALM

Sing praises to the Lord, O you his faithful ones,
and give thanks to his holy name.
For his anger is but for a moment;
his favor is for a lifetime.
Weeping may linger for the night,
but joy comes with the morning.

PSALM 30:4-5

MEDITATION

It was not merely in what we usually call great and important matters that
Christ followed the will of his Father, but also in even the most minute and
circumstantial events of his life.

ROBERT MILLIGAN, *Scheme of Redemption*, 246

SCRIPTURE

So if you have been raised with Christ, seek the things that are above, where Christ is,
seated at the right hand of God. Set your minds on things that are above, not on things
that are on earth, for you have died, and your life is hidden with Christ in God. When
Christ who is your life is revealed, then you also will be revealed with him in glory.

COLOSSIANS 3:1-4

PRAYER

God of joy, hide my life in Christ today. May I seek the things above, die to
myself, and live for you. Lord Jesus, come quickly and take me to be with you
in glory.

Obedience

Psalm

But the steadfast love of the Lord is from everlasting to everlasting
on those who fear him,
and his righteousness to children's children,
to those who keep his covenant
and remember to do his commandments.

Psalm 103:17-18

Meditation

Let us hear his sayings and do them, that he may liken us to wise people; let us keep his commandments, that we may enter in through the gate into the city, and have the right to the tree of life.

Benjamin Franklin, *The Gospel Preacher*, vol. 2, 53-54

Scripture

Everyone then who hears these words of mine and acts on them will be like a wise man who built his house on rock. The rain fell, the floods came, and the winds blew and beat on that house, but it did not fall, because it had been founded on rock.

Matthew 7:24-25

Prayer

Father, give me a heart of faith that will hear and obey your commandments. Lead me on the path of your covenant and your steadfast love, so I may share in your wisdom.

IDOLATRY

PSALM
If we had forgotten the name of our God,
or spread out our hands to a strange god,
would not God discover this?
For he knows the secrets of the heart.

PSALM 44:20-21

MEDITATION
The history of Israel and of all other nations that have fallen into idolatry proves beyond a doubt that idolatry is only another name for degeneration, degradation, and wretchedness.

ASHLEY S. JOHNSON, *The Life of Trust*, 24

SCRIPTURE
The Lord said to Moses, "Go down at once! Your people, whom you brought up out of the land of Egypt, have acted perversely; they have been quick to turn aside from the way that I commanded them; they have cast for themselves an image of a calf, and have worshiped it and sacrificed to it, and said, 'These are your gods, O Israel, who brought you up out of the land of Egypt!'"

EXODUS 32:7-8

PRAYER
Holy God, I live in a world of degeneration, degradation, and wretchedness. I confess that I am too much a part of that world. Keep me from idols—greed, power, pleasure, self—and turn my heart to worship you only.

May 4

LORD JESUS

PSALM

Your throne, O God, endures forever and ever.
Your royal scepter is a scepter of equity;
you love righteousness and hate wickedness.
Therefore God, your God, has anointed you
with the oil of gladness
beyond your companions.

PSALM 45:6-7

MEDITATION

He is now the Lord of hosts: legions of angels, the armies of the skies, are given to him—for what? That he might be able to do all for us that our condition needs. It was for us he became a Prophet, for us he became a Priest, for us he has been made Lord of Hosts, King of the Universe, Judge and avenger of all. He is Lord of life, Lord of the Spirit, Lord of all.

ALEXANDER CAMPBELL, *The Christian System*, 51

SCRIPTURE

For in him all the fullness of God was pleased to dwell, and through him God was
pleased to reconcile to himself all things, whether on earth or in heaven,
by making peace through the blood of his cross.

COLOSSIANS 1:19-20

PRAYER

Lord Jesus, be Lord of my life today. May I praise you as the fullness of God, Prophet, Priest, and King.

MONEY

PSALM

Do not be afraid when some become rich,
when the wealth of their houses increases.
For when they die they will carry nothing away;
their wealth will not go down after them.

PSALM 49:16-17

MEDITATION

Our Lord's example was certainly given for our imitation. He could have commanded the wealth of the universe; but he became poor, that we through his poverty might be made rich. The foxes had holes, the birds of the air had nests, but the Son of Man had no where to lay his head. His example was a veto against covetousness, and a rich ministry.

BARTON W. STONE, *Christian Messenger* (1843), 369

SCRIPTURE

If anyone strikes you on the cheek, offer the other also; and from anyone who takes away your coat do not withhold even your shirt. Give to everyone who begs from you; and if anyone takes away your goods, do not ask for them again. Do to others as you would have them do to you.

LUKE 6:29-31

PRAYER

God who gives all good gifts, may I trust you this day for daily bread. Free me from greed and covetousness. May I give freely to others as you have given to me.

May 6

THE WORD OF GOD

PSALM

But to the wicked God says:
"What right have you to recite my statutes,
or take my covenant on your lips?
For you hate discipline, and you cast my words behind you."

PSALM 50:16-17

MEDITATION

The faith of the child of God is not in humans, in the traditions, doctrines, and commandments of humans; nor in succession of human officers, churches, or ordinances, but in God, Christ, and the eternal Spirit, as revealed to us in the Scriptures.

BENJAMIN FRANKLIN, *The Gospel Preacher*, VOL. 2, 53

SCRIPTURE

We also constantly give thanks to God for this, that when you received the word of God
that you heard from us, you accepted it not as a human word but as what it really is,
God's word, which is also at work in you believers.

1 THESSALONIANS 2:13

PRAYER

Father, may I listen to your words in Scripture to increase my faith in the Word made flesh. Give me the discipline to keep your words ever before me.

TRUTH

PSALM

You desire truth in the inward being;
therefore teach me wisdom in my secret heart.
Purge me with hyssop, and I shall be clean;
wash me, and I shall be whiter than snow.

PSALM 51:6-7

MEDITATION

With what ardent desire, then, should the soul seek this ever-living and life-giving truth. With what readiness should it part with all that earth holds dear to secure the possession of this inestimable boon. And with what earnestness should it devote its powers and energies to the discovery and appreciation of that truth which is at once its light and life, its peace, its glory, and its joy.

ROBERT RICHARDSON, *Communings in the Sanctuary*, 68

SCRIPTURE

Let your word be "Yes, Yes" or "No, No"; anything more than this comes from the evil one.

MATTHEW 5:37

PRAYER

God of truth, implant your truth in my inner being. May I speak truth, think truth, and live truth. May Jesus who is the Truth live in me this day.

May 8

The Glory of the Lord

Psalm

All the kings of the earth shall praise you, O Lord,
for they have heard the words of your mouth.
They shall sing of the ways of the Lord,
for great is the glory of the Lord.

Psalm 138:4-5

Meditation

The human mind staggers at the thought of God. In the hour of solitude I contemplate Him until with heart over burdened and hand upon my mouth, I bow my head in the dust. O the greatness, the awfulness, the mystery of God; O the littleness, the weakness, the ignorance of humanity!

Ashley S. Johnson, *The Life of Trust*, 25

Scripture

Then the cloud covered the tent of meeting, and the glory of the Lord filled the tabernacle. Moses was not able to enter the tent of meeting because the cloud settled upon it, and the glory of the Lord filled the tabernacle.

Exodus 40:34-35

Prayer

Lord, I fall before you in awe of your glory. What words can tell your greatness? I contemplate you in silence, for there are no words that can describe you. May your glory fill me this day.

WORLDLINESS

PSALM

He who sits in the heavens laughs;
the Lord has them in derision.
Then he will speak to them in his wrath,
and terrify them in his fury, saying,
"I have set my king on Zion, my holy hill."

PSALM 2:4-6

MEDITATION

The god of this world has blinded the eyes of professed Christians and is fast leading them deceived into their ranks into captivity—into bondage and death. Christians are virtually forsaking the government and laws of heaven, to prop up and sustain the governments and laws of humanity, whether ecclesiastical or political.

BARTON W. STONE, *Christian Messenger* (1844), 226-227

SCRIPTURE

Enter through the narrow gate; for the gate is wide and the road is easy that leads to destruction, and there are many who take it. For the gate is narrow and the road is hard that leads to life, and there are few who find it.

MATTHEW 7:13-14

PRAYER

Father, lead me this day away from the easy path of conformity to this world. Give me clean hands and a pure heart.

May 10

PRAYER

PSALM

Praise is due to you, O God, in Zion;
and to you shall vows be performed,
O you who answer prayer!
To you all flesh shall come.

PSALM 65:1-2

MEDITATION

An hour in the closet may, therefore, do more to rectify and strengthen our religious impressions and moral faculties than many days of ordinary service in the public congregation.

ROBERT MILLIGAN, *A Brief Treatise on Prayer*, 16

SCRIPTURE

But whenever you pray, go into your room and shut the door and pray to your Father who is in secret; and your Father who sees in secret will reward you. When you are praying, do not heap up empty phrases as the Gentiles do; for they think that they will be heard because of their many words. Do not be like them, for your Father knows what you need before you ask him.

MATTHEW 6:6-8

PRAYER

God of love, strengthen my resolve to search for you with my whole heart. Give me the discipline to regularly spend time alone with you, knowing that you hear and answer.

May 11

ALONE WITH GOD

PSALM

For God alone my soul waits in silence;
from him comes my salvation.
He alone is my rock and my salvation,
my fortress; I shall never be shaken.

PSALM 62:1-2

MEDITATION

O the quiet holy joy of the silent hour, when the soul is alone with God! Have you learned to love it, dear reader? If not, you have yet to attain to one of the purest and sweetest pleasures possible to the Christian in this life.

J.H. GARRISON, *Alone with God*, 21

SCRIPTURE

For God has destined us not for wrath but for obtaining salvation through our Lord Jesus Christ, who died for us, so that whether we are awake or asleep we may live with him. Therefore encourage one another and build up each other, as indeed you are doing.

1 THESSALONIANS 5:9-11

PRAYER

My Lord and God, thank you for the joy of time spent alone with you. May I be shaped in that time into the image of Jesus, so I can faithfully wait on him and encourage others to do so.

May 12

The Poor

Psalm

For he delivers the needy when they call,
the poor and those who have no helper.
He has pity on the weak and the needy,
and saves the lives of the needy.

Psalm 72:12-13

Meditation

I think that sometimes in our great anxiety for the future of those about us that we forget that they have a present life. I would not hear less about the hereafter, but I would hear more of the present, the realities of food and raiment and shelter for those whose souls are no more precious in the sight of their Creator than their bodies!

Ashley S. Johnson, *The Life of Trust*, 171

Scripture

When you reap the harvest of your land, you shall not reap to the very edges of your field,
or gather the gleanings of your harvest. You shall not strip your vineyard bare, or gather
the fallen grapes of your vineyard; you shall leave them for the poor and the alien:
I am the Lord your God.

Leviticus 19:9-10

Prayer

Lord Jesus, you bring good news to the poor. Give me a heart of love to give freely to those in need.

May 13

MOUNT ZION

PSALM

O God, why do you cast us off for ever?
Why does your anger smoke against the sheep of your pasture?
Remember your congregation, which you acquired long ago,
which you redeemed to be the tribe of your heritage.
Remember Mount Zion, where you came to dwell.

PSALM 74:1-2

MEDITATION

Thus commenced the reign of Heaven, on the day of Pentecost, in the person
of the Messiah, the Son of God, and the anointed Monarch of the universe.
Under him his people, saved from their sins, have received a kingdom which
cannot be shaken or removed.

ALEXANDER CAMPBELL, *The Christian System*, 171

SCRIPTURE

For to this end Christ died and lived again,
so that he might be Lord of both the dead and the living.
Why do you pass judgment on your brother or sister? Or you, why do you despise your
brother or sister? For we will all stand before the judgment seat of God. For it is written,
"As I live, says the Lord, every knee shall bow to me,
and every tongue shall give praise to God."

ROMANS 14:9-11

PRAYER

Lord, may I bow the knee to you this day. Rule in my heart as you reign over all.

May 14

Judging Others

Psalm

Praise the Lord!
O give thanks to the Lord, for he is good;
for his steadfast love endures for ever.
Who can utter the mighty doings of the Lord,
or declare all his praise?
Happy are those who observe justice,
who do righteousness at all times.

Psalm 106:1-3

Meditation

We are also persuaded that as no one can be judged for a brother or sister, so no one can judge for a brother or sister: but that everyone must be allowed to judge, as everyone must bear his or her own judgment, and must give account to God.

Thomas Campbell, *The Declaration and Address*

Scripture

Let us therefore no longer pass judgment on one another, but resolve instead never to put a stumbling block or hindrance in the way of another.

Romans 14:13

Prayer

Lord God, you judge with righteous judgment. Help me not to judge my brothers and sisters, but to treat them the way I want to be treated.

May 15

LOVE OF NEIGHBOR

PSALM

I believe that I shall see the goodness of the Lord
in the land of the living.
Wait for the Lord;
be strong, and let your heart take courage;
wait for the Lord!

PSALM 27:13-14

MEDITATION

It is here within these sacred precincts that we should realize that divine spiritual unity which can be preserved only by the bond of peace. Partakers of one bread, we are one body. Animated by one spirit, cheered by one hope, led by one Lord, sustained by one God and Father of all, it is here we should ever feel the eternal ties which bind us to each other.

ROBERT RICHARDSON, *Communings in the Sanctuary*, 92

SCRIPTURE

We who are strong ought to put up with the failings of the weak,
and not to please ourselves. Each of us must please our neighbor
for the good purpose of building up the neighbor.

ROMANS 15:1-2

PRAYER

Jesus, my brother, open my eyes to the needs of my brothers, sisters, and neighbors. May I this day please them and not myself.

May 16

THE MYSTERY OF OUR RELIGION

PSALM

Ascribe to the Lord, O families of the peoples,
ascribe to the Lord glory and strength.
Ascribe to the Lord the glory due his name;
bring an offering, and come into his courts.

PSALM 96:7-8

MEDITATION

By this human nature he is our brother; bone of our bone and flesh of our flesh. He can approach the Father as a Son, and approach us as our brother. He loves the Father, and he also loves us.

BENJAMIN FRANKLIN, *The Gospel Preacher*, VOL. 2, 322-323

SCRIPTURE

Without any doubt, the mystery of our religion is great:
He was revealed in flesh,
vindicated in spirit,
seen by angels,
proclaimed among Gentiles,
believed in throughout the world,
taken up in glory.

1 TIMOTHY 3:16

PRAYER

God of glory, you took on our flesh in Jesus! Thank you for this amazing gift of revelation!

May 17

Overcoming Temptation

Psalm

But let your hand be upon the one at your right hand,
the one whom you made strong for yourself.
Then we will never turn back from you;
give us life, and we will call on your name.

Psalm 80:17-18

Meditation

In personal holiness, justice and the love of God, we have the outline of true character. With these we can hopefully wait the coming of our Lord Jesus Christ.

Walter Scott, *The Messiahship*, 338

Scripture

Blessed is anyone who endures temptation. Such a one has stood the test and will receive the crown of life that the Lord has promised to those who love him. No one, when tempted, should say, "I am being tempted by God"; for God cannot be tempted by evil and he himself tempts no one. But one is tempted by one's own desire, being lured and enticed by it; then, when that desire has conceived, it gives birth to sin, and that sin, when it is fully grown, gives birth to death. Do not be deceived, my beloved.

James 1:12-16

Prayer

Holy God, make me holy this day through the power of your Holy Spirit in me. Give me the power of overcoming temptation by calling on your name.

May 18

God's Gifts

Psalm

He divided the sea and let them pass through it,
and made the waters stand like a heap.
In the daytime he led them with a cloud,
and all night long with a fiery light.
He split rocks open in the wilderness,
and gave them drink abundantly as from the deep.
He made streams come out of the rock,
and caused waters to flow down like rivers.

Psalm 78:13-16

Meditation

These all seem to have sprung up instantly, in a state of perfection, at the command of God. Islands and continents, which, on the subsiding of the waters, seemed naked and barren as the flinty rock, were now adorned with all manner of trees, and fruits, and flowers. This is another fine illustration of the sublime and beautiful.

Robert Milligan, *Scheme of Redemption*, 29

Scripture

Every generous act of giving, with every perfect gift, is from above, coming down from
the Father of lights, with whom there is no variation or shadow due to change.
In fulfillment of his own purpose he gave us birth by the word of truth, so that we
would become a kind of first fruits of his creatures.

James 1:17-18

Prayer

Loving Creator, may I bask in the warmth of your good gifts this day. Make me ever thankful.

May 19

CONFESSION

PSALM

I hate the double-minded, but I love your law.
You are my hiding place and my shield;
I hope in your word.
Go away from me, you evildoers,
that I may keep the commandments of my God.

PSALM 119:113-115

MEDITATION

Holiness is wholeness. It is completeness, as relates to our ethical nature. It is spiritual sanity. It is moral health and soundness. It is our normal condition— that for which we were created. Sin is the abnormal, the destructive thing, that like an insidious poison has corrupted the fountains of our being and polluted all the streams of human life.

J.H. GARRISON, *The Holy Spirit*, 168

SCRIPTURE

Are any among you suffering? They should pray. Are any cheerful? They should sing songs of praise. Are any among you sick? They should call for the elders of the church and have them pray over them, anointing them with oil in the name of the Lord. The prayer of faith will save the sick, and the Lord will raise them up; and anyone who has committed sins will be forgiven. Therefore confess your sins to one another, and pray for one another, so that you may be healed. The prayer of the righteous is powerful and effective.

JAMES 5:13-16

PRAYER

Father, have mercy on me, a sinner! May I confess to you and to others so I may know your healing.

May 20

JESUS AND HUMANITY

PSALM

When I look at your heavens, the work of your fingers,
the moon and the stars that you have established;
what are human beings that you are mindful of them,
mortals that you care for them?

PSALM 8:3-4

MEDITATION

What a wonderful thought, that he, who was rich with the Father in heaven, should have become poor, that we, through his poverty, should be made rich! This our Lord did—become so poor that he had not where to lay his head, and that, too, when those he came to bless had plenty, and not only would not bestow anything for his support, but despised and rejected him.

BENJAMIN FRANKLIN, *The Gospel Preacher*, VOL. 1, 387

SCRIPTURE

It was fitting that God, for whom and through whom all things exist, in bringing many children to glory, should make the pioneer of their salvation perfect through sufferings. For the one who sanctifies and those who are sanctified all have one Father. For this reason Jesus is not ashamed to call them brothers and sisters.

HEBREWS 2:10-11

PRAYER

God of love, you so loved the world that you gave your Son! You think so highly of humanity, that you became one of us! Brother Jesus, may I show your love to all those around me.

May 21

THE TRANSFIGURATION

PSALM

You who live in the shelter of the Most High,
who abide in the shadow of the Almighty,
will say to the Lord, "My refuge and my fortress;
my God, in whom I trust."

PSALM 91:1-2

MEDITATION

But when our meditations overleap the negative, and by the Transfiguration ascend into the positive of eternal life, all is sunshine, unclouded glory, and eternal day. The problem of humanity is solved. Humans are immortal; and the principle end of our existence is "to glorify God and to enjoy him forever."

WALTER SCOTT, *The Messiahship*, 249

SCRIPTURE

Now about eight days after these sayings Jesus took with him Peter and John and James,
and went up on the mountain to pray. And while he was praying, the appearance of his
face changed, and his clothes became dazzling white. Suddenly they saw two men,
Moses and Elijah, talking to him.

LUKE 9:28-30

PRAYER

Lord Jesus, may I this day meditate on your glory. Reveal yourself to me as you did to those disciples, so I may praise you alone.

May 22

God Hears

Psalm

Make us glad for as many days as you have afflicted us,
and for as many years as we have seen evil.
Let your work be manifest to your servants,
and your glorious power to their children.
Let the favor of the Lord our God be upon us,
and prosper for us the work of our hands—
O prosper the work of our hands!

Psalm 90:15-17

Meditation

What of the lessons of redemption? Does God hear us? He heard his people in olden times. No one who believes the Bible disputes or doubts this, but does He hear us and hear us now? I want to emphasize the two words. Us! Now!!

Ashley S. Johnson, *The Life of Trust*, 19

Scripture

In the days of his flesh, Jesus offered up prayers and supplications, with loud cries and tears, to the one who was able to save him from death, and he was heard because of his reverent submission. Although he was a Son, he learned obedience through what he suffered; and having been made perfect, he became the source of eternal salvation for all who obey him, having been designated by God a high priest according to the order of Melchizedek.

Hebrews 5:7-10

Prayer

O Lord, hear my cry! Increase my trust that you indeed hear my prayers as you heard the cries of Jesus.

GRACE

PSALM

Come and hear, all you who fear God,
and I will tell what he has done for me.

PSALM 66:16

MEDITATION

Grace is a perfection of God. It is the beginning and ending of our salvation. From it bursts forth the ten thousand gifts to us—temporal and spiritual—called the gifts of grace, so often found in the scriptures.

BARTON W. STONE, *Christian Messenger* (1843), 296

SCRIPTURE

But God, who is rich in mercy, out of the great love with which he loved us even when we were dead through our trespasses, made us alive together with Christ—by grace you have been saved—and raised us up with him and seated us with him in the heavenly places in Christ Jesus, so that in the ages to come he might show the immeasurable riches of his grace in kindness toward us in Christ Jesus. For by grace you have been saved through faith, and this is not your own doing; it is the gift of God—not the result of works, so that no one may boast. For we are what he has made us, created in Christ Jesus for good works, which God prepared beforehand to be our way of life.

EPHESIANS 2:4-10

PRAYER

God of grace, open my heart to the amazing gifts of grace you have for me today. May I share your grace with others through the good works you have prepared for me to do.

May 24

DEDICATION

PSALM

How long, O Lord? Will you hide yourself forever?
How long will your wrath burn like fire?
Remember how short my time is—
for what vanity you have created all mortals.

PSALM 89:46-47

MEDITATION

One who lives for self has not yet learned the alphabet of Christianity. What an all-controlling influence, then, must the fact of real discipleship of Christ exert over the whole area of one's life, in all its aims and activities. Christ enthroned in the heart must be the regnant force in our lives, if we are indeed his disciples.

J.H. GARRISON, *Alone with God*, 65

SCRIPTURE

As they were going along the road, someone said to him, "I will follow you wherever you go." And Jesus said to him, "Foxes have holes, and birds of the air have nests; but the Son of Man has nowhere to lay his head." To another he said, "Follow me." But he said, "Lord, first let me go and bury my father." But Jesus said to him, "Let the dead bury their own dead; but as for you, go and proclaim the kingdom of God." Another said, "I will follow you, Lord; but let me first say farewell to those at my home." Jesus said to him, "No one who puts a hand to the plow and looks back is fit for the kingdom of God."

LUKE 9:57-62

PRAYER

Lord Jesus, forgive my feeble attempts to follow you. May I forsake all and follow you wherever you go, even to the cross!

HOPE

PSALM

If the Lord had not been my help,
my soul would soon have lived in the land of silence.
When I thought, "My foot is slipping,"
your steadfast love, O Lord, held me up.
When the cares of my heart are many,
your consolations cheer my soul.

PSALM 94:17-19

MEDITATION

Glory, honor, immortality, eternal life, and full and free salvation are by him offered to the world, on the condition that they believe in and obey the Savior. O glorious hope! And such is the hope, which the good and gracious God has set before the ruined world subjected by him to death.

BARTON W. STONE, *Christian Messenger* (1844), 157

SCRIPTURE

We have this hope, a sure and steadfast anchor of the soul, a hope that enters the inner shrine behind the curtain, where Jesus, a forerunner on our behalf, has entered, having become a high priest forever according to the order of Melchizedek.

HEBREWS 6:19-20

PRAYER

God of love, in the trials of life, in the daily sameness of life, give me hope.

May 26

THE POWER OF CHRIST

PSALM

With my mouth I will give great thanks to the Lord;
I will praise him in the midst of the throng.
For he stands at the right hand of the needy,
to save them from those who would condemn them to death.

PSALM 109:30-31

MEDITATION

With an ineffable sweetness of spirit he opened the human understanding or shut the heart; he could create bread, blast a tree, subdue a colt, open the blind eyes, unstop the deaf ears, unloose the dumb tongue, or recall the dead; create fish, provide a meal, or vanish from supper; discern the thoughts of the heart, detect the traitor, read his treason, and foretell his fate. These are some of his doings, but the full thunder of his power what heart can comprehend?

WALTER SCOTT, *The Messiahship*, 258

SCRIPTURE

At that same hour Jesus rejoiced in the Holy Spirit and said, "I thank you, Father,
Lord of heaven and earth, because you have hidden these things from the wise and the
intelligent and have revealed them to infants; yes, Father, for such was your gracious will.
All things have been handed over to me by my Father; and no one knows who the Son is
except the Father, or who the Father is except the Son and anyone to whom
the Son chooses to reveal him."

LUKE 10:21-22

PRAYER

Lord Jesus, whose hand worked wonders, open my eyes to your power in me today.

May 27

REDEMPTION

PSALM

For he remembered his holy promise,
and Abraham, his servant.
So he brought his people out with joy,
his chosen ones with singing.
He gave them the lands of the nations,
and they took possession of the wealth of the peoples,
that they might keep his statutes
and observe his laws. Praise the Lord!

PSALM 105:42-45

MEDITATION

O, that every one of us had a heart like that of our Redeemer, and that our lives corresponded in all possible respects with his life! Then, indeed, would the wilderness and solitary parts of the earth soon be glad, and the deserts would rejoice and blossom as the rose.

ROBERT MILLIGAN, *Scheme of Redemption*, 250

SCRIPTURE

Consequently he is able for all time to save those who approach God through him, since he always lives to make intercession for them. For it was fitting that we should have such a high priest, holy, blameless, undefiled, separated from sinners, and exalted above the heavens.

HEBREWS 7:25-26

PRAYER

Jesus, my Priest, intercede for me! May I in turn intercede for others in your holy name.

May 28

OUR SHEPHERD

PSALM

*Let the redeemed of the Lord say so, those he redeemed from trouble
and gathered in from the lands, from the east and from the west,
from the north and from the south.
Some wandered in desert wastes, finding no way to an inhabited town;
hungry and thirsty, their soul fainted within them.
Then they cried to the Lord in their trouble, and he delivered them from their distress;
he led them by a straight way, until they reached an inhabited town.*

PSALM 107:2-7

MEDITATION

As the sheep never lies down in the green and tender grass until its wants are
fully met and it is perfectly content, what a striking and beautiful picture this is
of the soul's peace and contentment in Christ. Faithful and tender shepherd
that he is, he will not desert us, though we walk through the valley and shadow
of death.

J.H. GARRISON, *Alone with God*, 32

SCRIPTURE

*I will set up over them one shepherd, my servant David, and he shall feed them: he shall
feed them and be their shepherd. And I, the Lord, will be their God, and my servant David
shall be prince among them; I, the Lord, have spoken.*

EZEKIEL 34:23-24

PRAYER

Jesus, great Shepherd of the sheep, guide me this day with your firm and
tender hand.

REDEMPTION

PSALM

I will give thanks to you, O Lord, among the peoples,
and I will sing praises to you among the nations.
For your steadfast love is higher than the heavens,
and your faithfulness reaches to the clouds.

PSALM 108:3-4

MEDITATION

I do not mean to say that the problem of redemption was then fully and perfectly understood. By no means. It is not even yet so understood. And it will, in all probability, require an eternity to trace out and comprehend all the effects of the blood of Christ on the government of God and the interests of humanity.

ROBERT MILLIGAN, *Scheme of Redemption*, 232

SCRIPTURE

For if the blood of goats and bulls, with the sprinkling of the ashes of a heifer, sanctifies those who have been defiled so that their flesh is purified, how much more will the blood of Christ, who through the eternal Spirit offered himself without blemish to God, purify our conscience from dead works to worship the living God!.

HEBREWS 9:13-14

PRAYER

Loving God, what a sacrifice you gave for me on the cross! This day make my conscience pure so I can serve you in love.

May 30

THE COMFORTER

PSALM

I will extol you, my God and King,
and bless your name forever and ever.
Every day I will bless you,
and praise your name forever and ever.
Great is the Lord, and greatly to be praised;
his greatness is unsearchable.

PSALM 145:1-3

MEDITATION

Notice, too, that this Comforter and personal helper who Jesus promised to send was not simply with them, as heretofore, but in them. Another contrast is, that while Jesus' presence with them was brief, this other Comforter was to abide with them forever.

J. H. GARRISON, *The Holy Spirit*, 115

SCRIPTURE

I have said these things to you while I am still with you. But the Advocate, the Holy Spirit, whom the Father will send in my name, will teach you everything, and remind you of all that I have said to you. Peace I leave with you; my peace I give to you. I do not give to you as the world gives. Do not let your hearts be troubled, and do not let them be afraid.

JOHN 14:25-27

PRAYER

Lord Jesus, thank you for being in me through your Holy Spirit. May your Spirit guide and comfort me this day.

May 31

New Creation

Psalm

By this I know that you are pleased with me; because my enemy has not triumphed over me.
But you have upheld me because of my integrity, and set me in your presence forever.

Psalm 41:11-12

Meditation

We need something more to make us happy than mere admission into a place of happiness. We must be regenerated, made new creatures, or we could not be happy among the happy, in heaven itself. Turn, then, to the Lord, enter the covenant, and live forever. Come with Christ, become conformed to him and made inexpressibly happy in him now and prepared to enjoy him forever and ever.

Benjamin Franklin, *The Gospel Preacher*, vol. 1, 303-304

Scripture

From now on, therefore, we regard no one from a human point of view;
even though we once knew Christ from a human point of view, we know him no longer in
that way. So if anyone is in Christ, there is a new creation: everything old has passed
away; see, everything has become new! All this is from God, who reconciled us to himself
through Christ, and has given us the ministry of reconciliation; that is, in Christ God was
reconciling the world to himself, not counting their trespasses against them, and
entrusting the message of reconciliation to us. So we are ambassadors for Christ, since
God is making his appeal through us; we entreat you on behalf of Christ,
be reconciled to God. For our sake he made him to be sin who knew no sin,
so that in him we might become the righteousness of God.

2 Corinthians 5:16-21

Prayer

Creator God, you have made me anew. Make me an ambassador with the message of reconciliation.

June 1

GOD'S TABLE

PSALM

Clap your hands, all you peoples;
shout to God with loud songs of joy.
For the Lord, the Most High, is awesome,
a great king over all the earth.
He subdued peoples under us,
and nations under our feet.
He chose our heritage for us,
the pride of Jacob whom he loves.

PSALM 47:1-4

MEDITATION

How precious the life which this spiritual food imparts. How just and striking the relation between this life and the food by which it is sustained. As the life must correspond with that by which it is maintained, celestial life can be nourished only by the bread of heaven.

ROBERT RICHARDSON, *Communings in the Sanctuary*, 19

SCRIPTURE

And you shall eat there in the presence of the Lord your God, you and your households together, rejoicing in all the undertakings in which the Lord your God has blessed you. You shall not act as we are acting here today, all of us according to our own desires, for you have not yet come into the rest and the possession that the Lord your God is giving you.

DEUTERONOMY 12:7-9

PRAYER

Father, give me this day my daily bread. Feed me at the table of Jesus with the living bread.

June 2

Room in Our Hearts

Psalm

Why should I fear in times of trouble,
when the iniquity of my persecutors surrounds me,
those who trust in their wealth
and boast of the abundance of their riches?

Psalm 49:5-6

Meditation

Humans charged with such responsibilities as that involved in the making known of the way of salvation, would not, could not, fail to realize their weakness and seek Divine help, and in view of the vastness, urgency, and almost boundlessness of the harvest, they would naturally feel their incapacity, their utter helplessness in view of the task, and cry to the Lord of the harvest for help.

Ashley S. Johnson, *The Life of Trust* , 140

Scripture

Make room in your hearts for us; we have wronged no one, we have corrupted no one, we have taken advantage of no one. I do not say this to condemn you, for I said before that you are in our hearts, to die together and to live together. I often boast about you; I have great pride in you; I am filled with consolation; I am overjoyed in all our affliction.

2 Corinthians 7:2-4

Prayer

Father, help me to open my heart and share the good news with others.

June 3

PRAYER

PSALM
Offer to God a sacrifice of thanksgiving,
and pay your vows to the Most High.
Call on me in the day of trouble;
I will deliver you, and you shall glorify me.

PSALM 50:14-15

MEDITATION
These Scriptures, and numerous others with which the word of God abounds, show that the followers of Christ, in this wilderness of sin through which they are passing, need every encouragement and support they can have; indeed, that they are in a dangerous land, making a perilous pilgrimage, and need help.

BENJAMIN FRANKLIN, *The Gospel Preacher*, VOL. 2, 179

SCRIPTURE
He also told this parable to some who trusted in themselves that they were righteous and regarded others with contempt: "Two men went up to the temple to pray, one a Pharisee and the other a tax collector. The Pharisee, standing by himself, was praying thus, 'God, I thank you that I am not like other people: thieves, rogues, adulterers, or even like this tax collector. I fast twice a week; I give a tenth of all my income.' But the tax collector, standing far off, would not even look up to heaven, but was beating his breast and saying, 'God, be merciful to me, a sinner!' I tell you, this man went down to his home justified rather than the other; for all who exalt themselves will be humbled, but all who humble themselves will be exalted."

LUKE 18:9-14

PRAYER
Lord Jesus Christ, Son of God, be merciful to me, a sinner.

June 4

CELEBRATION

PSALM

You have multiplied, O Lord my God,
your wondrous deeds and your thoughts toward us;
none can compare with you.
Were I to proclaim and tell of them,
they would be more than can be counted.

PSALM 40:5

MEDITATION

It also follows that whenever a company is called together, all of which are disciples of Christ, to eat and drink, and to be cheerful, such a feast is a system of means which is wisely adapted to enliven Christian affection, and prepare us for the entertainments of heaven.

ALEXANDER CAMPBELL, *Christian Baptist* (1826), 75

SCRIPTURE

"When the Egyptians treated us harshly and afflicted us, by imposing hard labor on us, we cried to the Lord, the God of our ancestors; the Lord heard our voice and saw our affliction, our toil, and our oppression. The Lord brought us out of Egypt with a mighty hand and an outstretched arm, with a terrifying display of power, and with signs and wonders; and he brought us into this place and gave us this land, a land flowing with milk and honey. So now I bring the first of the fruit of the ground that you, O Lord, have given me." You shall set it down before the Lord your God and bow down before the Lord your God. Then you, together with the Levites and the aliens who reside among you, shall celebrate with all the bounty that the Lord your God has given to you and to your house.

DEUTERONOMY 26:6-11

PRAYER

God of deliverance, may I celebrate your gifts to me with all who are around me this day.

June 5

CHILDREN

PSALM

Give ear to my prayer, O God; do not hide yourself from my supplication.
Attend to me, and answer me; I am troubled in my complaint.
I am distraught by the noise of the enemy, because of the clamor of the wicked.
For they bring trouble upon me, and in anger they cherish enmity against me.
Cast your burden on the Lord, and he will sustain you;
he will never permit the righteous to be moved.

PSALM 55:1-3, 22

MEDITATION

Let parents remember and do their duty, bring up their children in the nurture, fear, and admonition of the Lord, by teaching them his ways; and by their admonitions and example, encourage them to do them. Were they to spend the Lord's Day in this exercise, and in worship, they would see the fruits of their labors.

BARTON W. STONE, *Christian Messenger* (1835), 18

SCRIPTURE

People were bringing even infants to him that he might touch them; and when the disciples saw it, they sternly ordered them not to do it. But Jesus called for them and said, "Let the little children come to me, and do not stop them; for it is to such as these that the kingdom of God belongs. Truly I tell you, whoever does not receive the kingdom of God as a little child will never enter it."

LUKE 18:15-17

PRAYER

Lord Jesus, may I receive the kingdom as a child. Father God, may I lead children in the right paths as you have led me.

June 6

THE KINGDOM OF GOD

PSALM

The Lord sits enthroned over the flood;
the Lord sits enthroned as king forever.
May the Lord give strength to his people!
May the Lord bless his people with peace!

PSALM 29:10-11

MEDITATION

The supreme law of this kingdom is love—love to the King and love of each other. From this law all its religious homage and morality flow.

ALEXANDER CAMPBELL, THE CHRISTIAN SYSTEM, 157

SCRIPTURE

"Now have come the salvation and the power and the kingdom of our God
and the authority of his Messiah, for the accuser of our comrades has been thrown down,
who accuses them day and night before our God. But they have conquered him
by the blood of the Lamb and by the word of their testimony, for they did not
cling to life even in the face of death."

REVELATION 12:10-11

PRAYER

God of love, King of the universe, reign in my heart today. May I triumph over evil through the blood of the Lamb.

June 7

SIGHT

PSALM

Happy are those whom you choose and bring near
to live in your courts.
We shall be satisfied with the goodness of your house,
your holy temple.

PSALM 65:4

MEDITATION

Happy they who are permitted thus to approach to behold the glory of God in the face of Jesus Christ as he appears in his holy temple, and to dwell in the house of the Lord forever. Who can behold without loving him? Who can love him without joy?

ROBERT RICHARDSON, *Communings in the Sanctuary*, 62

SCRIPTURE

As he approached Jericho, a blind man was sitting by the roadside begging.
When he heard a crowd going by, he asked what was happening. They told him, "Jesus of
Nazareth is passing by." Then he shouted, "Jesus, Son of David, have mercy on me!" Those
who were in front sternly ordered him to be quiet; but he shouted even more loudly, "Son of
David, have mercy on me!" Jesus stood still and ordered the man to be brought to him;
and when he came near, he asked him, "What do you want me to do for you?" He said,
"Lord, let me see again." Jesus said to him, "Receive your sight; your faith has saved you."
Immediately he regained his sight and followed him, glorifying God;
and all the people, when they saw it, praised God.

LUKE 18:35-43

PRAYER

Lord Jesus, have mercy on me and let me see your face. Give me the joy of glorifying God.

June 8

The Word in Our Hearts

Psalm

On God rests my deliverance and my honor;
my mighty rock, my refuge is in God.
Trust in him at all times, O people;
pour out your heart before him;
God is a refuge for us.

Psalm 62:7-8

Meditation

All know that something wonderful exists in them—no matter what you call it—that never was fully satisfied with what they are and what they have. There is continually in them that craving, aspiring, and unsatisfied something, reaching forward. Looking ahead, anticipating, hoping for and desiring happiness never yet attained.

Benjamin Franklin, *The Gospel Preacher*, vol. 1, 155

Scripture

Surely, this commandment that I am commanding you today is not too hard for you, nor is it too far away. It is not in heaven, that you should say, "Who will go up to heaven for us, and get it for us so that we may hear it and observe it?" Neither is it beyond the sea, that you should say, "Who will cross to the other side of the sea for us, and get it for us so that we may hear it and observe it?" No, the word is very near to you; it is in your mouth and in your heart for you to observe.

Deuteronomy 30:11-14

Prayer

God of love, may your word rest continually in my heart today, through your Holy Spirit.

June 9

Suffering

Psalm

Give the king your justice, O God,
and your righteousness to a king's son.
May he judge your people with righteousness,
and your poor with justice.
May the mountains yield prosperity for the people,
and the hills, in righteousness.
May he defend the cause of the poor of the people,
give deliverance to the needy,
and crush the oppressor.

Psalm 72:1-4

Meditation

It is the mission of suffering not only to test faith, produce patience, work out probation, and intensify hope, but also to mellow the heart, widen our sympathies, burn out the dross in our nature and purify the gold, and qualify us for helpful ministries to all other suffering ones of earth.

J.H. Garrison, *Alone with God*, 109

Scripture

Again I saw that under the sun the race is not to the swift, nor the battle to the strong, nor bread to the wise, nor riches to the intelligent, nor favor to the skillful; but time and chance happen to them all. For no one can anticipate the time of disaster. Like fish taken in a cruel net, and like birds caught in a snare, so mortals are snared at a time of calamity, when it suddenly falls upon them.

Ecclesiastes 9:11-12

Prayer

Lord, save me when calamity falls upon me. Mellow my heart through suffering so I may be a help to others.

June 10

CRYING OUT TO GOD

PSALM

O God, do not be far from me;
O my God, make haste to help me!
Let my accusers be put to shame and consumed;
let those who seek to hurt me
be covered with scorn and disgrace.
But I will hope continually,
and will praise you yet more and more.

PSALM 71:12-14

MEDITATION

Prayer, I have said, is the voice of penitence, of helplessness, of wretchedness, crying to God for help, for deliverance. But it is infinitely more than this. It is the voice of faith pleading the promises of God. It is the voice of the child rehearsing to his Father the Father's own pledges of support, comfort, and peace.

ASHLEY S. JOHNSON, *The Life of Trust*, 158

SCRIPTURE

Therefore, to keep me from being too elated, a thorn was given me in the flesh, a messenger of Satan to torment me, to keep me from being too elated. Three times I appealed to the Lord about this, that it would leave me, but he said to me, "My grace is sufficient for you, for power is made perfect in weakness." So, I will boast all the more gladly of my weaknesses, so that the power of Christ may dwell in me. Therefore I am content with weaknesses, insults, hardships, persecutions, and calamities for the sake of Christ; for whenever I am weak, then I am strong.

2 CORINTHIANS 12:7-10

PRAYER

Lord, this day may I rely on your grace and power. I rejoice in my weakness, for then I am strong.

June 11

PRAYER

PSALM

My mouth will tell of your righteous acts,
of your deeds of salvation all day long,
though their number is past my knowledge.
I will come praising the mighty deeds of the Lord God,
I will praise your righteousness, yours alone.

PSALM 71:15-16

MEDITATION

So many and so great are the benefits of prayer, that no one who appreciates them can fail to be interested in the question as to what are some of the chief hindrances to its exercise. It is a common experience with most of us, that when we have tried to pray, there has been the absence of that joy, comfort and peace which true prayer always brings to the soul. For this there must be some cause, and the reason will always be found in us, not in God, who is always gracious, and whose ears are ever open to the cry of the righteous.

J.H. GARRISON, *Alone with God*, 81

SCRIPTURE

Then he entered the temple and began to drive out those who were selling things there;
and he said, "It is written, 'My house shall be a house of prayer';
but you have made it a den of robbers."

LUKE 19:45-46

PRAYER

Father, remove all barriers to prayer. May I approach you with a humble heart so my entire life will be a house of prayer, a living temple.

June 12

SELF-EXAMINATION

PSALM

Hear, O Lord, when I cry aloud,
be gracious to me and answer me!
"Come," my heart says, "seek his face!"
Your face, Lord, do I seek.
Do not hide your face from me.
Do not turn your servant away in anger,
you who have been my help.
Do not cast me off, do not forsake me,
O God of my salvation!

PSALM 27:7-9

MEDITATION

Let us live and walk in the Spirit every day, every hour, and then our labors
of love will prove effectual, not only to make proselytes, but also Christians.

BARTON W. STONE, *Christian Messenger* (1843), 37

SCRIPTURE

For he was crucified in weakness, but lives by the power of God. For we are
weak in him, but in dealing with you we will live with him by the power of God.
Examine yourselves to see whether you are living in the faith. Test yourselves. Do you not
realize that Jesus Christ is in you?—unless, indeed, you fail to meet the test!
I hope you will find out that we have not failed.

2 CORINTHIANS 13:4-6

PRAYER

Lord Jesus, through your Holy Spirit examine my heart. Live in me this day.
Do not hide your face from me.

June 13

HUMILITY

PSALM
Come, O children, listen to me;
I will teach you the fear of the Lord.

PSALM 34:11

MEDITATION

This humility is not a mere momentary accident of Christian character. It is not like a garment that can be put on, or that may be laid aside to suit the occasion. It must be a habit of mind, manifesting itself as a permanent characteristic of the heart and of the life of its possessor, or it is not worth a farthing.

ROBERT MILLIGAN, *A Brief Treatise on Prayer*, 86

SCRIPTURE

At that time the disciples came to Jesus and asked, "Who is the greatest in the kingdom of heaven?" He called a child, whom he put among them, and said, "Truly I tell you, unless you change and become like children, you will never enter the kingdom of heaven. Whoever becomes humble like this child is the greatest in the kingdom of heaven. Whoever welcomes one such child in my name welcomes me."

MATTHEW 18:1-5

PRAYER

Lord Jesus, teach me true humility, so I may receive the kingdom like a child. May I welcome children in your name this day.

June 14

THE ASCENSION

PSALM

He built his sanctuary like the high heavens,
like the earth, which he has founded for ever.

PSALM 78:69

MEDITATION

This is the great secret. A loving and obedient heart has eyes that can see and recognize Jesus, even when He comes to us as a spiritual and invisible Presence. The world is blind to such a manifestation of Christ, but not the loving, loyal heart.

J.H. GARRISON, *The Holy Spirit*, 116

SCRIPTURE

"But you will receive power when the Holy Spirit has come upon you; and you will be my witnesses in Jerusalem, in all Judea and Samaria, and to the ends of the earth." When he had said this, as they were watching, he was lifted up, and a cloud took him out of their sight. While he was going and they were gazing up towards heaven, suddenly two men in white robes stood by them. They said, "Men of Galilee, why do you stand looking up towards heaven? This Jesus, who has been taken up from you into heaven, will come in the same way as you saw him go into heaven."

ACTS 1:8-11

PRAYER

Lord Jesus, you ascended to give marvelous gifts, the greatest is your presence through the Holy Spirit. Open the eyes of my heart to see you today.

June 15

POVERTY

PSALM

You are the God who works wonders;
you have displayed your might among the peoples.

PSALM 77:14

MEDITATION

So the elect of God humbly and earnestly cry to him day and night, and perseveringly pray to their heavenly Father for constant supplies. They always feel their poverty, and that all help must come from God alone; therefore in him alone they trust.

BARTON W. STONE, *Christian Messenger* (1843), 205

SCRIPTURE

The Lord makes poor and makes rich;
he brings low, he also exalts.
He raises up the poor from the dust;
he lifts the needy from the ash heap,
to make them sit with princes
and inherit a seat of honor.
For the pillars of the earth are the Lord's,
and on them he has set the world.

1 SAMUEL 2:7-8

PRAYER

Father, help me know my poverty so I may rely on you alone.

June 16

SENDING OF THE SPIRIT

PSALM

Sing aloud to God our strength;
shout for joy to the God of Jacob.
Raise a song, sound the tambourine,
the sweet lyre with the harp.
Blow the trumpet at the new moon,
at the full moon, on our festal day.

PSALM 81:1-3

MEDITATION

The Spirit of God is therefore often used for his power; though it is not an impersonal power, but a living, energizing, active, personal existence.

ALEXANDER CAMPBELL, *The Christian System*, 24

SCRIPTURE

When the day of Pentecost had come, they were all together in one place. And suddenly from heaven there came a sound like the rush of a violent wind, and it filled the entire house where they were sitting. Divided tongues, as of fire, appeared among them, and a tongue rested on each of them. All of them were filled with the Holy Spirit and began to speak in other languages, as the Spirit gave them ability.

ACTS 2:1-4

PRAYER

Father, let me experience this day the personal energy of your Holy Spirit. Then I will sing aloud and shout for joy.

June 17

MONEY

PSALM

Incline your ear, O Lord, and answer me,
for I am poor and needy.

PSALM 86:1

MEDITATION

You may toil, as you think, for your children, and it will in all probability turn out that your savings will be a curse to them for time and for eternal years. It will be better far to teach them the life of trust and leave them with the rich heritage of the example of a father and a mother who were not afraid to bear witness in their lives, in temporal things, to the faithfulness of God to his promises in this generation even if the whole world goes the other way.

ASHLEY S. JOHNSON, *The Life of Trust*, 184

SCRIPTURE

He looked up and saw rich people putting their gifts into the treasury; he also saw a poor widow put in two small copper coins. He said, "Truly I tell you, this poor widow has put in more than all of them; for all of them have contributed out of their abundance, but she out of her poverty has put in all she had to live on."

LUKE 21:1-4

PRAYER

Father, increase my faith! Let me be like this poor widow and put my whole trust in you alone.

June 18

RENOVATION

PSALM
They are planted in the house of the Lord;
they flourish in the courts of our God.

PSALM 92:13

MEDITATION

But Christianity is very far from being a mere system of redemption from sin, or salvation from punishment, or selfish rewards for obedience. It designs not only to bestow remission of sins but to effect a renovation—a regeneration of the soul.

ROBERT RICHARDSON, *Communings in the Sanctuary*, 102

SCRIPTURE
They devoted themselves to the apostles' teaching and fellowship,
to the breaking of bread and the prayers.

Awe came upon everyone, because many wonders and signs were being done by the apostles. All who believed were together and had all things in common; they would sell their possessions and goods and distribute the proceeds to all, as any had need. Day by day, as they spent much time together in the temple, they broke bread at home and ate their food with glad and generous hearts, praising God and having the goodwill of all the people. And day by day the Lord added to their number those who were being saved.

ACTS 2:42-47

PRAYER
Lord Jesus, save me! Renovate my heart so I will share all I have with others.

June 19

SECOND COMING

PSALM

*Lord, you have been our dwelling-place
in all generations.
Before the mountains were brought forth,
or ever you had formed the earth and the world,
from everlasting to everlasting you are God.*

PSALM 90:1-2

MEDITATION

Thus will be consummated the work of human redemption; but the influence of the Scheme will be as enduring as the throne of God, and will, in all probability, be forever felt throughout his vast domains.

ROBERT MILLIGAN, *Scheme of Redemption*, 577

SCRIPTURE

"There will be signs in the sun, the moon, and the stars, and on the earth distress among nations confused by the roaring of the sea and the waves. People will faint from fear and foreboding of what is coming upon the world, for the powers of the heavens will be shaken. Then they will see 'the Son of Man coming in a cloud' with power and great glory. Now when these things begin to take place, stand up and raise your heads, because your redemption is drawing near."

LUKE 21:25-28

PRAYER

Lord Jesus, come quickly! Bring our full redemption so we can praise you forever.

June 20

Faith and Prayer

Psalm

But truly God has listened;
he has given heed to the words of my prayer.
Blessed be God,
because he has not rejected my prayer
or removed his steadfast love from me.

Psalm 66:19-20

Meditation

Can anyone believe with all the heart and not pray? Is not prayer a natural and necessary consequence of faith? Is it not as natural for the believer to adore and bless the Creator, Preserver, and Redeemer as it is to love him or to serve him in any other way?

Robert Milligan, *A Brief Treatise on Prayer*, 42

Scripture

If any of you is lacking in wisdom, ask God, who gives to all generously and ungrudgingly, and it will be given you. But ask in faith, never doubting, for the one who doubts is like a wave of the sea, driven and tossed by the wind; for the doubter, being double-minded and unstable in every way, must not expect to receive anything from the Lord.

James 1:5-8

Prayer

Generous God, give me the wisdom I so much need for this day. May I trust your steadfast love.

June 21

SIGNS AND WONDERS

PSALM

O Lord God of hosts,
who is as mighty as you, O Lord?
Your faithfulness surrounds you.

PSALM 89:8

MEDITATION

An apostle with the miraculous gifts of the Spirit could effect more in one day than all the missionaries in the field can for scores of years. I have for many years indulged in this cheering hope, that such gifts may yet be restored.

BARTON W. STONE, *Christian Messenger* (1843), 333

SCRIPTURE

Now many signs and wonders were done among the people through the apostles. And they were all together in Solomon's Portico. None of the rest dared to join them, but the people held them in high esteem. Yet more than ever believers were added to the Lord, great numbers of both men and women, so that they even carried out the sick into the streets, and laid them on cots and mats, in order that Peter's shadow might fall on some of them as he came by. A great number of people would also gather from the towns around Jerusalem, bringing the sick and those tormented by unclean spirits, and they were all cured.

ACTS 5:12-16

PRAYER

Father, increase my faith in your power, even when I do not see signs and wonders.

June 22

Death and Resurrection

Psalm

O Lord our God, you answered them;
you were a forgiving God to them,
but an avenger of their wrongdoings.
Extol the Lord our God,
and worship at his holy mountain;
for the Lord our God is holy.

Psalm 99:8-9

Meditation

In the flesh of Jesus, on the cross especially, we see the love of God preeminently displayed.

Barton W. Stone, *Christian Messenger* (1843), 113

Scripture

But Peter and the apostles answered, "We must obey God rather than any human
authority. The God of our ancestors raised up Jesus, whom you had killed by hanging him
on a tree. God exalted him at his right hand as Leader and Savior, so that he might give
repentance to Israel and forgiveness of sins. And we are witnesses to these things, and so is
the Holy Spirit whom God has given to those who obey him."

Acts 5:29-32

Prayer

God of resurrection, I praise you for your love and power, clearly shown in
Jesus. May I be a witness to your love along with your Holy Spirit.

June 23

PURITY

PSALM

I will sing of loyalty and of justice;
to you, O Lord, I will sing.
I will study the way that is blameless.
When shall I attain it?

PSALM 101:1-2

MEDITATION

In this there is no excuse for indifference, inefficiency, or carelessness in keeping the church in order, purging out the old leaven, or maintaining purity, but an encouragement to those who labor for the highest degree of purity and perfection but cannot reach it.

BENJAMIN FRANKLIN, *The Gospel Preacher*, VOL. 1, 419

SCRIPTURE

Then Samuel said to all the house of Israel, "If you are returning to the Lord with all your heart, then put away the foreign gods and the Astartes from among you. Direct your heart to the Lord, and serve him only, and he will deliver you out of the hand of the Philistines." So Israel put away the Baals and the Astartes, and they served the Lord only.

1 SAMUEL 7:3-4

PRAYER

Lord, remove every idol from my heart and my life, so that I serve you and you alone. Give me the gift of a pure heart.

June 24

SERVICE

PSALM

Remember the wonderful works he has done,
his miracles, and the judgments he has uttered,
O offspring of his servant Abraham,
children of Jacob, his chosen ones.

PSALM 105:5-6

MEDITATION

But if to enrich ourselves is the law of nature, the law of religion and society, Christ has showed us, is rather to enrich others; yea, and if necessary, to die for the brothers and sisters.

WALTER SCOTT, *The Messiahship*, 344

SCRIPTURE

A dispute also arose among them as to which one of them was to be regarded as the greatest. But he said to them, "The kings of the Gentiles lord it over them; and those in authority over them are called benefactors. But not so with you; rather the greatest among you must become like the youngest, and the leader like one who serves. For who is greater, the one who is at the table or the one who serves? Is it not the one at the table? But I am among you as one who serves."

LUKE 22:24-27

PRAYER

Lord Jesus, give me a servant heart, as you have yourself. May I keep your service to me constantly in mind this day, so I may serve others.

June 25

SIN AND FORGIVENESS

PSALM

For I eat ashes like bread,
and mingle tears with my drink,
because of your indignation and anger;
for you have lifted me up and thrown me aside.

PSALM 102:9-10

MEDITATION

The reason why we would have the reader to attend to this account of the state of misery is because it is a principle of the gospel, of which we shall immediately speak, to excise or cut out of the conscience this intolerable burden—the sense of guilt— and to replant in the human heart, as in its native seat, the joys of innocence, the joys of the Spirit of God.

WALTER SCOTT, *The Gospel Restored*, 38

SCRIPTURE

"Simon, Simon, listen! Satan has demanded to sift all of you like wheat, but I have prayed for you that your own faith may not fail; and you, when once you have turned back, strengthen your brothers." And he said to him, "Lord, I am ready to go with you to prison and to death!" Jesus said, "I tell you, Peter, the cock will not crow this day, until you have denied three times that you know me."

LUKE 22:31-34

PRAYER

Lord Jesus, like Peter, I have denied you with my words and life. Forgive! Restore me as your disciple.

June 26

GETHSEMANE

PSALM

Truly the eye of the Lord is on those who fear him,
on those who hope in his steadfast love,
to deliver their soul from death,
and to keep them alive in famine

PSALM 33:18-19

MEDITATION

Most assuredly has it been the work of Christ to deliver souls from death in this, its highest and true sense—a death in trespasses and sins—a state of separation of the soul from the favor and fellowship of God. This separation he endured on our account—a separation which probably took place from the moment in which he was "delivered up by the determinate and foreknowledge of God," and the near approach of which wrung from him the bloody sweat in the Garden of Gethsemane and the plaintive appeal: "O my Father! If it be possible, let this cup pass from me"; as well as that pathetic exclamation upon the cross: "My God! My God! Why hast thou forsaken me?"

ROBERT RICHARDSON, *Communings in the Sanctuary*, 123-124

SCRIPTURE

He came out and went, as was his custom, to the Mount of Olives; and the disciples followed him. When he reached the place, he said to them, "Pray that you may not come into the time of trial." Then he withdrew from them about a stone's throw, knelt down, and prayed, "Father, if you are willing, remove this cup from me; yet, not my will but yours be done."

LUKE 22:39-42

PRAYER

Lord Jesus, you endured so much for me. Through your obedience, God will hear my cries of pain and separation.

June 27

CHANGE OF HEART

PSALM

My mouth will speak the praise of the Lord,
and all flesh will bless his holy name forever and ever.

PSALM 145:21

MEDITATION

When our affections are won from sin to holiness, a love of Satan to God, and all the purposes of our hearts are submissive to the will of God as far as we know it, we have all the change of heart that God requires of us prior to obedience.

T.W. BRENTS, *The Gospel Plan of Salvation*, 225

SCRIPTURE

"What do you think? A man had two sons; he went to the first and said, 'Son, go and work in the vineyard today.' He answered, 'I will not'; but later he changed his mind and went. The father went to the second and said the same; and he answered, 'I go, sir'; but he did not go. Which of the two did the will of his father?" They said, "The first." Jesus said to them, "Truly I tell you, the tax collectors and the prostitutes are going into the kingdom of God ahead of you. For John came to you in the way of righteousness and you did not believe him, but the tax collectors and the prostitutes believed him; and even after you saw it, you did not change your minds and believe him."

MATTHEW 21:28-32

PRAYER

Loving Father, move my heart today to do your will. May I go beyond good intentions to actual obedience.

June 28

THE GLORY OF GOD

PSALM
Save us, O Lord our God,
and gather us from among the nations,
that we may give thanks to your holy name
and glory in your praise.

PSALM 106:47

MEDITATION

What a vision of immortal beauty awaits the transition of God's children from the body, with its pains and temptations, into the paradise of God! What radiant forms of celestial dignity shall pass before us! We shall see the King in his beauty, and look with unveiled faces upon the divine glory.

J.H. GARRISON, *Alone with God*, 111

SCRIPTURE

When they heard these things, they became enraged and ground their teeth at Stephen.
But filled with the Holy Spirit, he gazed into heaven and saw the glory of God and Jesus
standing at the right hand of God. "Look," he said, "I see the heavens opened and the Son
of Man standing at the right hand of God!" But they covered their ears, and with a loud
shout all rushed together against him. Then they dragged him out of the city and began to
stone him; and the witnesses laid their coats at the feet of a young man named Saul.
While they were stoning Stephen, he prayed, "Lord Jesus, receive my spirit." Then he knelt
down and cried out in a loud voice, "Lord, do not hold this sin against them."
When he had said this, he died.

ACTS 7:54-60

PRAYER

Lord, come quickly, so I may see your face and your glory. Receive me at the time of my death into that eternal vision of God.

June 29

The Holy Spirit

Psalm

The Lord has done great things for us, and we rejoiced.

Psalm 126:3

Meditation

As the apostles and first Christians received aid from the Holy Spirit for their special tasks and responsibilities in the times in which they lived, why may we not expect His gracious aid to quicken our spiritual powers and to fit us to do the particular work or bear the special burden which God has laid upon us? If the apostles and first Christians needed the divine Comforter to strengthen them in their struggles and to comfort them in their sorrows so that they might not feel like orphans in the world, why may we not expect the same gracious Spirit to comfort us in our sorrows, to strengthen us in our conflicts and to save us from the feeling of spiritual orphanage?

J.H. Garrison, *The Holy Spirit*, 90-91

Scripture

Now when the apostles at Jerusalem heard that Samaria had accepted the word of God, they sent Peter and John to them. The two went down and prayed for them that they might receive the Holy Spirit (for as yet the Spirit had not come upon any of them; they had only been baptized in the name of the Lord Jesus). Then Peter and John laid their hands on them, and they received the Holy Spirit.

Acts 8:14-17

Prayer

Lord Jesus, strengthen, comfort, and help me through your Holy Spirit. Let me know that you are with me and I am never orphaned.

June 30

INTERCESSORY PRAYER

PSALM
O Israel, hope in the Lord!
For with the Lord there is steadfast love,
and with him is great power to redeem.
It is he who will redeem Israel
from all its iniquities.

PSALM 130:7-8

MEDITATION

Who, then, can estimate the amount of good that has been secured to humanity through the humble, earnest, and penitential supplications of the closet? Who can recount the various individual, social, ecclesiastical, and national blessings that have been poured out of the windows of heaven in answer to secret prayer? Who can tell how many poor wandering prodigals have been brought back to their Father's house, and made heirs to immortality and eternal life, through the earnest and repeated prayers of a pious brother, or sister, or mother?

ROBERT MILLIGAN, *A Brief Treatise on Prayer*, 25

SCRIPTURE

Moreover as for me, far be it from me that I should sin against the Lord by ceasing to pray for you; and I will instruct you in the good and the right way. Only fear the Lord, and serve him faithfully with all your heart; for consider what great things he has done for you.

1 SAMUEL 12:23-24

PRAYER

Lord, this day I pray for those on my heart who particularly need your grace, comfort, and help. May others intercede for me!

July 1

Baptism

Psalm

Praise the Lord!
Praise the name of the Lord;
give praise, O servants of the Lord,
you that stand in the house of the Lord,
in the courts of the house of our God.
Praise the Lord, for the Lord is good;
sing to his name, for he is gracious.

PSALM 135:1-3

Meditation

Your hearts were sprinkled from evil consciences, when your bodies were washed in the cleansing water. Then into the kingdom of Jesus you entered. The King of righteousness, of peace and joy, extended his scepter over you, and sanctified in state and in your whole person, you rejoiced in the Lord with joy unspeakable and full of glory. Being washed, you were sanctified, as well as acquitted.

ALEXANDER CAMPBELL, *The Christian System*, 237-238

Scripture

Then Philip began to speak, and starting with this scripture, he proclaimed to him the good news about Jesus. As they were going along the road, they came to some water; and the eunuch said, "Look, here is water! What is to prevent me from being baptized?" He commanded the chariot to stop, and both of them, Philip and the eunuch, went down into the water, and Philip baptized him. When they came up out of the water, the Spirit of the Lord snatched Philip away; the eunuch saw him no more, and went on his way rejoicing.

ACTS 8:35-39

Prayer

Lord Jesus, I rejoice as one who is baptized, washed, forgiven, and sanctified. May I show that joy to all around me this day.

THE SPIRIT OF ADOPTION

PSALM

I call upon you, O Lord; come quickly to me;
give ear to my voice when I call to you.
Let my prayer be counted as incense before you,
and the lifting up of my hands as an evening sacrifice.

PSALM 141:1-2

MEDITATION

Hearing the gospel will not save; obeying the gospel will not save, only as the means of leading us to the Savior, who alone does save us from our sins by his Spirit. He sheds abroad his love into our hearts by the Holy Ghost given unto us—that perfect love of God, which casteth out tormenting fear. It is the Spirit of love, of power, and of a sound mind.

BARTON W. STONE, *Christian Messenger* (1844), 261

SCRIPTURE

For all who are led by the Spirit of God are children of God. For you did not receive a spirit of slavery to fall back into fear, but you have received a spirit of adoption. When we cry, "Abba! Father!" it is that very Spirit bearing witness with our spirit that we are children of God, and if children, then heirs, heirs of God and joint heirs with Christ—if, in fact, we suffer with him so that we may also be glorified with him.

ROMANS 8:14-17

PRAYER

Father, I thank you that through your Spirit I am your beloved child. Cast fear out of my life today

July 3

MERCY

PSALM

When you hide your face, they are dismayed;
when you take away their breath, they die
and return to their dust.
When you send forth your spirit, they are created;
and you renew the face of the ground.

PSALM 104:29-30

MEDITATION

He is merciful to all the unthankful the poor as well as the rich and grateful receiver. What can induce him thus to act? What but infinite benevolence? He does not hope nor expect to receive a compensation for these favors. If he did, we are too poor to give it. Be ye therefore merciful, as your Father is merciful.

BARTON W. STONE, *Christian Messenger* (1843), 50

SCRIPTURE

One of the criminals who were hanged there kept deriding him and saying, "Are you not the Messiah? Save yourself and us!" But the other rebuked him, saying, "Do you not fear God, since you are under the same sentence of condemnation? And we indeed have been condemned justly, for we are getting what we deserve for our deeds, but this man has done nothing wrong." Then he said, "Jesus, remember me when you come into your kingdom." He replied, "Truly I tell you, today you will be with me in Paradise."

LUKE 23:39-43

PRAYER

Lord Jesus, have mercy on me, a sinner! Accept me into paradise with you as you did the criminal on the cross.

PEACE

PSALM

He grants peace within your borders;
he fills you with the finest of wheat.
He sends out his command to the earth;
his word runs swiftly.

PSALM 147:14-15

MEDITATION

But the children of God, all his children, are the children of peace. They have peace with God through our Lord Jesus Christ—they have the peace of God ruling in them, and this leads them to live in peace with all, and to cause them to make peace among all as far as their influence extends, and to labor to put down wrath, strife, and division in the world.

BARTON W. STONE, *Christian Messenger* (1843), 232-233

SCRIPTURE

Therefore, since we are justified by faith, we have peace with God through our Lord Jesus Christ, through whom we have obtained access to this grace in which we stand; and we boast in our hope of sharing the glory of God. And not only that, but we also boast in our sufferings, knowing that suffering produces endurance, and endurance produces character, and character produces hope, and hope does not disappoint us, because God's love has been poured into our hearts through the Holy Spirit that has been given to us.

ROMANS 5:1-5

PRAYER

Almighty God, you have given me peace through the Lord Jesus Christ. This day, make me a peacemaker.

July 5

The Cross

Psalm

Why do the nations conspire, and the peoples plot in vain?
The kings of the earth set themselves, and the rulers take counsel together,
against the Lord and his anointed, saying,
"Let us burst their bonds asunder, and cast their cords from us."

Psalm 2:1-3

Meditation

Ought it not to be sacredly remembered by all who serve God in the gospel that "the cross of Christ" is that power which is to "slay" the natural "enmity" of the sinner's heart to God and to his law? With what holy reverence, then, ought Christ and him crucified to be preached to the world! What solemn themes are these! Ought they not be bathed in "many tears" by him whose sacred office it is to announce them?

Walter Scott, *The Messiahship*, 182

Scripture

It was now about noon, and darkness came over the whole land until three in the afternoon, while the sun's light failed; and the curtain of the temple was torn in two. Then Jesus, crying with a loud voice, said, "Father, into your hands I commend my spirit." Having said this, he breathed his last. When the centurion saw what had taken place, he praised God and said, "Certainly this man was innocent."

Luke 23:44-47

Prayer

With holy reverence, with tears, and with awe, I contemplate the cross of Christ today. Lord Jesus, you have given yourself for the world! Live in me, so I may bear your cross this day.

July 6

LOVE OF GOD

PSALM

But I, through the abundance of your steadfast love,
will enter your house,
I will bow down toward your holy temple
in awe of you.

PSALM 5:7

MEDITATION

We may not love as God loves, who is infinite in love as well as in wisdom and in power; but we may love as humans can love, who are so limited and feeble in all their capacities. And when one loves the Lord with all the heart and mind and soul and strength, one renders the least return that may be offered and the greatest that can be demanded.

ROBERT RICHARDSON, *Communings in the Sanctuary*, 14

SCRIPTURE

Who will separate us from the love of Christ? Will hardship, or distress, or persecution,
or famine, or nakedness, or peril, or sword? As it is written, "For your sake we are being
killed all day long; we are accounted as sheep to be slaughtered." No, in all these things we
are more than conquerors through him who loved us. For I am convinced that neither
death, nor life, nor angels, nor rulers, nor things present, nor things to come, nor powers,
nor height, nor depth, nor anything else in all creation, will be able to separate us
from the love of God in Christ Jesus our Lord.

ROMANS 8:35-39

PRAYER

God of love, today may I focus less on my hardships and more on your infinite love. May I ever be convinced of that love, through Christ.

July 7

THE PRESENCE OF GOD

PSALM

The Lord also thundered in the heavens,
and the Most High uttered his voice.
And he sent out his arrows, and scattered them;
he flashed forth lightnings, and routed them.
Then the channels of the sea were seen,
and the foundations of the world were laid bare
at your rebuke, O Lord,
at the blast of the breath of your nostrils.

PSALM 18:13-15

MEDITATION

No one would think of going into the presence of an earthly king or potentate, to seek a favor, without proper preparation of one's apparel, and a clear and distinct understanding of the request one was to make. Do we not ofttimes treat God with less respect, carrying into his presence sins unrepented of, hearts ungrateful for his daily mercies and minds preoccupied with worldly thoughts and cares, having only a vague and indistinct idea of the favors we need?

J.H. GARRISON, *Alone With God*, 58

SCRIPTURE

At that time, too, I entreated the Lord, saying: "O Lord God, you have only begun to show your servant your greatness and your might; what god in heaven or on earth can perform deeds and mighty acts like yours!"

DEUTERONOMY 3:23-24

PRAYER

Almighty God, I stand in awe of your power and glory! You have only begun to show me your greatness and might. Open my eyes to see your great deeds this day.

SEEING JESUS

PSALM

Open my eyes, so that I may behold
wondrous things out of your law.

PSALM 119:18

MEDITATION

All that love, mercy, grace, faithfulness, truth, power, benevolence, we see in Jesus, in his works, in his words, in his tears, in his sufferings, in his death and resurrection, is the true character of God manifested in the flesh—like a mirror, he presents the true image of the invisible God—the true form of God in all his divinity; for the fullness of it dwells in him; the full exhibition of the truth as it is in Jesus.

BARTON W. STONE, *Christian Messenger* (1843), 47

SCRIPTURE

When he was at the table with them, he took bread, blessed and broke it, and gave it to them. Then their eyes were opened, and they recognized him; and he vanished from their sight. They said to each other, "Were not our hearts burning within us while he was talking to us on the road, while he was opening the scriptures to us?" That same hour they got up and returned to Jerusalem; and they found the eleven and their companions gathered together. They were saying, "The Lord has risen indeed, and he has appeared to Simon!" Then they told what had happened on the road, and how he had been made known to them in the breaking of the bread.

LUKE 24:30-35

PRAYER

Lord Jesus, open my eyes so I can see you this day and in you see the amazing love of God.

July 9

THE HOLY SPIRIT

PSALM

You show me the path of life.
In your presence there is fullness of joy;
in your right hand are pleasures forevermore.

PSALM 16:11

MEDITATION

The Holy Spirit is the divine agent in our illumination, our spiritual quickening through faith, our penitence—in a word, in the whole process of bringing us to God. That is a fact to be everywhere and always recognized and emphasized. The failure to do this is sure to lead to superficial and legalistic views on the whole question of our conversion and salvation.

J.H. GARRISON, *The Holy Spirit*, 64

SCRIPTURE

While Peter was still speaking, the Holy Spirit fell upon all who heard the word. The circumcised believers who had come with Peter were astounded that the gift of the Holy Spirit had been poured out even on the Gentiles, for they heard them speaking in tongues and extolling God. Then Peter said, "Can anyone withhold the water for baptizing these people who have received the Holy Spirit just as we have?" So he ordered them to be baptized in the name of Jesus Christ. Then they invited him to stay for several days.

ACTS 10:44-48

PRAYER

Father, thank you for bringing me to new birth through the work of the Holy Spirit. Fill me with your Spirit this day so I may bear fruit for you.

FOLLOWING JESUS

PSALM
I love the Lord, because he has heard
my voice and my supplications.
Because he inclined his ear to me,
therefore I will call on him as long as I live.

PSALM 116:1-2

MEDITATION
So when one believes on the Savior, goes for him, and devotes himself to him, one goes for all he taught, whether one understands it or not. One is then a Christian—a disciple of Christ, and nothing else. It is the concentration, the embodiment of all Christianity in a person, a living and glorious person.

BENJAMIN FRANKLIN, *The Gospel Preacher*, VOL. 1, 50

SCRIPTURE
As Jesus passed along the Sea of Galilee, he saw Simon and his brother Andrew casting a net into the sea—for they were fishermen. And Jesus said to them, "Follow me and I will make you fish for people." And immediately they left their nets and followed him. As he went a little farther, he saw James son of Zebedee and his brother John, who were in their boat mending the nets. Immediately he called them; and they left their father Zebedee in the boat with the hired men, and followed him.

MARK 1:16-20

PRAYER
Jesus, this day make me a disciple, a follower, and a Christian. May I follow you wherever you go.

BE STRONG

PSALM

The Lord has been mindful of us; he will bless us;
he will bless the house of Israel;
he will bless the house of Aaron;
he will bless those who fear the Lord, both small and great.

PSALM 115:12-13

MEDITATION

It would, also, serve to develop, mold, and perfect our Christian character, by the frequent and systematic exercise of all our moral and religious faculties. This is essential to the proper development and discipline of both head and heart. It is the means ordained by God for educating our whole spiritual nature, and making it subservient to the Divine will.

ROBERT MILLIGAN, *Scheme of Redemption*, 528

SCRIPTURE

"Only be strong and very courageous, being careful to act in accordance with all the law that my servant Moses commanded you; do not turn from it to the right hand or to the left, so that you may be successful wherever you go. This book of the law shall not depart out of your mouth; you shall meditate on it day and night, so that you may be careful to act in accordance with all that is written in it. For then you shall make your way prosperous, and then you shall be successful. I hereby command you: Be strong and courageous; do not be frightened or dismayed, for the Lord your God is with you wherever you go."

JOSHUA 1:7-9

PRAYER

Father, let me meditate on your ways this day so I may be strong and courageous.

July 12

SURRENDER

PSALM

To you, O Lord, I lift up my soul.
O my God, in you I trust;
do not let me be put to shame;
do not let my enemies exult over me.

PSALM 25:1-2

MEDITATION

We are brought into this world without any desire or volition of our own,
and there are those who are responsible for our support and comfort while we
are helpless. In acknowledging Himself to be our Father—the Father of our
spirits—God commits Himself to our care and support when we are helpless,
and this does not apply to childhood simply, but to youth and even down to old
age, if we commit ourselves, in well doing to his care.

ASHLEY S. JOHNSON, *The Life of Trust*, 29

SCRIPTURE

Then Paul answered, "What are you doing, weeping and breaking my heart? For I am ready
not only to be bound but even to die in Jerusalem for the name of the Lord Jesus." Since he
would not be persuaded, we remained silent except to say, "The Lord's will be done."

ACTS 21:13-14

PRAYER

Loving Father, I place my life in your hands. May I daily surrender to your
will, not my own.

FAITH

PSALM

But as for me, I walk in my integrity;
redeem me, and be gracious to me.
My foot stands on level ground;
in the great congregation I will bless the Lord.

PSALM 26:11-12

MEDITATION

Any belief, then, that does not terminate in our personal confidence in Jesus as the Christ, and induce trustful submission to him, is not faith unfeigned; but a dead faith, and cannot save the soul.

ALEXANDER CAMPBELL, *The Christian System*, 53

SCRIPTURE

Then some people came, bringing to him a paralyzed man, carried by four of them. And when they could not bring him to Jesus because of the crowd, they removed the roof above him; and after having dug through it, they let down the mat on which the paralytic lay. When Jesus saw their faith, he said to the paralytic, "Son, your sins are forgiven."

MARK 2:3-5

PRAYER

Lord Jesus, increase my faith! May I trust in you, your goodness and power, so my sins will be forgiven.

July 14

Prayer and Praise

Psalm

But it is for you, O Lord, that I wait;
it is you, O Lord my God, who will answer.
For I pray, "Only do not let them rejoice over me,
those who boast against me when my foot slips."

Psalm 38:15-16

Meditation

Brothers and sisters, let us cultivate in our hearts more and more the spirit of prayer; let us pray without ceasing; let us in everything give thanks; let us often retire with our blessed Redeemer, to spend a few moments, at least, if not whole nights, in prayer to our Heavenly Father. In this way we shall be happier in life, more triumphant in death, and better prepared to join the general assembly and church of the first-born whose names are written in heaven, and who cease not day or night to worship God.

Robert Milligan, *A Brief Treatise on Prayer*, 54

Scripture

O the depth of the riches and wisdom and knowledge of God! How unsearchable are his judgments and how inscrutable his ways! "For who has known the mind of the Lord? Or who has been his counselor?" "Or who has given a gift to him, to receive a gift in return?" For from him and through him and to him are all things. To him be the glory forever. Amen.

Romans 11:33-36

Prayer

O God who is beyond my wisdom, knowledge, and imagination, I give you praise this day. May all the glory be yours!

July 15

LED BY THE SPIRIT

PSALM

Be still before the Lord, and wait patiently for him;
do not fret over those who prosper in their way,
over those who carry out evil devices.

PSALM 37:7

MEDITATION

Then they received the Holy Spirit of promise, whereby they were sealed
unto for the day of redemption. They were prepared as blank paper, not to be
inscribed with ink, but with the Spirit of the living God. So evident is the
inscription, that it is known and read of all. This is designed of God for the
good of all. For the manifestation of the Spirit is given to or for all that all may
be profited. This inscription written by the Spirit of God on the fleshly table of
the heart is that strong bias in the Christian to holiness.

BARTON W. STONE, *Christian Messenger* (1843), 366

SCRIPTURE

Now in the church at Antioch there were prophets and teachers: Barnabas, Simeon who
was called Niger, Lucius of Cyrene, Manaen a member of the court of Herod the ruler,
and Saul. While they were worshiping the Lord and fasting, the Holy Spirit said, "Set
apart for me Barnabas and Saul for the work to which I have called them." Then after
fasting and praying they laid their hands on them and sent them off.

ACTS 13:1-3

PRAYER

Lord Jesus, open the ears of my heart so I may hear your Spirit today. Holy
Spirit, lead me into holiness.

DELIVERANCE BY GOD

PSALM

Blessed be the Lord,
for he has wondrously shown his steadfast love to me
when I was beset as a city under siege.

PSALM 31:21

MEDITATION

We have given no time to meditation or to self-examination. We have been too slothful, mentally, to make an effort to fix in our minds, clearly, the essential truths on which prayer is based: God is. He is a Person. He is here. He has promised to hear me when I call on him. He cannot lie. He loves to give good gifts to his needy children. He has heard and answered prayer. He has answered my prayers. He has invited me to ask him for what I need.

J.H. GARRISON, *Alone With God,* 57

SCRIPTURE

Those twelve stones, which they had taken out of the Jordan, Joshua set up in Gilgal,
saying to the Israelites, "When your children ask their parents in time to come, 'What do
these stones mean?' then you shall let your children know, 'Israel crossed over the Jordan
here on dry ground.' For the Lord your God dried up the waters of the Jordan for you until
you crossed over, as the Lord your God did to the Red Sea, which he dried up for us until
we crossed over, so that all the peoples of the earth may know that the hand of the Lord is
mighty, and so that you may fear the Lord your God forever."

JOSHUA 4:20-24

PRAYER

Lord God, as you delivered Israel over the Jordan, so may I rely on you through prayer to deliver me this day from every evil.

July 17

THE FAMILY OF JESUS

PSALM

By day the Lord commands his steadfast love,
and at night his song is with me,
a prayer to the God of my life.

PSALM 42:8

MEDITATION

They are adopted into the family of God; made sons and daughters of the Lord Almighty, children of God, and heirs—joint heirs—with Christ. They have an Advocate in the heavens, through whom their persons and prayers are accepted. They all know the Lord. "All thy children shall be taught of God." The Holy Spirit of God writes the law of God upon their hearts, and inscribes it upon their understanding; so that they need not teach everyone his fellow citizen to know the Lord, "for they all know him, from the least to the greatest." They are sanctified through the truth—separated and consecrated to God.

ALEXANDER CAMPBELL, *The Christian System*, 156

SCRIPTURE

Then his mother and his brothers came; and standing outside, they sent to him and called him. A crowd was sitting around him; and they said to him, "Your mother and your brothers and sisters are outside, asking for you." And he replied, "Who are my mother and my brothers?" And looking at those who sat around him, he said, "Here are my mother and my brothers! Whoever does the will of God is my brother and sister and mother."

MARK 3:31-35

PRAYER

Lord God, you have made me your beloved child, adopted into your family. Lord Jesus, you are my brother! May I do the will of our Father.

July 18

ETERNAL REWARD

PSALM

For a day in your courts is better than a thousand elsewhere.
I would rather be a doorkeeper in the house of my God than live in the tents of wickedness.
For the Lord God is a sun and shield; he bestows favor and honor.
No good thing does the Lord withhold from those who walk uprightly.
O Lord of hosts, happy is everyone who trusts in you.

PSALM 84:10-12

MEDITATION

Those who loved him here will love him there, and will be like him; for they shall see him as he is. They shall need no light of the sun, nor any artificial light; for the Lord God and the Lamb shall be the light of the holy city. In effable bliss, inexpressible happiness, and joys that shall never end, they shall bask forever and ever.

BENJAMIN FRANKLIN, *The Gospel Preacher*, VOL. 1, 478

SCRIPTURE

Then the one who had received the five talents came forward, bringing five more talents, saying, "Master, you handed over to me five talents; see, I have made five more talents." His master said to him, "Well done, good and trustworthy slave; you have been trustworthy in a few things, I will put you in charge of many things; enter into the joy of your master."

MATTHEW 25:20-21

PRAYER

Father, may I put my trust in you and so be a faithful servant, so I might be with you forever!

July 19

REFORMATION OF THE HEART

PSALM

If we had forgotten the name of our God,
or spread out our hands to a strange god,
would not God discover this?
For he knows the secrets of the heart.

PSALM 44:20-21

MEDITATION

We need practical, heart searching truth, more than the speculative and philosophic doctrines of the age in which we live. We need a greater reformation of the heart, than of the head, in order to grow up into Christ Jesus, and be as he was, and still is—in order that we may be profitable to the unbelieving world, and at last obtain the eternal inheritance of the saints in light.

BARTON W. STONE, *Christian Messenger* (1843), 180

SCRIPTURE

"For so the Lord has commanded us, saying, 'I have set you to be a light for the Gentiles,
so that you may bring salvation to the ends of the earth.'" When the Gentiles heard this,
they were glad and praised the word of the Lord; and as many as had been destined
for eternal life became believers.

ACTS 13:47-48

PRAYER

Lord, reform my heart so I may praise your name and bring your light to all around me.

July 20

GLORY OF JESUS

PSALM

God is king over the nations;
God sits on his holy throne.

PSALM 47:8

MEDITATION

Could we ascend to the summit of glory and the universe, whether the stupendous and unparalleled miracles of his glorification and the Apocalyptic worship would impel us to go—could we, like the blessed Lord, enshrined in glory which no one can see, look down from the eternal throne, and behold the principalities, dominations, and powers of the universe, and the universe itself laid at our feet, we might, if our souls did not expire under the greatness of the scene, acquire, perhaps, some adequate idea of the boundless, ineffable, and otherwise incomprehensible and eternal greatness, grandeur, and glory to which our Lord was elevated when his Almighty Father set him at his own right hand in the heavens.

WALTER SCOTT, *The Messiahship*, 218

SCRIPTURE

Why do you pass judgment on your brother or sister? Or you, why do you despise your brother or sister? For we will all stand before the judgment seat of God. For it is written, "As I live, says the Lord, every knee shall bow to me, and every tongue shall give praise to God." So then, each of us will be accountable to God.

ROMANS 14:10-12

PRAYER

Lord Jesus, may I bow the knee to you today, as all eventually will bow. Let my tongue give you all praise this day!

MIRACLES OF JESUS

PSALM

But God will ransom my soul from the power of Sheol,
for he will receive me.

PSALM 49:15

MEDITATION

There is, therefore, an amazing concatenation of miracles drawn out in the gospel to keep before the public the person of whom it was said, "Behold my Son", miracle after miracle follows each other in rapid succession, surprisingly diversified in manner, kind, and form, till the mighty chain terminates in that amazing wonder of his resurrection from the dead—a miracle, which, for its transcendent peculiarities, the apostle (Eph. 1:19) singles out as affording the most illustrious display of the mighty power of God.

WALTER SCOTT, *The Gospel Restored*, 180

SCRIPTURE

A great windstorm arose, and the waves beat into the boat, so that the boat was already being swamped. But he was in the stern, asleep on the cushion; and they woke him up and said to him, "Teacher, do you not care that we are perishing?" He woke up and rebuked the wind, and said to the sea, "Peace! Be still!" Then the wind ceased, and there was a dead calm. He said to them, "Why are you afraid? Have you still no faith?" And they were filled with great awe and said to one another, "Who then is this, that even the wind and the sea obey him?"

MARK 4:37-41

PRAYER

Jesus, my teacher, grant this day that I might trust in your power over all the forces that threaten me. Keep me from fear. Increase my faith.

GRACE

PSALM

"Gather to me my faithful ones,
who made a covenant with me by sacrifice!"
The heavens declare his righteousness,
for God himself is judge.

PSALM 50:5-6

MEDITATION

The Messiah is a gift, sacrifice is a gift, justification is a gift, the Holy Spirit is a gift, eternal life is a gift, and even the means of our personal sanctification is a gift from God. Truly, we are saved by grace. We are only asked to accept a sacrifice which God has provided for our sins, and then the pardon of them, and to open the doors of our hearts, that the Spirit of God may come in and make its abode in us. God has provided all these blessings for us, and only requires us to accept of them freely, without any price or idea of merit on our part. But he asks us to receive them cordially, and to give up our hearts to him.

ALEXANDER CAMPBELL, *The Christian System*, 34

SCRIPTURE

"Now therefore why are you putting God to the test by placing on the neck of the disciples a yoke that neither our ancestors nor we have been able to bear? On the contrary, we believe that we will be saved through the grace of the Lord Jesus, just as they will."

ACTS 15:10-11

PRAYER

God of love, you have saved me by your grace. Open my heart to receive your grace this day.

July 23

LED BY THE SPIRIT

PSALM

Save me, O God, by your name,
and vindicate me by your might.
Hear my prayer, O God;
give ear to the words of my mouth.

PSALM 54:1-2

MEDITATION

The great secret of church government and organization has almost been overlooked. It is the indwelling of the Holy Spirit in each believer, and member of the church. The fruits of this Spirit are love, joy, peace, longsuffering, gentleness, goodness, meekness, fidelity, and temperance; against such there is no law. Such a church as is composed of such members, is easily governed by the law of Christ.

BARTON W. STONE, *Christian Messenger* (1844), 119

SCRIPTURE

I myself feel confident about you, my brothers and sisters, that you yourselves are full of goodness, filled with all knowledge, and able to instruct one another. Nevertheless on some points I have written to you rather boldly by way of reminder, because of the grace given me by God to be a minister of Christ Jesus to the Gentiles in the priestly service of the gospel of God, so that the offering of the Gentiles may be acceptable, sanctified by the Holy Spirit.

ROMANS 15:14-16

PRAYER

Holy God, pour your Holy Spirit into my heart today, so he will bear fruit in my life. Through the Spirit may I instruct and be instructed by my brothers and sisters.

July 24

GOD'S BLESSINGS

PSALM

I give you thanks, O Lord, with my whole heart; before the gods I sing your praise;
I bow down toward your holy temple
and give thanks to your name for your steadfast love and your faithfulness;
for you have exalted your name and your word above everything.
On the day I called, you answered me, you increased my strength of soul.

PSALM 138:1-3

MEDITATION

God our Father measures his blessings out to us on a liberal scale. What is his measure? Let us see! The merchant measures cloth by the yard, wheat by the bushel, sugar by the pound. A yard, a bushel, or a pound is a purely arbitrary arrangement, but when once agreed upon, all must abide by it. The Lord has established from his standpoint a standard of measurement by which he bestows his blessings on those who trust him: "But unto every one of us is given grace according to the measure of the gift of Christ" (Eph.4:7). What does this mean? Evidently that having given his Son, the best he had, he is willing to measure out all his gifts with the same liberal rule.

ASHLEY S. JOHNSON, *The Life of Trust*, 108-109

SCRIPTURE

"And now I am about to go the way of all the earth, and you know in your hearts and souls, all of you, that not one thing has failed of all the good things that the Lord your God promised concerning you; all have come to pass for you, not one of them has failed."

JOSHUA 23:14

PRAYER

Generous Father, you have overwhelmed me with blessings. None of your promises fail.

FAMILY OF GOD

PSALM

How lovely is your dwelling place, O Lord of hosts!
My soul longs, indeed it faints for the courts of the Lord;
my heart and my flesh sing for joy to the living God.

PSALM 84:1-2

MEDITATION

The Church of Christ is a family, and all its members are related to each other as brothers and sisters. And hence they should ever cherish for each other feelings of the most tender love and affection.

ROBERT MILLIGAN, *Scheme of Redemption*, 477

SCRIPTURE

Let love be genuine; hate what is evil, hold fast to what is good; love one another with mutual affection; outdo one another in showing honor. Do not lag in zeal, be ardent in spirit, serve the Lord. Rejoice in hope, be patient in suffering, persevere in prayer. Contribute to the needs of the saints; extend hospitality to strangers. Bless those who persecute you; bless and do not curse them. Rejoice with those who rejoice, weep with those who weep. Live in harmony with one another; do not be haughty, but associate with the lowly; do not claim to be wiser than you are.

ROMANS 12:9-16

PRAYER

Lord Jesus, teach me how to love my brothers and sisters. Show me how to love the world as you love it, even blessing those who make life hard for me.

OBEDIENCE

PSALM

My vows to you I must perform, O God;
I will render thank offerings to you.
For you have delivered my soul from death,
and my feet from falling,
so that I may walk before God
in the light of life.

PSALM 56:12-13

MEDITATION

Righteousness is both inward and outward conformity to the law of God. Inward righteousness is to love God with all the heart, mind, and strength, and our neighbor as ourselves. Outward righteousness is to keep his commandments, and to do to others as we would they should do unto us.

BARTON W. STONE, *Christian Messenger* (1843), 289-290

SCRIPTURE

Then Joshua said to the people, "You are witnesses against yourselves that you have chosen the Lord, to serve him." And they said, "We are witnesses." He said, "Then put away the foreign gods that are among you, and incline your hearts to the Lord, the God of Israel." The people said to Joshua, "The Lord our God we will serve, and him we will obey."

JOSHUA 24:22-24

PRAYER

Lord God, give me a heart and a will to obey you this day. May my obedience be both inward and outward, that I might truly love You and my neighbor.

THE HEART

PSALM

Hear my cry, O God; listen to my prayer.
From the end of the earth I call to you, when my heart is faint.
Lead me to the rock that is higher than I;
for you are my refuge, a strong tower against the enemy.

PSALM 61:1-3

MEDITATION

The faith of the Gospel is not, as we have shown, a mere logical assent of the understanding to the truth of the proposition that "Jesus is the Christ the Son of the living God"; but it is a living, active, fruit-bearing principle, which, while it has its root in the understanding, at the same time pervades the heart; and through the heart it influences the will; and through the will it controls the life.

ROBERT MILLIGAN, *Scheme of Redemption*, 467

SCRIPTURE

On the sabbath day we went outside the gate by the river, where we supposed there was a place of prayer; and we sat down and spoke to the women who had gathered there. A certain woman named Lydia, a worshiper of God, was listening to us; she was from the city of Thyatira and a dealer in purple cloth. The Lord opened her heart to listen eagerly to what was said by Paul. When she and her household were baptized, she urged us, saying, "If you have judged me to be faithful to the Lord, come and stay at my home." And she prevailed upon us.

ACTS 16:13-15

PRAYER

God of love, may I trust in you with my whole heart. May I show my faith, as Lydia did, through hospitality.

ASCENSION

PSALM

Blessed be the Lord, the God of Israel,
who alone does wondrous things.
Blessed be his glorious name forever;
may his glory fill the whole earth. Amen and Amen.

PSALM 72:18-19

MEDITATION

Jesus did not, it is true, baptize in the Holy Spirit during his earthly ministry. He was preparing the way for such work in the future. He was, by his life, by his teaching, by his works, and most of all by his death and resurrection from the dead, and his ascension to the right hand of God, making possible that faith in himself and in his Father, on the part of his disciples which would prepare them for receiving the Holy Spirit.

J.H. GARRISON, *The Holy Spirit*, 112-113

SCRIPTURE

"But you will receive power when the Holy Spirit has come upon you; and you will be my witnesses in Jerusalem, in all Judea and Samaria, and to the ends of the earth." When he had said this, as they were watching, he was lifted up, and a cloud took him out of their sight. While he was going and they were gazing up toward heaven, suddenly two men in white robes stood by them. They said, "Men of Galilee, why do you stand looking up toward heaven? This Jesus, who has been taken up from you into heaven, will come in the same way as you saw him go into heaven."

ACTS 1:8-11

PRAYER

Lord Jesus, thank you for the gift of your Spirit.

PURITY OF HEART

PSALM

Let all who seek you rejoice and be glad in you.
Let those who love your salvation say evermore, "God is great!"
But I am poor and needy; hasten to me, O God!
You are my help and my deliverer; O Lord, do not delay!

PSALM 70:4-5

MEDITATION

The pure in heart are those who ardently desire to do good, are aiming and striving to do good; who hunger and thirst after righteousness. They purpose good in their hearts, intend or design good. Their meditations are good, pure, and holy.

BENJAMIN FRANKLIN, *The Gospel Preacher*, VOL. 1, 283-284

SCRIPTURE

And he said, "It is what comes out of a person that defiles. For it is from within, from the human heart, that evil intentions come: fornication, theft, murder, adultery, avarice, wickedness, deceit, licentiousness, envy, slander, pride, folly. All these evil things come from within, and they defile a person."

MARK 7:20-23

PRAYER

Lord Jesus, purify my heart this day. May no evil intentions enter or come from my heart.

RESURRECTION

PSALM

Do not let the flood sweep over me,
or the deep swallow me up,
or the Pit close its mouth over me.

PSALM 69:15

MEDITATION

We shall die no more. But Messiah's own resurrection is the great turning point; this was as clearly predicted in the Old Testament as was the general resurrection, and, therefore, it is only on the fact that God has fulfilled his promise to the Messiah that we his people and disciples can hope to be raised.

WALTER SCOTT, *The Gospel Restored*, 563

SCRIPTURE

But the angel said to the women, "Do not be afraid; I know that you are looking for Jesus who was crucified. He is not here; for he has been raised, as he said. Come, see the place where he lay. Then go quickly and tell his disciples, 'He has been raised from the dead, and indeed he is going ahead of you to Galilee; there you will see him.' This is my message for you." So they left the tomb quickly with fear and great joy, and ran to tell his disciples. Suddenly Jesus met them and said, "Greetings!" And they came to him, took hold of his feet, and worshiped him.

MATTHEW 28:5-9

PRAYER

Father, you vindicated Jesus through the resurrection. Increase my faith in my own resurrection so not even death can separate me from you.

REIGN OF CHRIST

PSALM

Make vows to the Lord your God, and perform them;
let all who are around him bring gifts
to the one who is awesome,
who cuts off the spirit of princes,
who inspires fear in the kings of the earth.

PSALM 76:11-12

MEDITATION

Their laws and government were changed at last by God himself; he having appointed his Son, Jesus Christ, Lord of all: him we are now to hear and him to obey. He is Lord not only of the Jews but also of the Gentiles, of all nations. Our government is a pure monarchy; Jesus being appointed Lord of all, the only lawgiver of the world. While he reigned and ruled alone in the first centuries of the world, religion in her loveliest forms dwelt on earth.

BARTON W. STONE, *Christian Messenger* (1843), 124

SCRIPTURE

From one ancestor he made all nations to inhabit the whole earth, and he allotted the times of their existence and the boundaries of the places where they would live, so that they would search for God and perhaps grope for him and find him—though indeed he is not far from each one of us. For "In him we live and move and have our being"; as even some of your own poets have said, "For we too are his offspring."

ACTS 17:26-28

PRAYER

Lord Jesus, you are king of all the earth! Reign in my heart and in the hearts of all your offspring today.

MONEY

PSALM

You have given him his heart's desire,
and have not withheld the request of his lips.
For you meet him with rich blessings;
you set a crown of fine gold on his head.

PSALM 21:2-3

MEDITATION

But have not we in a Christian land our idols too? How many worshipers of the god mammon are there among us! How many admirers of gold and silver eagles, or their paper representatives! With how much toil, and labor are they sought! With what greedy grasp are they held when obtained! With what warm affections are they viewed and gazed upon! What pleasurable thoughts do they inspire! To part with them without value received, is like rending the heart-strings of life. The love of money is the root of all evil.

BARTON W. STONE, *Christian Messenger* (1843), 292

SCRIPTURE

The point is this: the one who sows sparingly will also reap sparingly, and the one who sows bountifully will also reap bountifully. Each of you must give as you have made up your mind, not reluctantly or under compulsion, for God loves a cheerful giver. And God is able to provide you with every blessing in abundance, so that by always having enough of everything, you may share abundantly in every good work.

2 CORINTHIANS 9:6-8

PRAYER

Father of Abundance, you provide everything I need. May I trust your provision and not trust money. May I cheerfully give to those in need.

August 2

CHRISTIAN COMMUNITY

PSALM

Help us, O God of our salvation, for the glory of your name;
deliver us, and forgive our sins, for your name's sake.

PSALM 79:9

MEDITATION

As Christians, in their individual and social capacity, are frequently exhorted by the apostles to contribute to the wants of the poor, to distribute to the necessities of the saints: as the congregation at Jerusalem continued steadfastly in this institution; and as other congregations elsewhere were commended for these acceptable sacrifices, it is easy to see and feel that it is incumbent on all Christians as they have ability, and as circumstances require, to follow their example to this benevolent institution of him who became poor that the poor might be made rich by him.

ALEXANDER CAMPBELL, *Christian Baptist*, (1826), 126

SCRIPTURE

They devoted themselves to the apostles' teaching and fellowship, to the breaking of bread and the prayers. Awe came upon everyone, because many wonders and signs were being done by the apostles. All who believed were together and had all things in common; they would sell their possessions and goods and distribute the proceeds to all, as any had need.

ACTS 2:42-44

PRAYER

Lord Jesus, help me to be one with my brothers and sisters, sharing everything as these early disciples did.

August 3

BLESSEDNESS

PSALM

He chose his servant David,
and took him from the sheepfolds;
from tending the nursing ewes he brought him
to be the shepherd of his people Jacob,
of Israel, his inheritance.

PSALM 78:70-71

MEDITATION

How precious to the heart of the Christian the high privilege of fellowship with God. How poor, in comparison, all the pleasures of sense and all the honors of the world. It is to meet with the King Eternal, Immortal, and Invisible, amid the sacred mysteries of his spiritual temple, that we are here assembled. We come to seek from that holy presence those elevating and consoling influences which impart a divine peace to the soul and purify the affections from the polluting touch of life's vain idols. We come to approach the fountain of being and blessedness, to drink of its ever-flowing streams of life and joy.

ROBERT RICHARDSON, *Communings in the Sanctuary*, 43

SCRIPTURE

"And now, O Lord God, you are God, and your words are true, and you have promised this good thing to your servant; now therefore may it please you to bless the house of your servant, so that it may continue forever before you; for you, O Lord God, have spoken, and with your blessing shall the house of your servant be blessed forever."

2 SAMUEL 7:28-29

PRAYER

Father, you have blessed me beyond my imagination. May I offer heartfelt thanks and worship to you.

August 4

FOLLOWING JESUS

PSALM

They have neither knowledge nor understanding,
they walk around in darkness;
all the foundations of the earth are shaken.

PSALM 82:5

MEDITATION

There is something in the demeanor and words of Jesus that captivates the human heart. He did not enter into any lengthy explanation of his mission or dissertation on what he expected of them, but simply in passing invited them to come, and they, as if drawn by a power which they neither could explain nor resist, arose, leaving all behind and followed him.

ASHLEY S. JOHNSON, *The Life of Trust*, 141

SCRIPTURE

The next day John again was standing with two of his disciples, and as he watched Jesus walk by, he exclaimed, "Look, here is the Lamb of God!"

The two disciples heard him say this, and they followed Jesus. When Jesus turned and saw them following, he said to them, "What are you looking for?" They said to him, "Rabbi" (which translated means Teacher), "where are you staying?" He said to them, "Come and see." They came and saw where he was staying, and they remained with him that day.

JOHN 1:35-39

PRAYER

Rabbi Jesus, allow me to follow you this day, to come and see how you live in the world so I might be your disciple.

LORDSHIP OF CHRIST

PSALM

Let them know that you alone, whose name is the Lord,
are the Most High over all the earth.

PSALM 83:18

MEDITATION

Hence, the Holy Spirit, and all the angels of Heaven are now at the disposal of our Savior. For in him all the promises of God are laid up; all the treasures of wisdom and knowledge, and all the fullness of the Deity, reside fully and truly in him. All these things, it is true, might be comprehended in one gift—the gift of Jesus as our Mediator; our Prophet, Priest, and King.

ALEXANDER CAMPBELL, *The Christian System*, 52

SCRIPTURE

Then Peter, filled with the Holy Spirit, said to them, "Rulers of the people and elders,
if we are questioned today because of a good deed done to someone who was sick and are
asked how this man has been healed, let it be known to all of you, and to all the people of
Israel, that this man is standing before you in good health by the name of Jesus Christ of
Nazareth, whom you crucified, whom God raised from the dead. This Jesus is 'the stone
that was rejected by you, the builders; it has become the cornerstone.' There is salvation
in no one else, for there is no other name under heaven given among mortals
by which we must be saved."

ACTS 4:8-12

PRAYER

Jesus, you are my Lord, my Priest, my King! May I always praise your powerful name that saves!

August 6

PRAYER AND FAITH

PSALM

O Lord, God of my salvation,
when, at night, I cry out in your presence,
let my prayer come before you;
incline your ear to my cry.

PSALM 88:1-2

MEDITATION

In no other act does the soul assert its divine paternity so clearly as in seeking communion with and blessings from the Father of Spirits. But the value, the dignity, and the power of prayer grow out of the fact, that it is the cry of a human soul uttered in the ear of the Almighty Father, who will withhold no good thing from them that walk uprightly.

J.H. GARRISON, *Alone with God*, 59

SCRIPTURE

Jesus asked the father, "How long has this been happening to him?" And he said, "From childhood. It has often cast him into the fire and into the water, to destroy him; but if you are able to do anything, have pity on us and help us." Jesus said to him, "If you are able! —All things can be done for the one who believes." Immediately the father of the child cried out, "I believe; help my unbelief!"

MARK 9:21-24

PRAYER

Jesus, help my unbelief! Increase my trust in your goodness and power! Let my prayer come before you. Listen to my cry.

GENEROSITY AND JUSTICE

PSALM
Glorious things are spoken of you, O city of God.
PSALM 87:3

MEDITATION
There is a fellowship in the Church of Christ which gives to all its members a right to whatever is really necessary to their comfort, and which, if properly understood, would render all secular policies of insurance wholly unnecessary. It is useless to recommend to others the religion of the Lord Jesus Christ while we are ourselves neglecting the principles of common justice.

ROBERT MILLIGAN, *Scheme of Redemption*, 526

SCRIPTURE
Now the whole group of those who believed were of one heart and soul, and no one claimed private ownership of any possessions, but everything they owned was held in common. With great power the apostles gave their testimony to the resurrection of the Lord Jesus, and great grace was upon them all. There was not a needy person among them, for as many as owned lands or houses sold them and brought the proceeds of what was sold. They laid it at the apostles' feet, and it was distributed to each as any had need. There was a Levite, a native of Cyprus, Joseph, to whom the apostles gave the name Barnabas (which means "son of encouragement"). He sold a field that belonged to him, then brought the money, and laid it at the apostles' feet.

ACTS 4:32-37

PRAYER
Let my testimony about Jesus be more than words, but also be filled with actions of generosity and love. Lord, make me like Barnabas!

August 8
CHRISTIAN UNITY

PSALM
May God be gracious to us and bless us
and make his face to shine upon us,
that your way may be known upon earth,
your saving power among all nations.
Let the peoples praise you, O God;
let all the peoples praise you.

PSALM 67:1-3

MEDITATION
That church does not worship acceptably, in which reconciliation amongst its members does not exist. It is not in a healthy state, nor does it exert a healthy influence on the unregenerated around. No refreshing seasons from the Lord will be experienced there while this state of things exist. What shall we say of the worship of the churches of every name, who not only are irreconciled one to another, but ever wrangling and hostilely opposing one another?

BARTON W. STONE, *Christian Messenger* (1843), 334-335

SCRIPTURE
May the God of steadfastness and encouragement grant you to live in harmony
with one another, in accordance with Christ Jesus, so that together you may with one voice
glorify the God and Father of our Lord Jesus Christ.

ROMANS 15:5-6

PRAYER
Lord, live in me so I may be reconciled to everyone, living in harmony so I might glorify you.

August 9

THE HOLY SPIRIT

PSALM

For who in the skies can be compared to the Lord?
Who among the heavenly beings is like the Lord,
a God feared in the council of the holy ones,
great and awesome above all that are around him?

PSALM 89:6-7

MEDITATION

This language refers to the Holy Spirit as opening up in the human heart, not a cistern, but a life-giving fountain, forever satisfying all its deepest desires. It may be said that Christ Himself alone satisfies the human heart, and becomes a fountain of perpetual joy to the soul. This is true, and it is only as the Holy Spirit communicates Christ to the soul that he opens up this fountain of life and joy in us.

J.H. GARRISON, *The Holy Spirit*, 145

SCRIPTURE

Jesus answered, "Very truly, I tell you, no one can enter the kingdom of God without being born of water and Spirit. What is born of the flesh is flesh, and what is born of the Spirit is spirit. Do not be astonished that I said to you, 'You must be born from above.' The wind blows where it chooses, and you hear the sound of it, but you do not know where it comes from or where it goes. So it is with everyone who is born of the Spirit."

JOHN 3:5-8

PRAYER

Jesus, you have given me birth through water and the Spirit. May the Spirit give me living water to satisfy my deepest desires.

August 10

JESUS AS KING

PSALM

The Lord is king! Let the earth rejoice;
let the many coastlands be glad!
Clouds and thick darkness are all around him;
righteousness and justice are the foundation of his throne.
Fire goes before him,
and consumes his adversaries on every side.
The heavens proclaim his righteousness;
and all the peoples behold his glory.

PSALM 97:1-3, 6

MEDITATION

As King, he is the oracle of God—to have disposal of the Holy Spirit—to be the Prophet and High Priest of the Temple of God—to have the throne of his Father—to be Governor of all nations on earth, and head of all hierarchs and powers in heaven—the supreme Lawgiver, the only Savior—the resurrection and the life, the ultimate and final Judge of all, and the Heir of all things.

ALEXANDER CAMPBELL, *The Christian System*, 154

SCRIPTURE

"'For the king will hear, and deliver his servant from the hand of the man who would cut both me and my son off from the heritage of God.' Your servant thought, 'The word of my lord the king will set me at rest'; for my lord the king is like the angel of God, discerning good and evil. The Lord your God be with you!"

2 SAMUEL 14:16-17

PRAYER

King Jesus, rule my life today. May I serve you with all my heart, showing your good to others.

CHRISTIAN FELLOWSHIP

PSALM

I will look with favor on the faithful in the land,
so that they may live with me;
whoever walks in the way that is blameless
shall minister to me.

PSALM 101:6

MEDITATION

Here, then, ends the whole matter of identifying the body of Christ, and the union of Christians. When we are turned to the Lord, reconciled to God, made one with him, we are united to all that are united to him. This is the genuine union, the genuine religion, and the genuine body in which to meet and worship.

BENJAMIN FRANKLIN, *The Gospel Preacher*, VOL. 2, 478

SCRIPTURE

Peter began to say to him, "Look, we have left everything and followed you." Jesus said, "Truly I tell you, there is no one who has left house or brothers or sisters or mother or father or children or fields, for my sake and for the sake of the good news, who will not receive a hundredfold now in this age—houses, brothers and sisters, mothers and children, and fields with persecutions—and in the age to come eternal life. But many who are first will be last, and the last will be first."

MARK 10:28-31

PRAYER

Christ Jesus, help me to leave all for you, knowing that you give me a new family in which to live.

August 12

BREAD OF LIFE

PSALM

They asked, and he brought quails,
and gave them food from heaven in abundance.
He opened the rock, and water gushed out;
it flowed through the desert like a river.

PSALM 105:40-41

MEDITATION

Thus it is "living," incorruptible food alone that can impart life and incorruptibility. And oh! How striking the literal fact which perfects the agreement of these truths, that when our Lord gave his flesh for the life of the world that "living food" saw no corruption. For he was the "true bread from heaven"; the celestial manna; the "bread of God which came from heaven to give life to the world." It was not possible that he should be held by death in the bondage of the grave.

ROBERT RICHARDSON, *Communings in the Sanctuary*, 19-20

SCRIPTURE

But he said to them, "I have food to eat that you do not know about." So the disciples said to one another, "Surely no one has brought him something to eat?" Jesus said to them, "My food is to do the will of him who sent me and to complete his work."

JOHN 4:32-34

PRAYER

Lord Jesus, you are living bread. Fill me with obedience to the will and work of the Father.

August 13

CALLING ON THE LORD

PSALM
Hear my prayer, O Lord;
let my cry come to you.
Do not hide your face from me
in the day of my distress.
Incline your ear to me;
answer me speedily in the day when I call.

PSALM 102:1-2

MEDITATION
By all his tender mercies, then; his goodness, his great love; his wonderful compassion; by the value of your precious souls; by the sufferings of the bleeding, dying Savior; the shame and indignation heaped upon him, when he bore our sins on the cross; by all that is lovely and endearing, be persuaded to turn to the Lord and live forever.

BENJAMIN FRANKLIN, *The Gospel Preacher*, VOL. 1, 152

SCRIPTURE
Then he said, "The God of our ancestors has chosen you to know his will, to see the Righteous One and to hear his own voice; for you will be his witness to all the world of what you have seen and heard. And now why do you delay? Get up, be baptized, and have your sins washed away, calling on his name."

ACTS 22:14-16

PRAYER
O Lord, hear my cry as I call upon you this day. You heard my cry in baptism and washed away my sins. May I live forever in your Name!

August 14

PRAISE AND WORSHIP

PSALM

Be exalted, O God, above the heavens,
and let your glory be over all the earth.
Give victory with your right hand, and answer me,
so that those whom you love may be rescued.

PSALM 108:5-6

MEDITATION

Those in heaven worship in truth—truth in the inward parts, and according to the prescribed truth in heaven. When they praise they do it from a sense of praise-worthiness; when they give thanks it flows from a sense of obligation for unmerited favor; when they bow before him, it is with a deep sense of their unworthiness and dependence. O for such worship to be on earth, as it is in heaven!

BARTON W. STONE, *Christian Messenger* (1844), 142

SCRIPTURE

Many people spread their cloaks on the road, and others spread leafy branches that they had cut in the fields. Then those who went ahead and those who followed were shouting,
"Hosanna!
Blessed is the one who comes in the name of the Lord!
Blessed is the coming kingdom of our ancestor David!
Hosanna in the highest heaven!"

MARK 11:8-10

PRAYER

May your name be exalted, O God! I bless the one who comes in the name of the Lord, Jesus, the one who saves!

REDEMPTION

PSALM

This is the day that the Lord has made;
let us rejoice and be glad in it.
Save us, we beseech you, O Lord!
O Lord, we beseech you, give us success!
Blessed is the one who comes in the name of the Lord.
We bless you from the house of the Lord.

PSALM 118:24-26

MEDITATION

But in no other way could the love of God be so fully, so directly, and so effica-
ciously manifested to us as in the gift of his own Son. True, indeed, to him
whom the Lamp of Truth illuminates, all nature is but an index or manifestation
of the goodness and benevolence of God, as well as of his wisdom and power.

ROBERT MILLIGAN, *Scheme of Redemption*, 242

SCRIPTURE

Christ redeemed us from the curse of the law by becoming a curse for us—for it is written,
"Cursed is everyone who hangs on a tree"—in order that in Christ Jesus the blessing of
Abraham might come to the Gentiles, so that we might receive the promise
of the Spirit through faith.

GALATIANS 3:13-14

PRAYER

Father, you redeemed me through the gift of your Son. Jesus, you became a
curse for me, and gave me your Holy Spirit. I bless God for his marvelous gifts!

August 16

Prayer

Psalm

Remember me, O Lord, when you show favor to your people;
help me when you deliver them;
that I may see the prosperity of your chosen ones,
that I may rejoice in the gladness of your nation,
that I may glory in your heritage.

Psalm 106:4-5

Meditation

Is not prayer, next to repentance, one of the first fruits of that all-pervading, soul-transforming and regenerating principle by which God purifies the heart, makes it a fit temple for his Spirit, and gives new life and energy to the soul?

Robert Milligan, *A Brief Treatise on Prayer*, 42

Scripture

Jesus answered them, "Have faith in God. Truly I tell you, if you say to this mountain, 'Be taken up and thrown into the sea,' and if you do not doubt in your heart, but believe that what you say will come to pass, it will be done for you. So I tell you, whatever you ask for in prayer, believe that you have received it, and it will be yours."

Mark 11:22-24

Prayer

Father, I thank you that you hear my prayers. Increase my faith in your goodness and power, so I may glory in your heritage.

SALVATION

PSALM

Blessed be the Lord, who has not given us as prey to their teeth.
We have escaped like a bird from the snare of the fowlers;
the snare is broken, and we have escaped.

PSALM 124:6-7

MEDITATION

While Christians are taught to expect and hope for a future salvation—a salvation from the power of death and the grave, a salvation to be revealed at the last time—they receive the first fruit of the Spirit, the salvation of the soul from guilt, pollution, and the dominance of sin, and come under the dominance of righteousness, peace, and joy.

ALEXANDER CAMPBELL, *The Christian System*, 186

SCRIPTURE

But when they believed Philip, who was proclaiming the good news about the kingdom of God and the name of Jesus Christ, they were baptized, both men and women. Even Simon himself believed. After being baptized, he stayed constantly with Philip and was amazed when he saw the signs and great miracles that took place.

ACTS 8:12-13

PRAYER

Father, you have saved me now and for eternity. May I know the joy and peace of salvation today and look forward to the salvation yet to come.

DAILY BREAD

PSALM
Happy is everyone who fears the Lord,
who walks in his ways.
You shall eat the fruit of the labor of your hands;
you shall be happy, and it shall go well with you.

PSALM 128:1-2

MEDITATION
Here is the beautiful spirit of dependence on, and trust in, a Father's love and care. When we can recognize all our daily blessings as gifts from the hand of our heavenly Father, the gratitude we feel will express itself in constant thanksgiving to him.

J.H. GARRISON, *Alone with God*, 116

SCRIPTURE
Then Jesus took the loaves, and when he had given thanks, he distributed them to those who were seated; so also the fish, as much as they wanted. When they were satisfied, he told his disciples, "Gather up the fragments left over, so that nothing may be lost." So they gathered them up, and from the fragments of the five barley loaves, left by those who had eaten, they filled twelve baskets. When the people saw the sign that he had done, they began to say, "This is indeed the prophet who is to come into the world."

JOHN 6:11-14

PRAYER
Father, give me this day my daily bread. Jesus, feed me as you did the crowd, with yourself the living bread.

August 19

Help in Hardships

Psalm
O Lord, remember in David's favor all the hardships he endured.

PSALM 132:1

Meditation
I have taken much pains to give you glimpses of his power and majesty, for I want you to know that our God has the power to help in time of need. I wish to bring him down, or rather bring us up to the point where our minds and hearts will take hold of him.

Is God our Father? Certainly. Even nature teaches that he is the Father of all the sons and daughters of earth. The adaptability and plenitude of the provisions of nature for human desires prove that he who made both had a Father's feeling.

ASHLEY S. JOHNSON, *The Life of Trust*, 28

Scripture
Then Job arose, tore his robe, shaved his head, and fell on the ground and worshiped. He said, "Naked I came from my mother's womb, and naked shall I return there; the Lord gave, and the Lord has taken away; blessed be the name of the Lord." In all this Job did not sin or charge God with wrong-doing.

JOB 1:20-22

Prayer
God of love, I am weak and helpless. My struggles and sorrows threaten to overwhelm me. Lord, hear my cry and hurry to help me!

August 20

GRIEF

PSALM

With my voice I cry to the Lord;
with my voice I make supplication to the Lord.
I pour out my complaint before him;
I tell my trouble before him.
When my spirit is faint,
you know my way.
In the path where I walk
they have hidden a trap for me.

PSALM 142:1-3

MEDITATION

O Lord, you are our refuge in every time of trouble and of danger. Though we forget you, too often, when our path is unshadowed, and all goes well with us, yet in the day of affliction, when clouds overspread our sky, you are remembered by us as our only refuge, and to you we flee.

J.H. GARRISON, *Alone with God*, 139

SCRIPTURE

So the victory that day was turned into mourning for all the troops; for the troops heard that day, "The king is grieving for his son." The troops stole into the city that day as soldiers steal in who are ashamed when they flee in battle. The king covered his face, and the king cried with a loud voice, "O my son Absalom, O Absalom, my son, my son!"

2 SAMUEL 19:2-4

PRAYER

Loving Father, listen to me as I pour out my grief and complaint to you. I flee to you for help, O Lord. Deliver me from evil.

August 21

HELP OF THE SPIRIT

PSALM

Stretch out your hand from on high;
set me free and rescue me from the mighty waters,
from the hand of aliens,
whose mouths speak lies,
and whose right hands are false.

PSALM 144:7-8

MEDITATION

Without the Spirit of God, how infirm, how weak, how helpless we are! He gives help to us in time of need. It was this Spirit in the apostles and martyrs that made them strong to endure persecution and death in its most horrid forms. It is this Spirit in Christians that supports them in all the ills of life, and causes them to triumph in death. Often this Spirit of prayer intercedes in groans unutterable—God understands the meaning and grants the grace we need.

BARTON W. STONE, *Christian Messenger* (1841), 240

SCRIPTURE

As for yourselves, beware; for they will hand you over to councils; and you will be beaten in synagogues; and you will stand before governors and kings because of me, as a testimony to them. And the good news must first be proclaimed to all nations. When they bring you to trial and hand you over, do not worry beforehand about what you are to say; but say whatever is given you at that time, for it is not you who speak, but the Holy Spirit.

MARK 13:9-11

PRAYER

Brother Jesus, this day may I rely on the help of the Holy Spirit, not on my own feeble wisdom and power. Give me words to say when others speak lies about me.

August 22

ONE IN CHRIST

PSALM

Praise the Lord!
I will give thanks to the Lord with my whole heart,
in the company of the upright, in the congregation.
Great are the works of the Lord,
studied by all who delight in them.

PSALM 111:1-2

MEDITATION

It is true, indeed, that for a short time the power of the Gospel seemed to neutralize and triumph over everything else. Under its potent influence some of the worst forms of human nature were molded into the image and likeness of Him who became flesh and dwelt among us.

ROBERT MILLIGAN, *Scheme of Redemption,* 501

SCRIPTURE

As many of you as were baptized into Christ have clothed yourselves with Christ.
There is no longer Jew or Greek, there is no longer slave or free, there is no longer male and
female; for all of you are one in Christ Jesus. And if you belong to Christ, then you are
Abraham's offspring, heirs according to the promise.

GALATIANS 3:27-29

PRAYER

Father, remove from my heart and life all prejudice and favoritism. May I embrace all your children, knowing that we all belong to Christ through grace.

LIVING FOOD

PSALM

Happy are those
who do not follow the advice of the wicked,
or take the path that sinners tread,
or sit in the seat of scoffers;
but their delight is in the law of the Lord,
and on his law they meditate day and night.

PSALM 1:1-2

MEDITATION

How important to realize that there is this necessary connection between life and its food, and that as mortality and corruption depend upon food that is itself perishable, so eternal life is equally dependent upon that food which endures forever. How happy the one who can truly realize by experience these precious spiritual truths.

ROBERT RICHARDSON, *Communings in the Sanctuary*, 20

SCRIPTURE

So Jesus said to them, "Very truly, I tell you, unless you eat the flesh of the Son of Man and drink his blood, you have no life in you. Those who eat my flesh and drink my blood have eternal life, and I will raise them up on the last day; for my flesh is true food and my blood is true drink."

JOHN 6:53-55

PRAYER

Jesus, let me eat of your flesh and drink your blood today, as I meditate on your life and death for me.

August 24

RESURRECTION

PSALM

Depart from me, all you workers of evil,
for the Lord has heard the sound of my weeping.
The Lord has heard my supplication; the Lord accepts my prayer.
All my enemies shall be ashamed and struck with terror;
they shall turn back, and in a moment be put to shame.

PSALM 6:8-10

MEDITATION

By the word of his power he created the heavens and the earth; by the word of his grace he reanimates the human soul; and by the word of his power he will again form our bodies anew, and reunite the spirit and the body in the bonds of an incorruptible and everlasting union.

ALEXANDER CAMPBELL, *The Christian System*, 271

SCRIPTURE

All the widows stood beside him, weeping and showing tunics and other clothing that Dorcas had made while she was with them. Peter put all of them outside, and then he knelt down and prayed. He turned to the body and said, "Tabitha, get up." Then she opened her eyes, and seeing Peter, she sat up. He gave her his hand and helped her up. Then calling the saints and widows, he showed her to be alive.

ACTS 9:39-41

PRAYER

Lord, deliver me from that ultimate enemy, death. May my weeping be turned to joy!

August 25

PRAYER IN TROUBLE

PSALM

You, O Lord, will protect us;
you will guard us from this generation forever.
On every side the wicked prowl,
as vileness is exalted among humankind.

PSALM 12:7-8

MEDITATION

To come to the Lord in faith, over the sick, and pray for the sick, not simply
in view of their being raised up, or recovered, but to invoke the divine blessing
on them, in full assurance that the Lord will hear, answer, and bless them—it
may be, not precisely as we meant it, or looked for it, but in a better way—is
the exercise of living faith.

BENJAMIN FRANKLIN, *The Gospel Preacher*, VOL. 2, 185

SCRIPTURE

"Do not human beings have a hard service on earth, and are not their days like the days
of a laborer? Like a slave who longs for the shadow, and like laborers who look for their
wages, so I am allotted months of emptiness, and nights of misery are apportioned to me.
When I lie down I say, 'When shall I rise?' But the night is long, and I am full of tossing
until dawn. My flesh is clothed with worms and dirt; my skin hardens, then breaks out
again. My days are swifter than a weaver's shuttle, and come to their end without hope."

JOB 7:1-6

PRAYER

Father, hear me when I cry out in pain for others and for myself. Give me
faith to trust your power to protect and heal.

August 26

DELIVERANCE

PSALM

The Lord lives! Blessed be my rock,
and exalted be the God of my salvation,
the God who gave me vengeance
and subdued peoples under me;
who delivered me from my enemies;
indeed, you exalted me above my adversaries;
you delivered me from the violent.
For this I will extol you, O Lord, among the nations,
and sing praises to your name.

PSALM 18:46-49

MEDITATION

Evil is the one thing to be feared, and we do well to ask our heavenly Father to "deliver us from evil"—the evil that is without, and the evil thoughts that may arise in our own hearts. God alone can deliver us from the dominion of evil or the "Evil One."

J.H. GARRISON, *Alone With God*, 117

SCRIPTURE

Now some of the people of Jerusalem were saying, "Is not this the man whom they are trying to kill? And here he is, speaking openly, but they say nothing to him! Can it be that the authorities really know that this is the Messiah? Yet we know where this man is from; but when the Messiah comes, no one will know where he is from."

JOHN 7:25-27

PRAYER

My Father, deliver me from evil this day. Lord Jesus, thank you for delivering me from the Evil One by the power of your death and resurrection.

August 27

GOD'S TEMPLE

PSALM

I will tell of your name to my brothers and sisters;
in the midst of the congregation I will praise you:
You who fear the Lord, praise him!
All you offspring of Jacob, glorify him;
stand in awe of him, all you offspring of Israel!

PSALM 22:22-23

MEDITATION

As God dwelt in his temple of old, so now he dwells in his church. As he manifested himself in that which was the type of his future church, so now he dwells in his church on earth by his Spirit, and shines through them to the world in darkness.

BARTON W. STONE, *Christian Messenger* (1841), 66

SCRIPTURE

"But now the Lord my God has given me rest on every side; there is neither adversary nor misfortune. So I intend to build a house for the name of the Lord my God, as the Lord said to my father David, 'Your son, whom I will set on your throne in your place, shall build the house for my name.'"

1 KINGS 5:4-5

PRAYER

Holy God, you had Solomon build you a temple. Today, build me and my sisters and brothers into a holy temple, so you will live in us.

JUDGMENT

PSALM

The Lord is at your right hand;
he will shatter kings on the day of his wrath.
He will execute judgment among the nations,
filling them with corpses;
he will shatter heads
over the wide earth.
He will drink from the stream by the path;
therefore he will lift up his head.

PSALM 110:5-7

MEDITATION

The Gospel is to kindreds, and tongues, and sects, and nations, as it is to individuals, a savor of life unto life or of death unto death. It either kills or cures. It is the ax that is even now laid at the root of every tree in Christendom, and every one which does not speedily bring forth good fruit must soon be cut down and cast into the fire.

ROBERT MILLIGAN, *Scheme of Redemption*, 555-556

SCRIPTURE

Jesus answered, "Even if I testify on my own behalf, my testimony is valid because I know where I have come from and where I am going, but you do not know where I come from or where I am going. You judge by human standards; I judge no one. Yet even if I do judge, my judgment is valid; for it is not I alone who judge, but I and the Father who sent me."

JOHN 8:14-16

PRAYER

Almighty God, deliver me from judgment through the love and power of your Son, Jesus. May I embrace the good news this day.

August 29

PRESENCE OF GOD

PSALM

Tremble, O earth, at the presence of the Lord,
at the presence of the God of Jacob,
who turns the rock into a pool of water,
the flint into a spring of water.

PSALM 114:7-8

MEDITATION

How many thus enter into the sanctuary of God without any realizing sense of the divine presence! How many, alas, from that sleep of error never waken! Yet the Lord is in his holy temple and will there reveal himself to his people; even to the seed of Israel, his servant—the children of Jacob, his chosen.

How fitting it is that we should enter into his gates with thanksgiving and into his courts with praise. How proper that we should here repress each worldly thought and yield our hearts up to those sacred communings in which faith lifts a ladder to the skies, that angels may descend to earth and God himself confirm his promises of grace.

ROBERT RICHARDSON, *Communings in the Sanctuary*, 1-2

SCRIPTURE

"Can you find out the deep things of God? Can you find out the limit of the Almighty?
It is higher than heaven—what can you do? Deeper than Sheol—what can you know?
Its measure is longer than the earth, and broader than the sea."

JOB 11:7-9

PRAYER

Lord God, welcome me into your presence this day, that I might enjoy sweet communion with you.

MERCY

PSALM

O Lord, who may abide in your tent?
Who may dwell on your holy hill?
Those who walk blamelessly, and do what is right,
and speak the truth from their heart;
who do not slander with their tongue,
and do no evil to their friends,
nor take up a reproach against their neighbors;
in whose eyes the wicked are despised,
but who honor those who fear the Lord;
who stand by their oath even to their hurt;
who do not lend money at interest,
and do not take a bribe against the innocent.
Those who do these things shall never be moved.

PSALM 15:1-5

MEDITATION

We ardently desire to see godliness, piety, and love keep pace with knowledge.

BARTON W. STONE, *Christian Messenger* (1844), 4

SCRIPTURE

So speak and so act as those who are to be judged by the law of liberty. For judgment will be without mercy to anyone who has shown no mercy; mercy triumphs over judgment.

JAMES 2:12-13

PRAYER

Lord Jesus, have mercy on me! May I have mercy on others. May I walk blamelessly before you this day.

August 31
GOD'S PROMISES

PSALM

Your steadfast love, O Lord, extends to the heavens,
your faithfulness to the clouds.
Your righteousness is like the mighty mountains,
your judgments are like the great deep;
you save humans and animals alike, O Lord.

PSALM 36:5-6

MEDITATION

It takes a lifetime for each individual to test the faithfulness of God for himself or herself, and if you are not willing to pledge your whole life, give your entire time to the work, you might as well not begin.

ASHLEY S. JOHNSON, *The Life of Trust*, 162

SCRIPTURE

Blessed be the Lord, who has given rest to his people Israel according to all that he promised; not one word has failed of all his good promise, which he spoke through his servant Moses. The Lord our God be with us, as he was with our ancestors; may he not leave us or abandon us, but incline our hearts to him, to walk in all his ways, and to keep his commandments, his statutes, and his ordinances, which he commanded our ancestors.

1 KINGS 8:56-58

PRAYER

Faithful God, teach me this day to trust in your promises, knowing that you will never leave or abandon me.

September 1
DEITY OF CHRIST

PSALM

Let your steadfast love come to me, O Lord,
your salvation according to your promise.
Then I shall have an answer for those who taunt me,
for I trust in your word.

PSALM 119:41-42

MEDITATION

The introduction of the worship of the Messiah into the church of the living God, forms a new era in the history of the true religion, and can be justified only on the hypothesis that our Lord Jesus Christ was divine—"God manifest in the flesh."

WALTER SCOTT, *The Messiahship*, 212

SCRIPTURE

Jesus answered, "If I glorify myself, my glory is nothing. It is my Father who glorifies me, he of whom you say, 'He is our God,' though you do not know him. But I know him; if I would say that I do not know him, I would be a liar like you. But I do know him and I keep his word. Your ancestor Abraham rejoiced that he would see my day; he saw it and was glad." Then the Jews said to him, "You are not yet fifty years old, and have you seen Abraham?" Jesus said to them, "Very truly, I tell you, before Abraham was, I am."

JOHN 8:54-58

PRAYER

Jesus, God made flesh, you are before Abraham. May I worship you today in both word and action.

September 2
The Crucifixion

PSALM

The wicked plot against the righteous,
and gnash their teeth at them;
but the Lord laughs at the wicked,
for he sees that their day is coming.

PSALM 37:12-13

MEDITATION

But you say did Christ die for me? The Scriptures aver that he "died for all"; not only those who already believe, or have in any age believed, but "for the sins of the whole world." If therefore you are in the form of flesh and blood, you are included in the great reconciliation by Jesus Christ.

WALTER SCOTT, *The Gospel Restored*, 516-517

SCRIPTURE

Pilate spoke to them again, "Then what do you wish me to do with the man you call the King of the Jews?" They shouted back, "Crucify him!" Pilate asked them, "Why, what evil has he done?" But they shouted all the more, "Crucify him!" So Pilate, wishing to satisfy the crowd, released Barabbas for them; and after flogging Jesus, he handed him over to be crucified.

MARK 15:12-15

PRAYER

Christ, you suffered unjust punishment for me. You trusted in your Father for resurrection. Grant that I may know the depth of your love for me.

September 3

REDEMPTION

PSALM

You have seen, O Lord; do not be silent!
O Lord, do not be far from me!
Wake up! Bestir yourself for my defense,
for my cause, my God and my Lord!
Vindicate me, O Lord, my God,
according to your righteousness,
and do not let them rejoice over me.

PSALM 35:22-24

MEDITATION

Adopted thus into the family of God, you have not only received the name, the rank, and the dignity, but also the spirit of a child of God, and find, as such, that you are kings, priests, and heirs of God. You now feel that all things are yours, because you are Christ's and Christ is God's. The hope of the coming regeneration of the heavens and the earth, at the resurrection of the just, animates you. You look for the redemption, the adoption of your bodies, and their transfiguration.

ALEXANDER CAMPBELL, *The Christian System*, 238

SCRIPTURE

For I know that my Redeemer lives, and that at the last he will stand upon the earth; and after my skin has been thus destroyed, then in my flesh I shall see God, whom I shall see on my side, and my eyes shall behold, and not another.

JOB 19:25-27

PRAYER

Jesus, my Redeemer, I bless your holy name! Vindicate me this day, O Lord, and protect me from all who would harm me.

September 4

RESURRECTION

PSALM

I will extol you, O Lord, for you have drawn me up,
and did not let my foes rejoice over me.
O Lord my God, I cried to you for help,
and you have healed me.
O Lord, you brought up my soul from Sheol,
restored me to life from among those gone down to the Pit.

PSALM 30:1-3

MEDITATION

The promises of God are these; that the Messiah was to be the first fruits of a resurrection; that his dead men should live, and their bones be made to flourish like a green herb; that he should see a seed, who would publish his praises; that as in Adam all die so in Messiah all should be made alive; that he would raise us up at the last day.

WALTER SCOTT, *The Gospel Restored*, 563

SCRIPTURE

When they had carried out everything that was written about him, they took him down from the tree and laid him in a tomb. But God raised him from the dead; and for many days he appeared to those who came up with him from Galilee to Jerusalem, and they are now his witnesses to the people.

ACTS 13:29-31

PRAYER

Loving God who raised Jesus from the dead, you have raised me from the dead to be in Christ. May I live that new life today.

September 5

DEATH IN THE LORD

PSALM

As for mortals, their days are like grass;
they flourish like a flower of the field;
for the wind passes over it, and it is gone,
and its place knows it no more.

PSALM 103:15-16

MEDITATION

The prize of the Christian calling can be nothing less than the complete transformation into Christ's likeness, both in moral and bodily perfection, and the subsequent entrance into all the blessedness of state and being which make heaven. How all the world's most coveted prizes dwindle into utter worthlessness when compared with this!

J.H. GARRISON, *Alone With God*, 67-68

SCRIPTURE

Here is a call for the endurance of the saints, those who keep the commandments of God and hold fast to the faith of Jesus. And I heard a voice from heaven saying, "Write this: Blessed are the dead who from now on die in the Lord." "Yes," says the Spirit, "they will rest from their labors, for their deeds follow them."

REVELATION 14:12-13

PRAYER

Father, redeem me from my fear of death so I might know how blessed it is to die in the Lord Jesus.

September 6

LOVE OF KNOWLEDGE

PSALM

In God we have boasted continually,
and we will give thanks to your name forever.

PSALM 44:8

MEDITATION

As for our love of knowledge, Christianity purposes to fill us with all the riches and treasures of Jesus Christ. She opens for us a field of inquiry and sacred meditation, which the literature of the nations knows nothing at all about; and by assuring us that all we see, the world, the universe, is of God, she inspires us with an ardent zeal to inquire into his glorious works; so that she brings the works and words of God alike before us, and fills us with the most excellent knowledge.

WALTER SCOTT, *The Gospel Restored*, 208-209

SCRIPTURE

And this is my prayer, that your love may overflow more and more with knowledge and
full insight to help you to determine what is best, so that in the day of Christ you may be
pure and blameless, having produced the harvest of righteousness that comes through
Jesus Christ for the glory and praise of God.

PHILIPPIANS 1:9-11

PRAYER

Father, I bless you. May my love overflow with insight this day that I might work together with you in helping those in need.

September 7

LIFE IN THE KINGDOM

PSALM

Walk about Zion, go all around it, count its towers,
consider well its ramparts; go through its citadels,
that you may tell the next generation
that this is God, our God forever and ever.
He will be our guide forever.

PSALM 48:12-14

MEDITATION

So believers are one in the same benevolent operation of saving the world.
They are "workers together with God"—they cooperate with God and one
another in all divine means, ordained of God to effect this great end. They
regard not their own things, exclusively, but also the things of others. They
divide their substance with the poor and needy—the widow and the fatherless;
nor do they withdraw the hand of mercy from giving the means of sending the
gospel to a world in darkness.

BARTON W. STONE, *Christian Messenger* (1840), 257

SCRIPTURE

There they strengthened the souls of the disciples and encouraged them to continue in the
faith, saying, "It is through many persecutions that we must enter the kingdom of God."
And after they had appointed elders for them in each church, with prayer and fasting they
entrusted them to the Lord in whom they had come to believe.

ACTS 14:22-23

PRAYER

Blessed are you, King of the Universe! May I work with you this day even if
hardships and persecutions come.

September 8

LIGHT

PSALM

But I will sing of your might;
I will sing aloud of your steadfast love in the morning.
For you have been a fortress for me
and a refuge in the day of my distress.
O my strength, I will sing praises to you,
for you, O God, are my fortress,
the God who shows me steadfast love.

PSALM 59:16-17

MEDITATION

O for a revival of God's own work in the world! O that we all may be Christians indeed—sacrifices salted with divine grace! O Lord, may thy truth shine as the sun upon our benighted, frozen world! May all that profess the name of Jesus be filled with the Spirit, and bring forth the fruits of love, joy, peace, longsuffering, gentleness, goodness, fidelity, meekness, and temperance.

BARTON W. STONE, *Christian Messenger* (1843), 180

SCRIPTURE

Do all things without murmuring and arguing, so that you may be blameless and innocent, children of God without blemish in the midst of a crooked and perverse generation, in which you shine like stars in the world.

PHILIPPIANS 2:14-15

PRAYER

Father, may I shine with the light of Jesus today, through the power of your Spirit. Keep me from murmuring and arguing.

September 9

The Holy Spirit

Psalm

You have dealt well with your servant,
O Lord, according to your word.
Teach me good judgment and knowledge,
for I believe in your commandments.

Psalm 119:65-66

Meditation

If the love of God for us, as manifested in Christ Jesus, awakens a responsive love for God in the human heart, along this line of reciprocal affection God sends his Spirit, and with Him the richest treasures of his grace and truth, and we are "filled with the fullness of God."

J.H. Garrison, *The Holy Spirit*, 73-74

Scripture

After there had been much debate, Peter stood up and said to them, "My brothers, you know that in the early days God made a choice among you, that I should be the one through whom the Gentiles would hear the message of the good news and become believers. And God, who knows the human heart, testified to them by giving them the Holy Spirit, just as he did to us; and in cleansing their hearts by faith he has made no distinction between them and us."

Acts 15:7-9

Prayer

God of love, you have poured your love into my heart through your Spirit! May I be filled with your love today so I might share it with others.

THE GOAL

PSALM
I delight to do your will,
O my God; your law is within my heart.

PSALM 40:8

MEDITATION

Christ is the goal. His perfect, sinless character is the mark toward which we are pressing. Such an aim and plan of life necessitate constant growth, both in grace and in the knowledge of our Lord Jesus Christ. It forbids that we should rest, contentedly, on a low plane of spiritual attainment. What an enchanting view of life does Christianity thus present to the young! It is not a system of dead forms and arbitrary rules, but a glorious life of unending progress in knowledge and virtue, with Christ as our leader and our goal.

J.H. GARRISON, *Alone with God*, 66-67

SCRIPTURE

Not that I have already obtained this or have already reached the goal; but I press on to make it my own, because Christ Jesus has made me his own. Beloved, I do not consider that I have made it my own; but this one thing I do: forgetting what lies behind and straining forward to what lies ahead, I press on toward the goal for the prize of the heavenly call of God in Christ Jesus.

PHILIPPIANS 3:12-14

PRAYER

Lord Jesus, you are the plan and goal of my life. May I not be discouraged but press on in my race.

CREATION

PSALM

God, who is enthroned from of old,
will hear, and will humble them—
because they do not change,
and do not fear God.

PSALM 55:19

MEDITATION

At the simple command of the Great Architect, suns, and moons, and stars, and systems sprang into existence. And though they were perhaps at first in a chaotic state, they immediately commenced their march sublime under the laws and forces of universal gravitation.

ROBERT MILLIGAN, *Scheme of Redemption*, 24

SCRIPTURE

Then the Lord answered Job out of the whirlwind: "Who is this that darkens counsel by words without knowledge? Gird up your loins like a man, I will question you, and you shall declare to me.

"Where were you when I laid the foundation of the earth? Tell me, if you have understanding. Who determined its measurements—surely you know! Or who stretched the line upon it? On what were its bases sunk, or who laid its cornerstone when the morning stars sang together and all the heavenly beings shouted for joy?"

JOB 38:1-7

PRAYER

Almighty God, Creator, I bow humbly before you and bless you as my Maker and the one who sustains me. May I know your greatness and beauty this day.

UNITY

PSALM
How very good and pleasant it is
when kindred live together in unity!

PSALM 133:1

MEDITATION

All must be holy, meek, and heavenly as the cornerstone, Jesus Christ. He is the true and perfect example for our imitation. The cement, by which the different members of the building are bound and united together, is the Spirit of Jesus in them. Without this cement the building would fall. Hence we see the absolute necessity that each member have the Spirit of Christ; without it, it is impossible to be united according to the express will of God.

BARTON W. STONE, *Christian Messenger* (1843), 84

SCRIPTURE

So when you are offering your gift at the altar, if you remember that your brother or sister has something against you, leave your gift there before the altar and go; first be reconciled to your brother or sister, and then come and offer your gift. Come to terms quickly with your accuser while you are on the way to court with him, or your accuser may hand you over to the judge, and the judge to the guard, and you will be thrown into prison. Truly I tell you, you will never get out until you have paid the last penny.

MATTHEW 5:23-26

PRAYER

Jesus, Savior, bind me this day with your strong love to my brothers and sisters. I ask this through your Holy Spirit who makes us one.

September 13

KNOWLEDGE AND THE SPIRIT

PSALM

People will say, "Surely there is a reward for the righteous;
surely there is a God who judges on earth."

PSALM 58:11

MEDITATION

I have said that I had rather enjoy the Spirit, dwelling in me one hour, than to dispute about the mode of its operation a thousand years. What can we, with such limited minds, comprehend of unrevealed things? It is enough for us to believe that we receive the Spirit through faith and obedience, and that the disobedient unbeliever has no scriptural authority to expect it.

BARTON W. STONE, *Christian Messenger* (1835), 110

SCRIPTURE

I give thanks to my God always for you because of the grace of God that has been
given you in Christ Jesus, for in every way you have been enriched in him, in speech and
knowledge of every kind—just as the testimony of Christ has been strengthened
among you—so that you are not lacking in any spiritual gift as you wait for the
revealing of our Lord Jesus Christ.

1 CORINTHIANS 1:4-7

PRAYER

Lord Jesus, may I enjoy your Holy Spirit today. May he give me gifts of knowledge and speech as I wait to see you.

REPENTANCE

PSALM
"Bless God in the great congregation,
the Lord, O you who are of Israel's fountain!"
There is Benjamin, the least of them, in the lead,
the princes of Judah in a body,
the princes of Zebulun, the princes of Naphtali.

PSALM 68:26-27

MEDITATION

How kind and compassionate is our heavenly Father, against who we have sinned, not only one year, but every year of our life, till we turned to the Lord, to forgive all our sins—blot them from the book of remembrance and remember them no more forever—not even permit them to be mentioned; and how wonderful must one be to refuse to come and accept this most gracious pardon, when freely and mercifully offered!

BENJAMIN FRANKLIN, *The Gospel Preacher*, VOL. 1, 151-152

SCRIPTURE

He left Nazareth and made his home in Capernaum by the sea, in the territory of Zebulun and Naphtali, so that what had been spoken through the prophet Isaiah might be fulfilled: "Land of Zebulun, land of Naphtali, on the road by the sea, across the Jordan, Galilee of the Gentiles—the people who sat in darkness have seen a great light, and for those who sat in the region and shadow of death light has dawned." From that time Jesus began to proclaim, "Repent, for the kingdom of heaven has come near."

MATTHEW 4:13-17

PRAYER

Heavenly Father, turn my heart toward you this day in repentance, through Jesus Christ, my Lord.

September 15

SPIRIT AND KNOWLEDGE

PSALM

I will never forget your precepts,
for by them you have given me life.

PSALM 119:93

MEDITATION

The scriptures will never keep together in union and fellowship members not in the spirit of the scriptures, which spirit is love, peace, unity, forbearance, and cheerful obedience. This is the spirit of the great Head of the body. I blush for my fellows who hold up the Bible as the bond of union yet make their opinions of it tests of fellowship; who plead for union of all Christians, yet refuse fellowship with such as dissent from their notions. Vain men! Their zeal is not according to knowledge, nor is their spirit that of Christ.

BARTON W. STONE, *Christian Messenger* (1835), 180

SCRIPTURE

But, as it is written, "What no eye has seen, nor ear heard, nor the human heart conceived, what God has prepared for those who love him"—these things God has revealed to us through the Spirit; for the Spirit searches everything, even the depths of God. For what human being knows what is truly human except the human spirit that is within? So also no one comprehends what is truly God's except the Spirit of God. Now we have received not the spirit of the world, but the Spirit that is from God, so that we may understand the gifts bestowed on us by God. And we speak of these things in words not taught by human wisdom but taught by the Spirit, interpreting spiritual things to those who are spiritual.

1 CORINTHIANS 2:9-13

PRAYER

Lord, open my heart through your Spirit so I might comprehend what you have prepared for those who love you.

September 16

LIGHT

PSALM

The law of the Lord is perfect, reviving the soul;
the decrees of the Lord are sure, making wise the simple;
the precepts of the Lord are right, rejoicing the heart;
the commandment of the Lord is clear, enlightening the eyes;
the fear of the Lord is pure, enduring forever;
the ordinances of the Lord are true and righteous altogether.
More to be desired are they than gold, even much fine gold;
sweeter also than honey, and drippings of the honeycomb.

PSALM 19:7-10

MEDITATION

No other man had ever made such a claim as this, but he, unlike all others, was able to back up his claims by the life he lived and by the wonders which he performed. He claimed without hesitancy or qualification to be the light of the world: "As long as I am in the world, I am the light of the world" (John 9: 5).

ASHLEY S. JOHNSON, *The Life of Trust*, 42

SCRIPTURE

Jesus said to them, "The light is with you for a little longer. Walk while you
have the light, so that the darkness may not overtake you. If you walk in the darkness,
you do not know where you are going. While you have the light, believe in the light,
so that you may become children of light."

JOHN 12:35-36

PRAYER

Jesus, be my light this day. Let me live as a child of light, so others may see the path to God.

September 17

JUDGMENT

PSALM
Truly God is good to the upright,
to those who are pure in heart.
But as for me, my feet had almost stumbled;
my steps had nearly slipped.

PSALM 73:1-2

MEDITATION

How utterly wonderful, when the waywardness of the human race in all the past generations is considered, that the forbearance and long-suffering of God should have extended six thousand years; that the love of God to us, as displayed through our Lord Jesus the Christ, should have been extended for eighteen long centuries, while our God has been all the time extending his hands in mercy and in infinite compassion, in gracious invitations to return and live.

BENJAMIN FRANKLIN, *The Gospel Preacher*, VOL. 1, 454

SCRIPTURE

But with me it is a very small thing that I should be judged by you or by any human court. I do not even judge myself. I am not aware of anything against myself, but I am not thereby acquitted. It is the Lord who judges me. Therefore do not pronounce judgment before the time, before the Lord comes, who will bring to light the things now hidden in darkness and will disclose the purposes of the heart. Then each one will receive commendation from God.

1 CORINTHIANS 4:3-5

PRAYER

Lord, help me not to judge myself but to leave you to graciously judge me. In turn, may I not judge others, but trust them to your judgment.

September 18

The Great Shepherd

Psalm

The Lord is my shepherd, I shall not want.
He makes me lie down in green pastures; he leads me beside still waters;
he restores my soul. He leads me in right paths for his name's sake.
Even though I walk through the darkest valley, I fear no evil;
for you are with me; your rod and your staff—they comfort me.
You prepare a table before me in the presence of my enemies;
you anoint my head with oil; my cup overflows.
Surely goodness and mercy shall follow me all the days of my life,
and I shall dwell in the house of the Lord my whole life long.

PSALM 23

Meditation

What a beautiful picture of Christ's love and care for his disciples. How tenderly the shepherd guards the young and feeble of his flock, often carrying the lambs in his bosom.

J.H. GARRISON, *Alone with God*, 31-32

Scripture

The one who enters by the gate is the shepherd of the sheep. The gatekeeper opens the gate for him, and the sheep hear his voice. He calls his own sheep by name and leads them out. When he has brought out all his own, he goes ahead of them, and the sheep follow him because they know his voice.

JOHN 10:2-4

Prayer

Lord, you are my shepherd. Protect, carry, and feed me this day.

September 19

TURNING TO GOD

PSALM

When the righteous cry for help, the Lord hears,
and rescues them from all their troubles.
The Lord is near to the brokenhearted,
and saves the crushed in spirit.

PSALM 34:17-18

MEDITATION

Think of these things and turn, while it is called today. Be entreated by all the tender mercies of our God, his goodness and compassion, to turn and live. Today, if you will hear his voice, harden not your hearts, but bow your will to the will of God.

BENJAMIN FRANKLIN, *The Gospel Preacher*, VOL. 1, 127

SCRIPTURE

When Mordecai learned all that had been done, Mordecai tore his clothes and put on sackcloth and ashes, and went through the city, wailing with a loud and bitter cry; he went up to the entrance of the king's gate, for no one might enter the king's gate clothed with sackcloth. In every province, wherever the king's command and his decree came, there was great mourning among the Jews, with fasting and weeping and lamenting, and most of them lay in sackcloth and ashes.

ESTHER 4:1-3

PRAYER

Father, hear my cry of mourning, mend my broken heart, heal my crushed spirit, so I might turn to you and be saved.

September 20

GOD

PSALM

I will call to mind the deeds of the Lord;
I will remember your wonders of old.
I will meditate on all your work,
and muse on your mighty deeds.

PSALM 77:11-12

MEDITATION

How holy and how reverend is the name of God! How awful the deep mysteries of the Divine nature! That name, that nature, constitute the study of life. Even amidst the darkness of heathenism, some strove to grope their way to God, and the multitude of their idols, while it shows the failure, proclaims also the earnestness of their search.

ROBERT RICHARDSON, *Communings in the Sanctuary*, 43-44

SCRIPTURE

So he went down and immersed himself seven times in the Jordan, according to the word of the man of God; his flesh was restored like the flesh of a young boy, and he was clean.

Then he returned to the man of God, he and all his company; he came and stood before him and said, "Now I know that there is no God in all the earth except in Israel; please accept a present from your servant."

2 KINGS 5:14-15

PRAYER

God of love, there is no God in all the earth but you! I praise your Name, remember your deeds, and meditate on your works.

September 21

CARE FOR THE POOR

PSALM

I know that the Lord maintains the cause of the needy,
and executes justice for the poor.
Surely the righteous shall give thanks to your name;
the upright shall live in your presence.

PSALM 140:12-13

MEDITATION

How much true riches we may secure and lay up in heaven, while we dwell on earth, by wisely and piously distributing our goods and money to the glory of God. Wealth rightly and religiously used is a great blessing, but if improperly and irreligiously used, is a great curse. O that this world would lay these things to heart, especially the professors of Christianity! Covetousness is idolatry, and no idolater hath any inheritance in the kingdom of heaven.

BARTON W. STONE, *Christian Messenger* (1840), 249

SCRIPTURE

Therefore because you trample on the poor and take from them levies of grain,
you have built houses of hewn stone, but you shall not live in them; you have planted
pleasant vineyards, but you shall not drink their wine. For I know how many are your
transgressions, and how great are your sins—you who afflict the righteous,
who take a bribe, and push aside the needy in the gate.

AMOS 5:11-12

PRAYER

Lord Jesus, you freely gave all for me. Open my heart so I might share what you have given me with those in need. Keep me from covetousness.

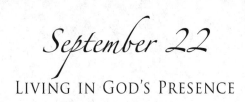

September 22

LIVING IN GOD'S PRESENCE

PSALM

I will give to the Lord the thanks due to his righteousness,
and sing praise to the name of the Lord, the Most High.

PSALM 7:17

MEDITATION

The presence of God in the soul is like the presence of God in heaven—full of glory and joy. Our life is divine only as we dwell in his presence and walk in him—the invisible God. Our religious character resolves itself into our mental devotion in the first instance, which will be characterized by poverty or fullness according to the nature of our faith.

WALTER SCOTT, *The Messiahship*, 354

SCRIPTURE

For the grace of God has appeared, bringing salvation to all, training us to renounce impiety and worldly passions, and in the present age to live lives that are self-controlled, upright, and godly, while we wait for the blessed hope and the manifestation of the glory of our great God and Savior, Jesus Christ. He it is who gave himself for us that he might redeem us from all iniquity and purify for himself a people of his own who are zealous for good deeds.

TITUS 2:11-14

PRAYER

Loving God, may I be aware of your presence today so that I might live a self-controlled, upright, and godly life.

September 23

PRAISE

PSALM

Come, bless the Lord, all you servants of the Lord,
who stand by night in the house of the Lord!
Lift up your hands to the holy place, and bless the Lord.
May the Lord, maker of heaven and earth, bless you from Zion.

PSALM 134

MEDITATION

Therefore, to make use of ourselves and the goods we possess, to any other
purpose than to glorify God, is a sin of no small magnitude. As our great High
Priest, we must pray for all—for kings and all in authority—we must make
strong cries and supplications to him that is able to save—we must offer praise
and thanksgiving, the calves of our lips. All our offerings must be seasoned
with salt, and on a pure altar, on which the sacred fire of the spirit of burning,
must continually be found, in the flames of which our offerings ascend to God
with acceptance.

BARTON W. STONE, *Christian Messenger* (1840), 333

SCRIPTURE

Then Deborah and Barak son of Abinoam sang on that day, saying: "When locks are long
in Israel, when the people offer themselves willingly—bless the Lord! "Hear, O kings; give
ear, O princes; to the Lord I will sing, I will make melody to the Lord, the God of Israel."

JUDGES 5:1-3

PRAYER

Bless the Lord! May all my life and breath give glory to God! Lord, accept my
sacrifice of praise this day.

September 24

TRUTH

PSALM

In my distress I cry to the Lord, that he may answer me:
"Deliver me, O Lord, from lying lips, from a deceitful tongue."

PSALM 120:1-2

MEDITATION

But Christ did not deliver all of that message to humans while here in the flesh. There were certain truths which he desired to speak which they were not able at that time to receive. This condition of things was provided for in sending the Holy Spirit to abide in the Church as its guide until it shall come into the fullness of the knowledge of Christ.

J.H. GARRISON, *The Holy Spirit*, 203

SCRIPTURE

Beloved, I pray that all may go well with you and that you may be in good health, just as it is well with your soul.

I was overjoyed when some of the friends arrived and testified to your faithfulness to the truth, namely how you walk in the truth. I have no greater joy than this, to hear that my children are walking in the truth.

3 JOHN 2-4

PRAYER

Father, may I love and speak your truth. Lord Jesus, continue to guide me in the truth through your Holy Spirit. Let me live the truth, not merely speak it.

WISDOM

PSALM

Fools say in their hearts, "There is no God."
They are corrupt, they do abominable deeds;
there is no one who does good.
The Lord looks down from heaven on humankind
to see if there are any who are wise,
who seek after God.

PSALM 14:1-2

MEDITATION

Fill me with your Holy Spirit, increase my faith, intensify my zeal for you and the souls of others; press on me the weight of the world's woe; keep me in your love; satisfy my reasonable wants, and place in my hands much of this world's goods, and then give me the wisdom that comes alone from you, that I may manage your work to the smallest detail, unto your glory.

ASHLEY S. JOHNSON, *The Life of Trust*, 90

SCRIPTURE

God answered Solomon, "Because this was in your heart, and you have not asked for possessions, wealth, honor, or the life of those who hate you, and have not even asked for long life, but have asked for wisdom and knowledge for yourself that you may rule my people over whom I have made you king, wisdom and knowledge are granted to you. I will also give you riches, possessions, and honor, such as none of the kings had who were before you, and none after you shall have the like."

2 CHRONICLES 1:11-12

PRAYER

Father, give me wisdom as you did to Solomon. May I always seek you and glorify you.

September 26

FASTING

PSALM

Unless the Lord builds the house, those who build it labor in vain.
Unless the Lord guards the city, the guard keeps watch in vain.
It is in vain that you rise up early and go late to rest, eating the bread of anxious toil;
for he gives sleep to his beloved.

PSALM 127:1-2

MEDITATION

One now chooses to go to the house of fasting rather than to the house of
feasting, in order that one give full scope and free exercise to the swellings and
impulses of the soul. And hence it is that on great and solemn occasions fasting
has ordinarily, in all ages and all nations, been connected with prayer as a
means of spiritual strength and religious discipline.

ROBERT MILLIGAN, *Scheme of Redemption*, 388

SCRIPTURE

Sanctify a fast, call a solemn assembly. Gather the elders and all the inhabitants of the
land to the house of the Lord your God, and cry out to the Lord.

JOEL 1:14

PRAYER

God of plenty, who provides my daily bread, as I fast, may I hunger for you
and you alone.

LIFE IS SHORT

PSALM

"Lord, let me know my end, and what is the measure of my days;
let me know how fleeting my life is.
You have made my days a few handbreadths,
and my lifetime is as nothing in your sight.
Surely everyone stands as a mere breath."

PSALM 39:4-5

MEDITATION

How short our life! How vast is eternity! We have but a little time allowed us to make preparations for an eternal home—but a little time to profit our fellow creatures. We have no time allowed for angry debates, wrangling, and disputation. It is high time to awake out of sleep, and to shake ourselves from the defiling dust of past ages. Let us endeavor to pluck our poor, blind fellows, as brands from the burning. Let self sink at the feet of Jesus. Let him, and his glory, and the salvation of souls be your polar star.

BARTON W. STONE, *Christian Messenger* (1841), 260

SCRIPTURE

A voice says, "Cry out!" And I said, "What shall I cry?" All people are grass, their constancy is like the flower of the field. The grass withers, the flower fades, when the breath of the Lord blows upon it; surely the people are grass. The grass withers, the flower fades; but the word of our God will stand forever.

ISAIAH 40:6-8

PRAYER

Lord, let me know the brevity of my life so I might live to the fullest! This day may I fill each moment with service to you and to others.

September 28

COMMUNION WITH GOD

PSALM

To you I lift up my eyes,
O you who are enthroned in the heavens!
As the eyes of servants
look to the hand of their master,
as the eyes of a maid
to the hand of her mistress,
so our eyes look to the Lord our God,
until he has mercy upon us.

PSALM 123:1-2

MEDITATION

To establish and maintain this communion is the great end of religion. To unite the soul to God; to erect in the human heart a living temple for his abode; to secure the enjoyment of that Divine presence which is the earnest of eternal blessedness: these are its noble and exalted aims—its truest, holiest purposes.

ROBERT RICHARDSON, *Communings in the Sanctuary*, 45

SCRIPTURE

His divine power has given us everything needed for life and godliness, through the knowledge of him who called us by his own glory and goodness. Thus he has given us, through these things, his precious and very great promises, so that through them you may escape from the corruption that is in the world because of lust, and may become participants of the divine nature.

2 PETER 1:3-4

PRAYER

Lord Jesus, you have made me a participant in the very life of God. Open my eyes to your presence this day.

September 29

JERUSALEM

PSALM

Pray for the peace of Jerusalem: "May they prosper who love you.
Peace be within your walls, and security within your towers."
For the sake of my relatives and friends I will say, "Peace be within you."
For the sake of the house of the Lord our God, I will seek your good.

PSALM 122:6-9

MEDITATION

This is a beautiful illustration of the sanctifying and soul-redeeming influences of the Gospel. Humanity is dead in trespasses and in sins. But a fountain has been opened in the house of David; a living stream has gone forth from the side of our Redeemer. It has purified the sanctuary; it has cleansed the temple of God. But it cannot be confined within the limits of any one town, city, or continent. It is the remedy which God has provided to supply the wants of a fallen world, and hence he has made it as free as the air or the sunlight of heaven.

ROBERT MILLIGAN, *Scheme of Redemption*, 563

SCRIPTURE

You are beautiful as Tirzah, my love, comely as Jerusalem,
terrible as an army with banners.

SONG OF SOLOMON 6:4

PRAYER

O Lord, Jerusalem was beautiful because of your presence there. May I show the beauty of your presence this day, as I wait for the New Jerusalem where I will be with you forever.

September 30

Faithfulness

Psalm

I cry to God Most High,
to God who fulfills his purpose for me.
He will send from heaven and save me,
he will put to shame those who trample on me.
God will send forth his steadfast love and his faithfulness.

Psalm 57:2-3

Meditation

How would a man feel towards a wife, whose heart was divided between her husband and other lovers? God "our Maker, is our husband." How will he feel towards us, if our heart be divided between him and the world? Compared with the love we must have for God, all other love to the dearest objects on earth is a nothing—as hatred. We leave all and cleave to him as our chief beloved.

Barton W. Stone, *Christian Messenger* (1843), 290-291

Scripture

"Come, let us return to the Lord; for it is he who has torn, and he will heal us; he has struck down, and he will bind us up. After two days he will revive us; on the third day he will raise us up, that we may live before him. Let us know, let us press on to know the Lord; his appearing is as sure as the dawn; he will come to us like the showers, like the spring rains that water the earth."

Hosea 6:1-3

Prayer

My God, you have been faithful to me. May I show complete faithfulness to you, loving you alone.

October 1

RESTORATION

PSALM

O God, you have rejected us, broken our defenses;
you have been angry; now restore us!

PSALM 60:1

MEDITATION

A restoration of the ancient order of things is all that is necessary to the happiness and usefulness of Christians. Just in so far as the ancient order of things, or the religion of the New Testament, is restored, just so far has the Millennium commenced, and so far have its blessings been enjoyed. For to the end of time, we shall have no other revelation of the Spirit, no other New Testament, no other Savior, and no other religion than we now have, when we understand, believe, and practice the doctrine of Christ delivered to us by his apostles.

ALEXANDER CAMPBELL, *Christian Baptist* (1825), 136

SCRIPTURE

But you, O Lord, reign forever; your throne endures to all generations. Why have you forgotten us completely? Why have you forsaken us these many days? Restore us to yourself, O Lord, that we may be restored; renew our days as of old—unless you have utterly rejected us, and are angry with us beyond measure.

LAMENTATIONS 5:19-22

PRAYER

Father, I pray for that greatest of restorations, that you will restore me to yourself through Jesus Christ, my Lord.

October 2

GOD OUR REFUGE

PSALM
Let the righteous rejoice in the Lord and take refuge in him.
Let all the upright in heart glory.

PSALM 64:10

MEDITATION
With what heartfelt assurance, then, we should make his sheltering wings our refuge. With what reverential joy we should approach the sacred memorials of his grace here presented before us and "banquet on love's repast." Behold these emblems. They speak to the heart. They tell of God's love—the love of him from whom all love proceeds.

ROBERT RICHARDSON, *Communings in the Sanctuary*, 2-3

SCRIPTURE
On that day you shall not be put to shame because of all the deeds by which you have rebelled against me; for then I will remove from your midst your proudly exultant ones, and you shall no longer be haughty in my holy mountain. For I will leave in the midst of you a people humble and lowly. They shall seek refuge in the name of the Lord—the remnant of Israel; they shall do no wrong and utter no lies, nor shall a deceitful tongue be found in their mouths. Then they will pasture and lie down, and no one shall make them afraid.

ZEPHANIAH 3:11-13

PRAYER
Lord, shelter me beneath your wings as a hen shelters her chicks. Be my refuge this day, tomorrow, and forever.

October 3

GOD'S LOVE

PSALM

O give thanks to the Lord, for he is good;
his steadfast love endures forever!
Let Israel say,
"His steadfast love endures forever."
Let the house of Aaron say,
"His steadfast love endures forever."
Let those who fear the Lord say,
"His steadfast love endures forever."

PSALM 118:1-4

MEDITATION

In redemption God manifests his love. His condescension and mercy also establishes a line of communication between earth and heaven; at the end of which is the earnest, believing, Christian heart, and at the other end of which sits our God in his own uncreated splendor, and glory indescribable, ready to hear and help.

ASHLEY S. JOHNSON, *The Life of Trust*, 20

SCRIPTURE

I said, "O Lord God of heaven, the great and awesome God who keeps covenant and
steadfast love with those who love him and keep his commandments; let your ear be
attentive and your eyes open to hear the prayer of your servant that I now pray before you
day and night for your servants, the people of Israel, confessing the sins of the people of
Israel, which we have sinned against you."

NEHEMIAH 1:5-6

PRAYER

God of love, your love for me is steadfast and true. Fill me with that love this day so I might fear and love you.

THANKSGIVING

PSALM

Blessed be the Lord, the God of Israel,
from everlasting to everlasting.
And let all the people say, "Amen."
Praise the Lord!

PSALM 106:48

MEDITATION

As the poor use entreaties, so the poor in spirit, sensible of their wants, are often at the throne using entreaties, and making fervent prayer for grace. They are a thankful people; for they, feeling their unworthiness, and that all they receive is of free favor, feel obligations unknown to any other character. How humble his heart in the presence of his God!

BARTON W. STONE, *Christian Messenger* (1835), 73

SCRIPTURE

O give thanks to the Lord, for he is good; for his steadfast love endures forever.
Say also: "Save us, O God of our salvation, and gather and rescue us from among the
nations, that we may give thanks to your holy name, and glory in your praise.
Blessed be the Lord, the God of Israel, from everlasting to everlasting."
Then all the people said "Amen!" and praised the Lord.

1 CHRONICLES 16:34-36

PRAYER

God, giver of life and all good things, I thank you for your steadfast love. I bless your holy name! Amen. Praise the Lord!

October 5

ENTERING THE HOUSE OF THE LORD

PSALM

I was glad when they said to me,
"Let us go to the house of the Lord!"

PSALM 122:1

MEDITATION

We come to Jesus and he meets us here—"The King himself draws near to feast with his saints today." In the awful mysteries of life and death we hold communion. With the spiritual unseen we live and move. Into the dwelling of the Most High we enter to take the cup of salvation—to pay our vows in the presence of his people.

ROBERT RICHARDSON, *Communings in the Sanctuary*, 3

SCRIPTURE

When the builders laid the foundation of the temple of the Lord, the priests in their vestments were stationed to praise the Lord with trumpets, and the Levites, the sons of Asaph, with cymbals, according to the directions of King David of Israel; and they sang responsively, praising and giving thanks to the Lord, "For he is good, for his steadfast love endures forever toward Israel." And all the people responded with a great shout when they praised the Lord, because the foundation of the house of the Lord was laid.

EZRA 3:10-11

PRAYER

Lord God, you have made your people into a holy temple. May I enter your presence this day with humble, heartfelt praise.

October 6

WORLDLINESS

PSALM

"Often have they attacked me from my youth"
—let Israel now say—
"often have they attacked me from my youth,
yet they have not prevailed against me."

PSALM 129:1-2

MEDITATION

The friendship of the world is enmity to God. To seek the friendship of the world, and the friendship of God at the same time, cannot be done consistently with truth—it is a vain work; yet this work, vain as it is, seems to mark the professors of Christianity at the present day; almost an armistice seems to be concluded between the world and professed Christianity.

BARTON W. STONE, *Christian Messenger* (1844), 226-227

SCRIPTURE

But the Lord is with me like a dread warrior; therefore my persecutors will stumble, and they will not prevail. They will be greatly shamed, for they will not succeed. Their eternal dishonor will never be forgotten. O Lord of hosts, you test the righteous, you see the heart and the mind; let me see your retribution upon them, for to you I have committed my cause.

JEREMIAH 20:11-12

PRAYER

Father, mold my mind and life so I will be free of the control of the world. Test my heart and mind this day to prove my love for you.

October 7

Love for the Saints

Psalm

For the Lord has chosen Zion;
he has desired it for his habitation:
"This is my resting place forever;
here I will reside, for I have desired it.
I will abundantly bless its provisions;
I will satisfy its poor with bread."

Psalm 132:13-15

Meditation

Their own hearts will then be filled with love to God, and with an ardent sympathy for our race, while the world will look on and exclaim, "Behold how good and how pleasant it is for brothers and sisters to dwell together in unity."

Robert Milligan, *Scheme of Redemption*, 535

Scripture

When I remember you in my prayers, I always thank my God because I hear of your love for all the saints and your faith toward the Lord Jesus. I pray that the sharing of your faith may become effective when you perceive all the good that we may do for Christ. I have indeed received much joy and encouragement from your love, because the hearts of the saints have been refreshed through you, my brother.

Philemon 4-7

Prayer

Lord, may I show genuine love to my brothers and sisters in Christ, refreshing their hearts. Let me know that we are your chosen ones, the place where you live.

Judgment

Psalm

The nations have sunk in the pit that they made;
in the net that they hid has their own foot been caught.
The Lord has made himself known, he has executed judgment;
the wicked are snared in the work of their own hands.
The wicked shall depart to Sheol,
all the nations that forget God.
For the needy shall not always be forgotten,
nor the hope of the poor perish forever.

Psalm 9:15-18

Meditation

Shall their eyes be closed against the calamities that have been brought on the ungodly in past ages, not knowing that the terrible judgment of all is approaching? Be warned and entreated, then, to turn to the Lord before the day of vengeance shall come.

Benjamin Franklin, *The Gospel Preacher*, vol. 1, 455

Scripture

For the day of the Lord is near against all the nations. As you have done,
it shall be done to you; your deeds shall return on your own head.

Obadiah 15

Prayer

Lord God, bring justice to our land, so the poor may have hope and the needy be vindicated. May I leave vengeance in your gracious hands, O Lord, and not take it into my own.

October 9

GOD PROVIDES

PSALM

You cause the grass to grow for the cattle,
and plants for people to use,
to bring forth food from the earth,
and wine to gladden the human heart,
oil to make the face shine,
and bread to strengthen the human heart.
The trees of the Lord are watered abundantly,
the cedars of Lebanon that he planted.

PSALM 104:14-16

MEDITATION

How he bears with our infirmities. "He knoweth our frame, that we are dust."
What a scene of pastoral beauty and loveliness is here brought before us, with
its "still waters" and "green pastures." How bountiful the provision for our
soul's needs suggested by verdant fields and the deep, quiet pools.

J.H. GARRISON, *Alone with God*, 32

SCRIPTURE

When he saw the crowds, he had compassion for them, because they were harassed
and helpless, like sheep without a shepherd. Then he said to his disciples,
"The harvest is plentiful, but the laborers are few; therefore ask the Lord of the harvest
to send out laborers into his harvest."

MATTHEW 9:36-38

PRAYER

Father, you provide all I need. Give me today my daily bread and make me
ever thankful. Lord Jesus, have compassion on me as your helpless sheep.

October 10

WORSHIP

PSALM

He sent redemption to his people;
he has commanded his covenant forever.
Holy and awesome is his name.
The fear of the Lord is the beginning of wisdom;
all those who practice it have a good understanding.
His praise endures forever.

PSALM 111:9-10

MEDITATION

There can be no doubt to those who drink deep into the spirit of the New Testament, but that the aspect of a society of primitive worshipers was essentially different from ours. The hope, and joy, and love, and confidence in God, which their views of Jesus inspired, animated their countenances and their deportment, and shone forth in their whole demeanor.

ALEXANDER CAMPBELL, *Christian Baptist* (1826), 73

SCRIPTURE

Then those who revered the Lord spoke with one another. The Lord took note and listened, and a book of remembrance was written before him of those who revered the Lord and thought on his name. They shall be mine, says the Lord of hosts, my special possession on the day when I act, and I will spare them as parents spare their children who serve them.

MALACHI 3:16-17

PRAYER

Lord, may I show genuine reverence for your name this day. May I worship you with every aspect of my life.

October 11

LOVE

PSALM

I will give thanks to you, O Lord, among the peoples;
I will sing praises to you among the nations.
For your steadfast love is as high as the heavens;
your faithfulness extends to the clouds.

PSALM 57:9-10

MEDITATION

This may be called properly the golden chain of divine truth. The end of it is charity, or love—the beginning is unfeigned faith—and the middle is a good conscience, and a pure heart. Faith produces, or leads to a good conscience—this to purity of heart—and this to love, or universal benevolence. This is the sum of Christianity, without which none can be perfect or complete Christians.

BARTON W. STONE, *Christian Messenger* (1834), 74

SCRIPTURE

Love is patient; love is kind; love is not envious or boastful or arrogant or rude. It does not insist on its own way; it is not irritable or resentful; it does not rejoice in wrongdoing, but rejoices in the truth. It bears all things, believes all things, hopes all things, endures all things

1 CORINTHIANS 13:4-7

PRAYER

God of love, pour your love into my heart so I might bear, believe, hope, and endure all things.

October 12

RESURRECTION

PSALM

Rise up, O Lord; O God, lift up your hand;
do not forget the oppressed.
Why do the wicked renounce God,
and say in their hearts, "You will not call us to account"?
But you do see! Indeed you note trouble and grief,
that you may take it into your hands;
the helpless commit themselves to you;
you have been the helper of the orphan.

PSALM 10:12-14

MEDITATION

Let us now look at this beautiful creation by the Spirit, when emancipated from the frailty of death, the travail and groans of the present order of things, and ushered into the glorious liberty of the angels, being now both children of God and of the resurrection.

WALTER SCOTT, *The Gospel Restored*, 567

SCRIPTURE

They were all weeping and wailing for her; but he said, "Do not weep; for she is not dead but sleeping." And they laughed at him, knowing that she was dead. But he took her by the hand and called out, "Child, get up!" Her spirit returned, and she got up at once. Then he directed them to give her something to eat. Her parents were astounded; but he ordered them to tell no one what had happened.

LUKE 8:52-56

PRAYER

God of life, as you gave this young girl new life through the power of Jesus, so let me by the power of the Spirit be born anew, looking forward to the resurrection of my body.

October 13

PARDON

PSALM

But you, O Lord, are a God merciful and gracious,
slow to anger and abounding in steadfast love and faithfulness.
Turn to me and be gracious to me;
give your strength to your servant;
save the child of your serving girl.

PSALM 86:15-16

MEDITATION

What is pardon? This is the one great question to the alien or the erring heir of the Lord. I answer: Pardon is the act of an injured party; in this case the act of God, by which the offense or offenses are effaced from memory, and the offender treated by the offended as though the offense had never been committed. Does God exercise such mercy to those who have offended him or do offend him? Indisputably. The language of Scripture on this point is very full and explicit, and also very encouraging. Indeed, mercy is one of his great attributes. The proof is so abundant that I scarcely know where to begin.

ASHLEY S. JOHNSON, *The Life of Trust*, 90-91

SCRIPTURE

"The Lord is slow to anger, and abounding in steadfast love, forgiving iniquity and transgression, but by no means clearing the guilty, visiting the iniquity of the parents upon the children to the third and the fourth generation."

NUMBERS 14:18

PRAYER

Lord, by your grace pardon my sins, give me full forgiveness, erase my trespasses from memory. Let me live in full assurance that you are slow to anger.

October 14

MERCY

PSALM

The Lord is gracious and merciful,
slow to anger and abounding in steadfast love.
The Lord is good to all,
and his compassion is over all that he has made.

PSALM 145:8-9

MEDITATION

"Blessed are the merciful." They sympathize with their suffering fellow creatures, and are influenced to relieve them. They visit the widow and fatherless in their afflictions, to do them good. They are of a forgiving disposition, and are easy to be entreated. In this, they bear the image of the heavenly.

BARTON W. STONE, *Christian Messenger* (1841), 25

SCRIPTURE

But this was very displeasing to Jonah, and he became angry. He prayed to the Lord and said, "O Lord! Is not this what I said while I was still in my own country? That is why I fled to Tarshish at the beginning; for I knew that you are a gracious God and merciful, slow to anger, and abounding in steadfast love, and ready to relent from punishing. And now, O Lord, please take my life from me, for it is better for me to die than to live." And the Lord said, "Is it right for you to be angry?"

JONAH 4:1-4

PRAYER

Lord Jesus, have mercy on me. May I never be angry at the mercy you show to others. Let me be merciful as you are merciful.

October 15

GRACE

PSALM

The Lord is my chosen portion and my cup;
you hold my lot.
The boundary lines have fallen for me in pleasant places;
I have a goodly heritage.

PSALM 16:5-6

MEDITATION

That all that are enabled through grace to make such a profession, and to manifest the reality of it in their tempers and conduct, should consider each other as the precious saints of God, should love each other as brothers and sisters, children of the same family and Father, temples of the same Spirit, members of the same body, subjects of the same grace, objects of the same Divine love, bought with the same price, and joint-heirs of the same inheritance. Whom God hath thus joined together no one should dare to put asunder.

THOMAS CAMPBELL, *The Declaration and Address*

SCRIPTURE

Last of all, as to one untimely born, he appeared also to me. For I am the least of the apostles, unfit to be called an apostle, because I persecuted the church of God. But by the grace of God I am what I am, and his grace toward me has not been in vain. On the contrary, I worked harder than any of them—though it was not I, but the grace of God that is with me.

1 CORINTHIANS 15:8-10

PRAYER

God of grace, I thank you for making me what I am by your grace. By your grace may I work hard in your service this day and treat others with graciousness.

October 16

SILENCE

PSALM

For God alone my soul waits in silence,
for my hope is from him.
He alone is my rock and my salvation,
my fortress; I shall not be shaken.
On God rests my deliverance and my honor;
my mighty rock, my refuge is in God.
Trust in him at all times, O people;
pour out your heart before him;
God is a refuge for us.

PSALM 62:5-8

MEDITATION

Every day should have its quiet moments when, alone with God, the soul may meditate, with deep and silent awe, on everlasting things, and unbosom itself before the Father of spirits. This habit of reverential intimacy with God imparts that spiritual tone, that sensitiveness of conscience, that realization of the divine presence, so essential to moral beauty and symmetry of character. Shut in from the noise and scenes of the busy world, in the solitude of our chamber, we can the better examine our hearts and give ourselves up to holier thoughts.

J.H. GARRISON, *Alone With God*, 22

SCRIPTURE

But the Lord is in his holy temple; let all the earth keep silence before him!

HABAKKUK 2:20

PRAYER

Lord God, may I daily wait for you in silence, knowing that you are in your holy temple. Open the ears of my heart to listen.

October 17

KINGDOM OF HEAVEN

PSALM

When Israel went out from Egypt,
the house of Jacob from a people of strange language,
Judah became God's sanctuary,
Israel his dominion.

PSALM 114:1-2

MEDITATION

Such a kingdom must ultimately banish all discord, strife, and war on the earth. Well may we pray, thy kingdom come! We have seen its rise, but its completion is reserved for the future, when Christ shall personally reign on earth for a thousand years, and forever and ever.

BARTON W. STONE, *Christian Messenger* (1843), 206

SCRIPTURE

Simon Peter answered, "You are the Messiah, the Son of the living God." And Jesus
answered him, "Blessed are you, Simon son of Jonah! For flesh and blood has not revealed
this to you, but my Father in heaven. And I tell you, you are Peter, and on this rock I will
build my church, and the gates of Hades will not prevail against it. I will give you the keys
of the kingdom of heaven, and whatever you bind on earth will be bound in heaven, and
whatever you loose on earth will be loosed in heaven."

MATTHEW 16:16-19

PRAYER

Father, may your kingdom come! May I participate in your kingdom this day and be your holy sanctuary.

October 18

WEALTH AND POVERTY

PSALM

They will abide in prosperity,
and their children shall possess the land.
The friendship of the Lord is for those who fear him,
and he makes his covenant known to them.

PSALM 25:13-14

MEDITATION

Our Lord's example was certainly given for our imitation. He could have commanded the wealth of the universe; but he became poor, that we through his poverty might be made rich. The foxes had holes, the birds of the air had nests, but the Son of Man had not where to lay his head. His example was a veto against covetousness, and a rich ministry.

BARTON W. STONE, *Christian Messenger* (1843), 369

SCRIPTURE

For thus says the Lord of hosts: Once again, in a little while, I will shake the heavens and the earth and the sea and the dry land; and I will shake all the nations, so that the treasure of all nations shall come, and I will fill this house with splendor, says the Lord of hosts. The silver is mine, and the gold is mine, says the Lord of hosts. The latter splendor of this house shall be greater than the former, says the Lord of hosts; and in this place I will give prosperity, says the Lord of hosts.

HAGGAI 2:6-9

PRAYER

Lord of hosts, all in heaven and earth belongs to you! Lord Jesus, you gave up such wealth to become poor for my sake. May I generously give to others as you gave to me.

October 19

PEACE

PSALM

Too long have I had my dwelling
among those who hate peace.
I am for peace;
but when I speak,
they are for war.

PSALM 120:6-7

MEDITATION

If genuine Christianity were to overspread the earth, wars would cease, and the world would be bound together in the bonds of peace. A nation professing Christianity, yet teaching, learning and practicing the arts of war cannot be the kingdom of Christ, nor do they live in obedience to the laws of Christ—the government is anti-Christian, and must reap the fruits of their infidelity at some future day.

BARTON W. STONE, *Christian Messenger* (1844), 65

SCRIPTURE

Look! On the mountains the feet of one who brings good tidings, who proclaims peace!
Celebrate your festivals, O Judah, fulfill your vows, for never again shall the wicked
invade you; they are utterly cut off.

NAHUM 1:15

PRAYER

Prince of Peace, come quickly, so wars may cease and all peoples bow before you. Make me a peacemaker this day.

October 20

MEDITATION

PSALM

I find my delight in your commandments,
because I love them.
I revere your commandments, which I love,
and I will meditate on your statutes.

PSALM 119:47-48

MEDITATION

Nor can it be denied that many professed Christians are living poor, lean, unspiritual lives, without any real relish for God's word, or for prayer, because of their habitual neglect of private meditation, self-examination, and secret communings with God. And for this neglect, few of them can give any better excuse than the lack of time. There is time to look after the condition of the farm, the stock, the shop, the office, and the markets, but no time to inquire into the condition of the soul and its fitness for eternity!

J.H. GARRISON, *Alone With God*, 23

SCRIPTURE

Then turning to the disciples, Jesus said to them privately, "Blessed are the eyes that see what you see! For I tell you that many prophets and kings desired to see what you see, but did not see it, and to hear what you hear, but did not hear it."

LUKE 10:23-24

PRAYER

Father, may I meditate on your law and commandments, so I may see the greatness of your works and hear the beauty of your words.

October 21

CARING FOR THE NEEDY

PSALM

Happy are those who consider the poor;
the Lord delivers them in the day of trouble.
The Lord protects them and keeps them alive;
they are called happy in the land.
You do not give them up to the will of their enemies.

PSALM 41:1-2

MEDITATION

"Labor for the things that are good"—for what purpose? Is it that we may be esteemed great and honorable among others? Is it that we may adorn ourselves and children with wearing gold and costly apparel? Is it to hoard up much treasure? No! But it is that we may have to give to others who may need. Whenever we feel reluctant to give to the glory of God—whenever we say in our hearts, all these are mine; it shows plainly what god we serve.

BARTON W. STONE, *Christian Messenger* (1836), 13

SCRIPTURE

"But a Samaritan while traveling came near him; and when he saw him, he was moved with pity. He went to him and bandaged his wounds, having poured oil and wine on them. Then he put him on his own animal, brought him to an inn, and took care of him. The next day he took out two denarii, gave them to the innkeeper, and said, 'Take care of him; and when I come back, I will repay you whatever more you spend.' Which of these three, do you think, was a neighbor to the man who fell into the hands of the robbers?" He said, "The one who showed him mercy." Jesus said to him, "Go and do likewise."

LUKE 10:33-37

PRAYER

God of love, open my heart so I may be a generous giver. May I show mercy to others because of the great mercy you have shown me.

October 22

TRUST GOD, NOT MONEY

PSALM

But I trust in you, O Lord;
I say, "You are my God."
My times are in your hand;
deliver me from the hand of my enemies and persecutors.
Let your face shine upon your servant;
save me in your steadfast love.

PSALM 31:14-16

MEDITATION

We are positively commanded not to lay up treasures or riches on earth; the reason of which is at hand, for it is impossible for one to walk by faith, live the life of trust, who has a bank account awaiting his needs. I think I read in your faces that you think it right to lay up something for old age. Do you prefer not to walk by faith when you are old? Is not God the God of old age as well as the God of youth? Do you think he would take the almost infinite pains to count the hairs on your head and then let you suffer for what you need in your old age?

ASHLEY S. JOHNSON, *The Life of Trust*, 180

SCRIPTURE

As for those who in the present age are rich, command them not to be haughty, or to set their hopes on the uncertainty of riches, but rather on God who richly provides us with everything for our enjoyment. They are to do good, to be rich in good works, generous, and ready to share, thus storing up for themselves the treasure of a good foundation for the future, so that they may take hold of the life that really is life.

1 TIMOTHY 6:17-19

PRAYER

God of all, may I trust in you, not in my bank account.

October 23

COMFORT

PSALM

You have turned my mourning into dancing;
you have taken off my sackcloth and clothed me with joy,
so that my soul may praise you and not be silent.
O Lord my God, I will give thanks to you forever.

PSALM 30:11-12

MEDITATION

The comforts afforded them by their Lord in time, will more than compensate for their mourning here; but the comforts to be afforded in his everlasting kingdom will cause sorrow and sighing, pain and death and sin forever to flee away, never more to be felt or feared again. Happy mourners! You shall be comforted.

BARTON W. STONE, *Christian Messenger* (1843), 207

SCRIPTURE

When Jesus saw the crowds, he went up the mountain; and after he sat down, his disciples
came to him. Then he began to speak, and taught them, saying:
"Blessed are the poor in spirit, for theirs is the kingdom of heaven. "Blessed are those who
mourn, for they will be comforted. "Blessed are the meek, for they will inherit the earth."

MATTHEW 5:1-5

PRAYER

Father, you turn my mourning into dancing! May I celebrate your grace today with praise and thanksgiving.

October 24

JOY IN THE SPIRIT

PSALM

Make a joyful noise to the Lord, all the earth;
break forth into joyous song and sing praises.
Sing praises to the Lord with the lyre,
with the lyre and the sound of melody.

PSALM 98:4-5

MEDITATION

In view of the prominence we have given to the plea for Christian unity, it would follow that we ought to give equal prominence to the mission and power of the Holy Spirit in Christian lives. It is more than probable that we have given an undue proportion of emphasis to the doctrinal basis of unity, to the neglect of what is even more vital—the possession of the Spirit.

J.H. GARRISON, *The Holy Spirit*, 100-101

SCRIPTURE

Paul said, "John baptized with the baptism of repentance, telling the people to believe in the one who was to come after him, that is, in Jesus." On hearing this, they were baptized in the name of the Lord Jesus. When Paul had laid his hands on them, the Holy Spirit came upon them, and they spoke in tongues and prophesied—altogether there were about twelve of them.

ACTS 19:4-7

PRAYER

Lord I praise you this day for the unity of the Spirit, that unity given in baptism in the blessed name of Jesus.

October 25

PROSPERITY AND NEED

PSALM

*Better is a little that the righteous person has
than the abundance of many wicked.
For the arms of the wicked shall be broken,
but the Lord upholds the righteous.*

PSALM 37:16-17

MEDITATION

How easy it is to take hold of the horns of the very altar of God and plead
that God may help us because of his promises to us, and because we are in the
line of duty. What if I plead in vain? But I do not; I may have to wait, but plead
in vain, never! By waiting I renew my zeal, for my mind is, by the grace of God,
made up, and my life is consecrated to his work, in prosperity or adversity, in
life or in death. The act of persisting in my efforts under apparently
unpromising circumstances is of itself strengthening to both faith and purpose.

ASHLEY S. JOHNSON, *The Life of Trust*, 159

SCRIPTURE

*Therefore, thus says the Lord, I have returned to Jerusalem with compassion; my house
shall be built in it, says the Lord of hosts, and the measuring line shall be stretched out
over Jerusalem. Proclaim further: Thus says the Lord of hosts: My cities shall again
overflow with prosperity; the Lord will again comfort Zion and again choose Jerusalem.*

ZECHARIAH 1:16-17

PRAYER

My Father, may I be faithful to you in prosperity or adversity, in life or death.
Increase my trust in you.

October 26

PRAISE

PSALM

God has gone up with a shout,
the Lord with the sound of a trumpet.
Sing praises to God, sing praises;
sing praises to our King, sing praises.
For God is the king of all the earth;
sing praises with a psalm.

PSALM 47:5-7

MEDITATION

But his saints will glorify and extol his great name and hold him in eternal admiration. He will be admired by all them that believe.

WALTER SCOTT, *The Gospel Restored*, 569

SCRIPTURE

And the four living creatures, each of them with six wings, are full of eyes all around and inside. Day and night without ceasing they sing, "Holy, holy, holy, the Lord God the Almighty, who was and is and is to come." And whenever the living creatures give glory and honor and thanks to the one who is seated on the throne, who lives forever and ever, the twenty-four elders fall before the one who is seated on the throne and worship the one who lives forever and ever; they cast their crowns before the throne, singing, "You are worthy, our Lord and God, to receive glory and honor and power, for you created all things, and by your will they existed and were created."

REVELATION 4:8-11

PRAYER

Holy God, I look forward to that day when I see you face to face and glorify you forever. Even now, grant that I might catch a glimpse of your glory and live this day in praise.

October 27

RANSOM

PSALM

Truly, no ransom avails for one's life,
there is no price one can give to God for it.
For the ransom of life is costly, and can never suffice
that one should live on forever and never see the grave.

PSALM 49:7-9

MEDITATION

Look at Jesus weeping over a lost world—this is the very temper of the Father himself—see him bleeding and dying on Calvary—you see the very compassion and love of God manifested. See his tender solicitude for the salvation of sinners—it is the very heart of the Father.

BARTON W. STONE, *Christian Messenger* (1841), 44

SCRIPTURE

They sing a new song: "You are worthy to take the scroll and to open its seals,
for you were slaughtered and by your blood you ransomed for God saints from every tribe
and language and people and nation; you have made them to be a kingdom and priests
serving our God, and they will reign on earth."

REVELATION 5:9-10

PRAYER

Loving Father, I could not ransom myself and make my life eternal. I bless you for so loving the world that you gave your Son. Lord Jesus, you are worthy as the Lamb who ransomed me, made me a priest, and invited me into your kingdom. Praise be to God!

October 28

TURN TO GOD

PSALM

You have set up a banner for those who fear you,
to rally to it out of bowshot.
Give victory with your right hand, and answer us,
so that those whom you love may be rescued.

PSALM 60:4-5

MEDITATION

Be entreated, then, by all that is good, and pure, and lovely; by the love of Christ, the mercy of God, and the sufferings of the Savior; be warned by the threatenings of heaven, the terrors of the Lord, and the danger of being lost forevermore, to turn to the Lord and live; be persuaded by the tender mercies of our God, by all his goodness, by the value of the unfading heavens, and the value of precious souls yet to come, while it is called today, and be happy forever and ever.

BENJAMIN FRANKLIN, *The Gospel Preacher*, VOL. 1, 55-56

SCRIPTURE

Remember the word that you commanded your servant Moses, "If you are unfaithful, I will scatter you among the peoples; but if you return to me and keep my commandments and do them, though your outcasts are under the farthest skies, I will gather them from there and bring them to the place at which I have chosen to establish my name." They are your servants and your people, whom you redeemed by your great power and your strong hand.

NEHEMIAH 1:8-10

PRAYER

Father, I turn to you in repentance. Accept my broken heart and restore me to your presence, through Jesus Christ, my Lord.

October 29

A new Song

Psalm

I waited patiently for the Lord; he inclined to me and heard my cry.
He drew me up from the desolate pit, out of the miry bog,
and set my feet upon a rock, making my steps secure.
He put a new song in my mouth, a song of praise to our God.
Many will see and fear, and put their trust in the Lord.

Psalm 40:1-3

Meditation

It was not intended as an attraction, an entertainment, or amusement; but as homage, adoration, praise and thanksgiving, from those who were lost and have been found; who were fallen, but are lifted up; were enemies, but are now reconciled; were separated from God, but have been united with him; were in bondage under sin, but are now redeemed by the blood of Jesus. They do not sing because they love to sing, or because they love music, but because they love God and delight to do those things that are pleasing in his sight.

Benjamin Franklin, *The Gospel Preacher*, vol. 2, 415

Scripture

And I heard a voice from heaven like the sound of many waters and like the sound of loud thunder; the voice I heard was like the sound of harpists playing on their harps, and they sing a new song before the throne and before the four living creatures and before the elders. No one could learn that song except the one hundred forty-four thousand who have been redeemed from the earth.

Revelation 14:2-3

Prayer

Lord, you have given me a song of redemption. Let me sing it with joy this day!

October 30

KNOWING GOD

PSALM

Such knowledge is too wonderful for me;
it is so high that I cannot attain it.
Where can I go from your spirit?
Or where can I flee from your presence?
If I ascend to heaven, you are there;
if I make my bed in Sheol, you are there.
If I take the wings of the morning
and settle at the farthest limits of the sea,
even there your hand shall lead me,
and your right hand shall hold me fast.

PSALM 139:6-10

MEDITATION

And oh! How precious are the influences of that spiritual fellowship which we are permitted to enjoy. How dear to the soul should be every opportunity of cultivating that sacred intimacy, that divine acquaintanceship. How greatly we should desire to draw more closely still the ties that attach us to the heavens.

ROBERT RICHARDSON, *Communings in the Sanctuary*, 45

SCRIPTURE

For this reason, since the day we heard it, we have not ceased praying for you and asking that you may be filled with the knowledge of God's will in all spiritual wisdom and understanding, so that you may lead lives worthy of the Lord, fully pleasing to him, as you bear fruit in every good work and as you grow in the knowledge of God.

COLOSSIANS 1:9-10

PRAYER

God of love, let me know you more intimately today, so I might become more like you in your love and holiness.

October 31

FORGIVENESS AND UNITY

PSALM

Gladden the soul of your servant,
for to you, O Lord, I lift up my soul.
For you, O Lord, are good and forgiving,
abounding in steadfast love to all who call on you.
Give ear, O Lord, to my prayer;
listen to my cry of supplication.

PSALM 86:4-6

MEDITATION

Let every Christian begin the work of Union in himself or herself. Wait upon God, and pray for the promise of the Spirit. Rest not until you are filled with the Spirit. Then, and not till then, will you love your God and Savior—then and not till then will you love the brothers and sisters, who bear the image of the heavenly—then you will have the Spirit of Jesus to love the fallen world, and like him to sacrifice for their salvation.

BARTON W. STONE, *Christian Messenger* (1840), 334

SCRIPTURE

Then Peter came and said to him, "Lord, if another member of the church sins against me, how often should I forgive? As many as seven times?" Jesus said to him, "Not seven times, but, I tell you, seventy-seven times."

MATTHEW 18:21-22

PRAYER

Lord Jesus, give me your Spirit so I might forgive as I have been forgiven. Begin the work of Christian union in me.

GOD'S GIFTS

PSALM
Then everyone will fear;
they will tell what God has brought about,
and ponder what he has done.

PSALM 64:9

MEDITATION

It was through this variety of gifts that the unity of the body is conserved. As the diverse functions of the several members of the human body, all cooperating together, are necessary to the welfare of the body, so the variety of gifts possessed by different members in the body of Christ, is essential to the growth and unity of that body.

J.H. GARRISON, *The Holy Spirit*, 152

SCRIPTURE

Now you are the body of Christ and individually members of it. And God has appointed in the church first apostles, second prophets, third teachers; then deeds of power, then gifts of healing, forms of assistance, forms of leadership, various kinds of tongues. Are all apostles? Are all prophets? Are all teachers? Do all work miracles? Do all possess gifts of healing? Do all speak in tongues? Do all interpret? But strive for the greater gifts. And I will show you a still more excellent way.

1 CORINTHIANS 12:27-31

PRAYER

Lord, I praise you for the gifts you have given your body. May I use the gifts you have given me to bless others.

November 2

GOD OUR REFUGE

PSALM

Let me abide in your tent forever,
find refuge under the shelter of your wings.
For you, O God, have heard my vows;
you have given me the heritage of those who fear your name.

PSALM 61:4-5

MEDITATION

When the heart is beset with anxieties, and burdened with care, it cannot well wait for relief until the regular hour for prayer arrives, but goes at once to God for his strength and guidance. To all such hearts, the habit of ejaculatory prayer is a blessing of inestimable value. By means of it, they are enabled, right in the stress of the emergency, to enter into the closet of their own heart, shut the door, and speak into the ear of a sympathetic and Infinite Father. Here they find refuge in the midst of the storm, and a haven in which they may anchor and find rest and peace.

J.H. GARRISON, *Alone With God*, 92-93

SCRIPTURE

In the same way, when God desired to show even more clearly to the heirs of the promise the unchangeable character of his purpose, he guaranteed it by an oath, so that through two unchangeable things, in which it is impossible that God would prove false, we who have taken refuge might be strongly encouraged to seize the hope set before us.

HEBREWS 6:17-18

PRAYER

Father, in times of trouble and distress, may I always find refuge in you.

November 3

COMFORT

PSALM

I know, O Lord, that your judgments are right,
and that in faithfulness you have humbled me.
Let your steadfast love become my comfort
according to your promise to your servant.
Let your mercy come to me, that I may live;
for your law is my delight.

PSALM 119:75-77

MEDITATION

O, for a faith, that in sorrow will give me comfort; in trouble will give me peace; in loss will give me consolation; in poverty will give me contentment; in trial will give me strength; in persecution will give me joy; in death will give me heaven!

ASHLEY S. JOHNSON, *The Life of Trust*, 118

SCRIPTURE

You will say in that day: I will give thanks to you, O Lord, for though you were angry with me, your anger turned away, and you comforted me. Surely God is my salvation; I will trust, and will not be afraid, for the Lord God is my strength and my might; he has become my salvation. With joy you will draw water from the wells of salvation.

ISAIAH 12:1-3

PRAYER

God, you are my strength, my might, and my salvation. May I find comfort in your faithfulness and steadfast love.

November 4

DAY AND NIGHT

PSALM

Yours is the day, yours also the night;
you established the luminaries and the sun.
You have fixed all the bounds of the earth;
you made summer and winter.

PSALM 74:16-17

MEDITATION

Let all Christians join with us, in crying to God day and night, to remove the obstacles which stand in the way of his work, and give him no rest till he makes Jerusalem a praise in the earth. We heartily unite with our Christian brothers and sisters of every name, in thanksgiving to God for the display of his goodness in the glorious work he is carrying on in our Western country, which we hope will terminate in the universal spread of the gospel, and the unity of the church.

The Last Will and Testament of the Springfield Presbytery (1804)

SCRIPTURE

"For this reason they are before the throne of God, and worship him day and night within his temple, and the one who is seated on the throne will shelter them. They will hunger no more, and thirst no more; the sun will not strike them, nor any scorching heat; for the Lamb at the center of the throne will be their shepherd, and he will guide them to springs of the water of life, and God will wipe away every tear from their eyes."

REVELATION 7:15-17

PRAYER

Father, I worship you day and night, crying out for the spread of the gospel and the unity of the church.

November 5

Turning to Christ

Psalm

Nevertheless I am continually with you;
you hold my right hand.
You guide me with your counsel,
and afterward you will receive me with honor.

Psalm 73:23-24

Meditation

Be entreated by your best friends, by the love of Christ, by the tender mercies of God, by all that is sacred, lovely, and endearing, to turn to the Lord while it is an accepted time and day of salvation. Commit your all into the gracious and merciful hands of him who has loved you, endured the cross, despised the shame, and laid down his life for you. He is your best friend, your only Savior and Redeemer, and if, in madness, you turn away from him and dash the cup of salvation from your lips, despise his goodness, love and mercy, you will lament your folly forever.

Benjamin Franklin, *The Gospel Preacher*, vol. 1, 177

Scripture

"Jerusalem, Jerusalem, the city that kills the prophets and stones those who are sent to it!
How often have I desired to gather your children together as a hen gathers her brood
under her wings, and you were not willing! See, your house is left to you. And I tell you,
you will not see me until the time comes when you say, 'Blessed is the one
who comes in the name of the Lord.'"

Luke 13:34-35

Prayer

Precious Jesus, make me willing to turn to you, so you can mother me as a hen does her chicks.

November 6

HUMILITY AND EXALTATION

PSALM

For he will hide me in his shelter
in the day of trouble;
he will conceal me under the cover of his tent;
he will set me high on a rock.

PSALM 27:5

MEDITATION

Who, believing with all his heart that Jesus is the Christ, the Son of God, will not bow in humble submission to his will? Who will not be influenced by such faith to come to God in his own appointed way, and receive his Holy Spirit? Who, having received the Spirit through faith, does not love the brothers and sisters, and become one, even as the Father and Son are one?

BARTON W. STONE, *Christian Messenger* (1840), 238

SCRIPTURE

"But when you are invited, go and sit down at the lowest place, so that when your host comes, he may say to you, 'Friend, move up higher'; then you will be honored in the presence of all who sit at the table with you. For all who exalt themselves will be humbled, and those who humble themselves will be exalted."

LUKE 14:10-11

PRAYER

Father, I bow in humility before you this day, knowing that you will shelter me in times of trouble and exalt me in your presence.

November 7

CHRIST THE KING

PSALM

Worship the Lord in holy splendor;
tremble before him, all the earth.
Say among the nations, "The Lord is king!
The world is firmly established; it shall never be moved.
He will judge the peoples with equity."

PSALM 96:9-10

MEDITATION

Ever since the commencement of this kingdom, the governments of this world have either been directly opposed to it, or, at best, pretended friends; and therefore their influence has always been opposed to the true spirit and genius of the Christian institution. Christians have nothing to expect from them except liberty of conscience and protection from violence, while leading peaceable and quiet lives, in all godliness and honesty, till Jesus take to himself his great power, and hurl those potentates from their thrones and make his cause triumphant—a consummation devoutly to be wished, and which cannot now be regarded as far distant.

ALEXANDER CAMPBELL, *The Christian System*, 159-160

SCRIPTURE

But our citizenship is in heaven, and it is from there that we are expecting a Savior, the Lord Jesus Christ. He will transform the body of our humiliation that it may be conformed to the body of his glory, by the power that also enables him to make all things subject to himself.

PHILIPPIANS 3:20-21

PRAYER

Jesus, King of Kings, come quickly and reign over all the earth. Remind me today of my true citizenship.

November 8

FASTING AND PRAYER

PSALM

Restore us, O God of hosts;
let your face shine, that we may be saved.

PSALM 80:7

MEDITATION

Were we individually as Nehemiah, to fast, confess, and pray, were we as congregations to proclaim a fast and meet together in the house of God in humble confession and prayer, were we as a people widely scattered abroad to agree to meet in our various houses of worship on the same day with fasting and prayer, were professors of Christianity of the various denominations to do the same—who can tell what floods of glory would roll through our land, through Christendom, throughout the world? God is faithful who has promised.

BARTON W. STONE, *Christian Messenger* (1844), 174

SCRIPTURE

Now on the twenty-fourth day of this month the people of Israel were assembled with fasting and in sackcloth, and with earth on their heads. Then those of Israelite descent separated themselves from all foreigners, and stood and confessed their sins and the iniquities of their ancestors. They stood up in their place and read from the book of the law of the Lord their God for a fourth part of the day, and for another fourth they made confession and worshiped the Lord their God.

NEHEMIAH 9:1-3

PRAYER

Father, help me to learn how to be hungry for you alone. I confess my sins to you and rely on your grace, forgiveness, and glory.

November 9

SUPPER OF THE LAMB

PSALM

Their heart was not steadfast toward him;
they were not true to his covenant.
Yet he, being compassionate,
forgave their iniquity, and did not destroy them;
often he restrained his anger,
and did not stir up all his wrath.

PSALM 78:37-38

MEDITATION

In the gospel feast, all things are prepared by the King of heaven, and the sinner furnishes no part of the entertainment. In accepting the divine invitation one has but to comply with the established usages of the banquet and enjoy the rich provisions so bountifully supplied.

ROBERT RICHARDSON, *Communings in the Sanctuary*, 53-54

SCRIPTURE

Then I heard what seemed to be the voice of a great multitude, like the sound of many waters and like the sound of mighty thunderpeals, crying out, "Hallelujah! For the Lord our God the Almighty reigns. Let us rejoice and exult and give him the glory, for the marriage of the Lamb has come, and his bride has made herself ready; to her it has been granted to be clothed with fine linen, bright and pure"—for the fine linen is the righteous deeds of the saints. And the angel said to me, "Write this: Blessed are those who are invited to the marriage supper of the Lamb."

REVELATION 19:6-9

PRAYER

Lord God Almighty, I accept your invitation to the great feast. Lord Jesus, Lamb of God, may your church be a bride covered with the righteous deeds of the saints.

November 10

GOD FEEDS

PSALM

I am the Lord your God,
who brought you up out of the land of Egypt.
Open your mouth wide and I will fill it.

PSALM 81:10

MEDITATION

Feed me with the heavenly manna. Gird me with your everlasting arm. Shelter me under the shadow of your wing. Fold me to your loving breast. Fill me with your Holy Spirit. Help me to abide in you as the branch abides in the vine. Give me daily a deeper and more vital union with yourself, and grant that I may never lose the blessed consciousness that you are mine and that I am yours.

J. H. GARRISON, *Alone With God*, 137

SCRIPTURE

But she came and knelt before him, saying, "Lord, help me." He answered, "It is not fair to take the children's food and throw it to the dogs." She said, "Yes, Lord, yet even the dogs eat the crumbs that fall from their masters' table." Then Jesus answered her, "Woman, great is your faith! Let it be done for you as you wish." And her daughter was healed instantly.

MATTHEW 15:25-28

PRAYER

Father, give me this day my daily bread. Lord Jesus, fill me with your very self, the living bread.

November 11

FASTING

PSALM

Steadfast love and faithfulness will meet;
righteousness and peace will kiss each other.
Faithfulness will spring up from the ground,
and righteousness will look down from the sky.
The Lord will give what is good,
and our land will yield its increase.
Righteousness will go before him,
and will make a path for his steps.

PSALM 85:10-13

MEDITATION

Surely, then, we need no further evidence that fasting is a means ordained by God for the purpose of preparing the soul, on all solemn occasions, for all manner of religious exercise and spiritual enjoyment.

ROBERT MILLIGAN, *Scheme of Redemption*, 390

SCRIPTURE

Yet even now, says the Lord, return to me with all your heart, with fasting, with weeping, and with mourning; rend your hearts and not your clothing. Return to the Lord, your God, for he is gracious and merciful, slow to anger, and abounding in steadfast love, and relents from punishing. Who knows whether he will not turn and relent, and leave a blessing behind him, a grain offering and a drink offering for the Lord, your God? Blow the trumpet in Zion; sanctify a fast; call a solemn assembly; gather the people. Sanctify the congregation; assemble the aged; gather the children, even infants at the breast.

JOEL 2:12-16

PRAYER

O Lord, as you feed me when I am hungry, help me to fast so I might know it is you who fully satisfies. Move me to return to you with my whole heart.

November 12

PURE RELIGION

PSALM

Those who love me, I will deliver;
I will protect those who know my name.
When they call to me, I will answer them;
I will be with them in trouble,
I will rescue them and honor them.
With long life I will satisfy them,
and show them my salvation.

PSALM 91:14-16

MEDITATION

Many boast of having the Spirit, who are destitute of it. Have they the Spirit of grace and supplication? Do they pray in secret, and with their families night and morning? If not, is not their religion vain? Is it better than the moral infidel's? Do they bear the fruits of the Spirit, love, joy, peace, long-suffering, gentleness, goodness, fidelity, meekness, temperance? The tree is known by its fruits.

BARTON W. STONE, *Christian Messenger* (1836), 120

SCRIPTURE

But those who look into the perfect law, the law of liberty, and persevere, being not hearers who forget but doers who act—they will be blessed in their doing. If any think they are religious, and do not bridle their tongues but deceive their hearts, their religion is worthless. Religion that is pure and undefiled before God, the Father, is this: to care for orphans and widows in their distress, and to keep oneself unstained by the world.

JAMES 1:25-27

PRAYER

Lord Jesus, give me of your Spirit, so I will bear fruit, serving those in need.

November 13

Giving Thanks

Psalm

O give thanks to the Lord, for he is good,
for his steadfast love endures forever.
O give thanks to the God of gods,
for his steadfast love endures forever.
O give thanks to the Lord of lords,
for his steadfast love endures forever.

Psalm 136:1-3

Meditation

To what Christian, given to prayer and communion with God, does there not come, often during the busiest days, a sweet remembrance of God's loving kindness, and merciful providence? How delightful it is, at such times, to lift the heart to God in a moment of thanksgiving and adoration. And this habit tends to bring to our remembrance the unnumbered benefits which we receive from the hand of God, and which we are too prone to forget. Thankfulness for mercies received is the best preparation of heart for seeking additional favors.

J.H. Garrison, *Alone With God*, 94

Scripture

Rejoice always, pray without ceasing, give thanks in all circumstances;
for this is the will of God in Christ Jesus for you.

1 Thessalonians 5:16-18

Prayer

Father, I give you thanks for all your mercies, your steadfast love, and your infinite patience. I do not deserve these gifts, but I praise you for them!

November 14

JOYFUL SINGING

PSALM

Make a joyful noise to God, all the earth;
sing the glory of his name;
give to him glorious praise.
Say to God, "How awesome are your deeds!
Because of your great power, your enemies cringe before you.
All the earth worships you; they sing praises to you,
sing praises to your name."

PSALM 66:1-4

MEDITATION

Now should it appear that the open, but unostentatious display of all the Christian affections, feelings, sympathies, joys, and delights, in our meetings—in our songs, prayers, and Christian feasts, are parts of God's appointed means of quickening and exalting our piety, and of producing it in others, might it not in that case be made evident to all, that they are all more or less culpable who conceal their joys in the Lord, or refuse to appear as spiritually and heavenly minded as they are?

ALEXANDER CAMPBELL, *Millennial Harbinger* (1836), 181

SCRIPTURE

Do not get drunk with wine, for that is debauchery; but be filled with the Spirit,
as you sing psalms and hymns and spiritual songs among yourselves, singing and making
melody to the Lord in your hearts, giving thanks to God the Father at all times and for
everything in the name of our Lord Jesus Christ.

EPHESIANS 5:18-20

PRAYER

I sing the glory of your name, O Lord! Filled with the Spirit, I give thanks to you.

November 15

JUDGMENT

PSALM

For you are the glory of their strength;
by your favor our horn is exalted.
For our shield belongs to the Lord,
our king to the Holy One of Israel.

PSALM 89:17-18

MEDITATION

Be warned and entreated, then, to turn to the Lord before the day of
vengeance shall come—before the terrible announcement shall be made that
"time shall be no longer," but eternity, with all its solemnities and realities,
shall be ushered in. May we find mercy of the Lord in that day!

BENJAMIN FRANKLIN, *The Gospel Preacher*, VOL. 1, 455

SCRIPTURE

Then I saw a great white throne and the one who sat on it; the earth and the heaven fled
from his presence, and no place was found for them. And I saw the dead, great and small,
standing before the throne, and books were opened. Also another book was opened, the
book of life. And the dead were judged according to their works, as recorded in the books.
And the sea gave up the dead that were in it, Death and Hades gave up the dead that were
in them, and all were judged according to what they had done. Then Death and Hades
were thrown into the lake of fire. This is the second death, the lake of fire; and anyone
whose name was not found written in the book of life was thrown into the lake of fire.

REVELATION 20:11-15

PRAYER

Father, I thank you for your mercy through Jesus the Christ, that he came to
save the world and not to condemn. Your mercy triumphs over judgment!

November 16

FAITH

PSALM

The Lord loves those who hate evil;
he guards the lives of his faithful;
he rescues them from the hand of the wicked.
Light dawns for the righteous,
and joy for the upright in heart.
Rejoice in the Lord, O you righteous,
and give thanks to his holy name!

PSALM 97:10-12

MEDITATION

There is nothing theoretical in the faith recommended in the scriptures. It is wholly of a practical nature, and demonstrates its genuineness by its effects. In purifying the heart, and reconciling us to God and by means of these virtues enabling us to overcome the world, faith is most triumphant and victorious.

WALTER SCOTT, *The Gospel Restored*, 295-296

SCRIPTURE

And Jesus rebuked the demon, and it came out of him, and the boy was cured instantly.
Then the disciples came to Jesus privately and said, "Why could we not cast it out?" He
said to them, "Because of your little faith. For truly I tell you, if you have faith the size of a
mustard seed, you will say to this mountain, 'Move from here to there,'
and it will move; and nothing will be impossible for you."

MATTHEW 17:18-21

PRAYER

Jesus, I believe, but increase my faith. May I live faithfully this day, trusting you to guard me.

November 17

Trust God, Not Money

Psalm

Let them be before the Lord continually, and may his memory be cut off from the earth. For he did not remember to show kindness, but pursued the poor and needy and the brokenhearted to their death.

Psalm 109:15-16

Meditation

First, riches accumulated in defiance of the laws of God and society are a curse to the possessor, and the only way for one to get rid of the curse is to get rid of the unrighteous mammon! Second, the life of trust is a slow but sure growth; the only way to attain to or do great things is to be faithful in that which is least. Do not withhold God's part because it is small, the longer you hold to it the harder it will be for you to let it go.

Ashley S. Johnson, *The Life of Trust*, 182

Scripture

Come now, you rich people, weep and wail for the miseries that are coming to you. Your riches have rotted, and your clothes are moth-eaten. Your gold and silver have rusted, and their rust will be evidence against you, and it will eat your flesh like fire. You have laid up treasure for the last days. Listen! The wages of the laborers who mowed your fields, which you kept back by fraud, cry out, and the cries of the harvesters have reached the ears of the Lord of hosts. You have lived on the earth in luxury and in pleasure; you have fattened your hearts in a day of slaughter. You have condemned and murdered the righteous one, who does not resist you.

James 5:1-6

Prayer

Father, I thank you for my riches and pray you will give me the strength to give them away. May I trust you, not money, for security and worth.

November 18

JOY

PSALM

He is the Lord our God;
his judgments are in all the earth.
He is mindful of his covenant forever,
of the word that he commanded, for a thousand generations.

PSALM 105:7-8

MEDITATION

Joy in the Holy Spirit is another property and mark of the kingdom of God. We rejoice in God through our Lord Jesus Christ—in his power to protect and bless us—in his wisdom to guide and direct us—in his love, truth, and goodness—in his faithfulness to his promises—in all his perfections, and promises of the life that now is, and of that which is to come.

BARTON W. STONE, *Christian Messenger* (1840), 28-29

SCRIPTURE

Though the fig tree does not blossom, and no fruit is on the vines; though the produce of the olive fails and the fields yield no food; though the flock is cut off from the fold and there is no herd in the stalls, yet I will rejoice in the Lord; I will exult in the God of my salvation. God, the Lord, is my strength; he makes my feet like the feet of a deer, and makes me tread upon the heights.

HABAKKUK 3:17-19

PRAYER

Lord God, I rejoice in you, even when times are hard. I trust in your unfailing love. I thank you for the joy I have through your Holy Spirit.

November 19

PRAYER

PSALM

For the Lord will build up Zion;
he will appear in his glory.
He will regard the prayer of the destitute,
and will not despise their prayer.

PSALM 102:16-17

MEDITATION

Prayer is the offering up of our desires to God for things agreeable to his will, by faith in Jesus Christ, the mediator betwixt God and men, with a humble confidence of obtaining the things prayed for.

BARTON W. STONE, *Christian Messenger* (1835), 55

SCRIPTURE

Then Jesus told them a parable about their need to pray always and not to lose heart. He said, "In a certain city there was a judge who neither feared God nor had respect for people. In that city there was a widow who kept coming to him and saying, 'Grant me justice against my opponent.' For a while he refused; but later he said to himself, 'Though I have no fear of God and no respect for anyone, yet because this widow keeps bothering me, I will grant her justice, so that she may not wear me out by continually coming.'" And the Lord said, "Listen to what the unjust judge says. And will not God grant justice to his chosen ones who cry to him day and night? Will he delay long in helping them? I tell you, he will quickly grant justice to them. And yet, when the Son of Man comes, will he find faith on earth?"

LUKE 18:1-8

PRAYER

Father, hear the prayers I offer. May I not lose heart but trust in your justice, faithfulness, and love.

November 20

PRAISE IN THE ASSEMBLY

PSALM

Let them thank the Lord for his steadfast love,
for his wonderful works to humankind.
Let them extol him in the congregation of the people,
and praise him in the assembly of the elders.

PSALM 107:31-32

MEDITATION

What a wise, benevolent, and independent institution, a Christian congregation is! Nothing is left out of view which can contribute to the temporal and spiritual weal of the brotherhood. They meet in full assembly once every week to remember, praise, and adore the Lord; to share in the participation of his favors.

ALEXANDER CAMPBELL, *Christian Baptist* (1827), 212

SCRIPTURE

Then the angel showed me the river of the water of life, bright as crystal, flowing from the throne of God and of the Lamb through the middle of the street of the city. On either side of the river is the tree of life with its twelve kinds of fruit, producing its fruit each month; and the leaves of the tree are for the healing of the nations. Nothing accursed will be found there any more. But the throne of God and of the Lamb will be in it, and his servants will worship him; they will see his face, and his name will be on their foreheads. And there will be no more night; they need no light of lamp or sun, for the Lord God will be their light, and they will reign forever and ever.

REVELATION 22:1-5

PRAYER

Almighty God, I praise you in the congregation of the saints, looking forward to that day when we praise you face to face.

November 21

UNITY

PSALM

The Lord is my strength and my might;
he has become my salvation.
There are glad songs of victory in the tents of the righteous:
"The right hand of the Lord does valiantly;
the right hand of the Lord is exalted;
the right hand of the Lord does valiantly."

PSALM 118:14-16

MEDITATION

That the Church of Christ upon earth is essentially, intentionally, and constitutionally one; consisting of all those in every place that profess their faith in Christ and obedience to him in all things according to the Scriptures, and that manifest the same by their tempers and conduct, and of none else; as none else can be truly and properly called Christians.

THOMAS CAMPBELL, *The Declaration and Address*

SCRIPTURE

May the God of steadfastness and encouragement grant you to live in harmony
with one another, in accordance with Christ Jesus, so that together you may with one voice
glorify the God and Father of our Lord Jesus Christ.

ROMANS 15:5-6

PRAYER

Lord Jesus, as you prayed that all who believe in you might be one, let me work for that unity through the power of the God of steadfastness and encouragement.

November 22

A Pleasant Land

Psalm

Then they despised the pleasant land,
having no faith in his promise.
They grumbled in their tents,
and did not obey the voice of the Lord.

Psalm 106:24-25

Meditation

Give the earth peace, O God, and crown the year with increase. Fill our land with piety, virtue, and contentment. Rule, in your fear, the hearts of those who are our rulers. Be pleased to guide the young in your ways of pleasantness. Let the parched places of your church be revived with grace. Widen the boundaries of your kingdom.

J.H. Garrison, *Alone With God*, 168

Scripture

In that day the mountains shall drip sweet wine, the hills shall flow with milk, and all the stream beds of Judah shall flow with water; a fountain shall come forth from the house of the Lord and water the Wadi Shittim. Egypt shall become a desolation and Edom a desolate wilderness, because of the violence done to the people of Judah, in whose land they have shed innocent blood. But Judah shall be inhabited forever, and Jerusalem to all generations.

Joel 3:18-20

Prayer

God of the nations, lead your people throughout the earth into the pleasant land of your kingdom.

November 23

RANSOM

PSALM

The Lord will keep you from all evil;
he will keep your life.
The Lord will keep your
going out and your coming in
from this time on and forevermore.

PSALM 121:7-8

MEDITATION

God proposes, first of all, as introductory to the saving of humanity, his own and well beloved and only begotten Son, a personal Savior. He does not propose to bring us in touch with a system of abstractions or a set of arbitrary rules imposed simply because he has the power, but to bring us, sin-stained, polluted, lost, in contact with one whose virtue cures by the touch! Jesus is a personal Savior, he treats his patients as individuals, one by one and not in the aggregate. What has our Savior done for us already? He says he came to ransom us by exchanging his life for ours.

ASHLEY S. JOHNSON, *The Life of Trust*, 94

SCRIPTURE

You know that you were ransomed from the futile ways inherited from your ancestors, not with perishable things like silver or gold, but with the precious blood of Christ, like that of a lamb without defect or blemish. He was destined before the foundation of the world, but was revealed at the end of the ages for your sake.

1 PETER 1:18-20

PRAYER

Holy God, you gave your Son for me. Jesus, Son of God, you gave your precious blood to ransom me. May I live in freedom!

November 24

PRAYER

PSALM

I rise before dawn and cry for help;
I put my hope in your words.
My eyes are awake before each watch of the night,
that I may meditate on your promise.

PSALM 119:147-148

MEDITATION

These reflections, it is hoped, will help us to understand better what the apostle means by his exhortation to "pray without ceasing." Prayer, it is seen, is not a thing to be shut up in one corner of the day, or limited to a brief space in the morning and evening; but it is a pervading habit of the soul which is to shed its holy and hallowing influence over all the hours, and to maintain unbroken communion with God.

J.H. GARRISON, *Alone With God*, 94

SCRIPTURE

I have heard of your faith in the Lord Jesus and your love toward all the saints, and for this reason I do not cease to give thanks for you as I remember you in my prayers. I pray that the God of our Lord Jesus Christ, the Father of glory, may give you a spirit of wisdom and revelation as you come to know him, so that, with the eyes of your heart enlightened, you may know what is the hope to which he has called you, what are the riches of his glorious inheritance among the saints, and what is the immeasurable greatness of his power for us who believe, according to the working of his great power.

EPHESIANS 1:15-19

PRAYER

Father, I bow before you morning and night, crying for help, knowing that you hear. May I always pray so that I might begin to grasp the extent of your love.

November 25

UNITY AND SERVICE

PSALM

How very good and pleasant it is
when kindred live together in unity!
It is like the precious oil on the head,
running down upon the beard,
on the beard of Aaron,
running down over the collar of his robes.
It is like the dew of Hermon,
which falls on the mountains of Zion.
For there the Lord ordained his blessing, life forevermore.

PSALM 133

MEDITATION

All preachers will labor to reconcile jarring Christians, instead of, as we often see them, laboring to excite the angry passions, one against the other. Such plainly show that they have not received the ministry of reconciliation, and it is very doubtful whether they have received the Spirit of Christianity.

BARTON W. STONE, *Christian Messenger* (1841), 25

SCRIPTURE

But Jesus called them to him and said, "You know that the rulers of the Gentiles lord it over them, and their great ones are tyrants over them. It will not be so among you; but whoever wishes to be great among you must be your servant, and whoever wishes to be first among you must be your slave; just as the Son of Man came not to be served but to serve, and to give his life a ransom for many."

MATTHEW 20:25-28

PRAYER

Brother Jesus, make me a servant as you made yourself. May I live in unity and peace with my brothers and sisters in Christ.

November 26

WORSHIP

PSALM

I remember the days of old,
I think about all your deeds,
I meditate on the works of your hands.
I stretch out my hands to you;
my soul thirsts for you like a parched land.

PSALM 143:5-6

MEDITATION

How precious are the hours appropriated to the worship of the Most High. In the assembly of the saints a heavenly peace diffuses itself over the soul. The swelling anthem of praise bears, upon wings of melody, into the deepest recesses of our nature the transporting truths of revelation, awakens the dearest memories of the past, or marshals in bright array the crowding visions of the future.

ROBERT RICHARDSON, *Communings in the Sanctuary*, 109

SCRIPTURE

For thus it shall be on the earth and among the nations, as when an olive tree is beaten, as at the gleaning when the grape harvest is ended. They lift up their voices, they sing for joy; they shout from the west over the majesty of the Lord. Therefore in the east give glory to the Lord; in the coastlands of the sea glorify the name of the Lord, the God of Israel.

ISAIAH 24:13-15

PRAYER

Father, I think of all your kindnesses of the past. I sing for joy. I imagine the brightness of your future. I thirst for you. Blessed be the Lord!

HUMILITY

PSALM

O Lord, what are human beings that you regard them,
or mortals that you think of them?
They are like a breath;
their days are like a passing shadow.

PSALM 144:3-4

MEDITATION

Show how opposite to truth is sectarianism, and preach union, not of the sects as such, but of Christians, not a union founded on the wisdom or devices of humans, but that based upon the word of God, not only of the letter, but of the spirit of the word. Be careful to avoid all offensive language as much as possible. Let all your things be done with charity, humility, and meekness, but with boldness in the faith.

BARTON W. STONE, *Christian Messenger* (1843), 35

SCRIPTURE

"Will the Lord be pleased with thousands of rams, with ten thousands of rivers of oil?
Shall I give my firstborn for my transgression, the fruit of my body for the sin of my soul?"
He has told you, O mortal, what is good; and what does the Lord require of you but to do
justice, and to love kindness, and to walk humbly with your God?

MICAH 6:7-8

PRAYER

Father, forgive my pride that divides me from you and your people. May I do justice, love kindness, and walk humbly with you.

November 28

Our Creator

Psalm

By the word of the Lord the heavens were made,
and all their host by the breath of his mouth.
He gathered the waters of the sea as in a bottle;
he put the deeps in storehouses.
Let all the earth fear the Lord;
let all the inhabitants of the world stand in awe of him.
For he spoke, and it came to be;
he commanded, and it stood firm.

Psalm 33:6-9

Meditation

Almighty God, Creator of heaven and earth, who from the beginning did appoint the day and the night to succeed each other, and have now by your providence brought us once again through the hours of toil to the time of resting; be with us, we pray you, during the season of darkness, and cause the light of your countenance to shine upon our souls.

J.H. Garrison, *Alone With God*, 173

Scripture

In the beginning when God created the heavens and the earth,
the earth was a formless void and darkness covered the face of the deep,
while a wind from God swept over the face of the waters.
Then God said, "Let there be light"; and there was light.

Genesis 1:1-3

Prayer

Almighty Creator, you spoke the world into existence, you formed humans from the dust, and you brought us light. Lord give me the light of your presence this day.

November 29

THE HOLY SPIRIT

PSALM

O guard my life, and deliver me;
do not let me be put to shame, for I take refuge in you.
May integrity and uprightness preserve me,
for I wait for you.
Redeem Israel, O God,
out of all its troubles.

PSALM 25:20-22

MEDITATION

The Spirit of the Father, flows through the Son into every member of his spiritual body. Though humans may, and do possess this Spirit, if one be a Christian, yet we do not call it the human spirit, but the Spirit of God in us; the Spirit received by faith. When we receive this Spirit we are made "partakers of the divine nature." This is the Spirit that groans and prays, as it did in the great head of the body, the son of God.

BARTON W. STONE, *Christian Messenger* (1835), 166

SCRIPTURE

But you are not in the flesh; you are in the Spirit, since the Spirit of God dwells in you.
Anyone who does not have the Spirit of Christ does not belong to him.
But if Christ is in you, though the body is dead because of sin, the Spirit is life because of
righteousness. If the Spirit of him who raised Jesus from the dead dwells in you, he who
raised Christ from the dead will give life to your mortal bodies also
through his Spirit that dwells in you.

ROMANS 8:9-11

PRAYER

God of love, fill me with your Spirit, so I may have life this day. You have given me of yourself, dear God. May I share in your very life.

November 30

UNITY

PSALM

O sing to the Lord a new song,
for he has done marvelous things.
His right hand and his holy arm
have gotten him victory.

PSALM 98:1

MEDITATION

Who does not see in this petition, that the words or testimony of the apostles, the unity of the disciples, and the conviction of the world are bound together by the wisdom and the love of the Father, by the devotion and philanthropy of the Son.

ALEXANDER CAMPBELL, *Christian Baptist* (1825), 156

SCRIPTURE

"I ask not only on behalf of these, but also on behalf of those who will believe in me through their word, that they may all be one. As you, Father, are in me and I am in you, may they also be in us, so that the world may believe that you have sent me. The glory that you have given me I have given them, so that they may be one, as we are one, I in them and you in me, that they may become completely one, so that the world may know that you have sent me and have loved them even as you have loved me."

JOHN 17:20-23

PRAYER

Lord Jesus, as you prayed for unity among Christians, so I also pray this day. Make us one as you and the Father are one.

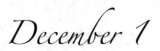

December 1

WATCHING

PSALM

Do not put your trust in princes,
In mortals, in whom there is no help.
When their breath departs, they return to the earth;
On that very day, their plans perish.

PSALM 146:3

MEDITATION

We are commanded to watch for the Coming of the Son of Man, the great event of the future, and to be ready, lest he find us slumbering, or with lamps untrimmed or unsupplied with oil. The best state of readiness for the coming of Christ is eagerness to know and readiness to do his will.

J.H. GARRISON, *Alone With God*, 102

SCRIPTURE

And while they went to buy it, the bridegroom came, and those who were ready went with him into the wedding banquet; and the door was shut. Later, the other bridesmaids came also, saying, "Lord, lord, open to us." But he replied, "Truly I tell you, I do not know you." Keep awake therefore, for you know neither the day nor the hour.

MATTHEW 25: 10-13

PRAYER

Good and faithful God, still my heart with patience. May I be ever watchful for your presence and the coming of your Son. Make me vigilant in time of temptation. Open my eyes to the needs of those around us. May I wait in silence for you, O God.

December 2

GOD ANSWERS

PSALM

I lie down and sleep;
I wake again, for the Lord sustains me.
I am not afraid of ten thousands of people
who have set themselves against me all around.

PSALM 3:5-6

MEDITATION

Does God really answer prayer in this age as he did in the ages when the Bible was being written? By the help of God and his word I can demonstrate fully, clearly, irresistibly, that God does hear and answer, and that our greatest need is the deep conviction that this is true, and thus one moves out into the bright, clear atmosphere of God's love and promises.

ASHLEY S. JOHNSON, *The Life of Trust*, 11

SCRIPTURE.

We always give thanks to God for all of you and mention you in our prayers, constantly remembering before our God and Father your work of faith and labor of love and steadfastness of hope in our Lord Jesus Christ.

1 THESSALONIANS 1:2-3

PRAYER

Lord God, answer me from your holy hill! Increase my trust in you and bring me to the clear atmosphere of your love.

December 3

PRAYER

PSALM

Answer me when I call, O God of my right!
You gave me room when I was in distress.
Be gracious to me and hear my prayer.

PSALM 4:1

MEDITATION

A prayerless Christian is, to the eye of reason, an absurdity, as it is to the eye of faith an impossibility. I could not imagine a prayerless Christian, any more than a breathless person. Prayer is but the Christian's breath. Without it, one cannot live or be happy a single day.

ALEXANDER CAMPBELL, *Millennial Harbinger* (1854), 552

SCRIPTURE

Then Jesus entered the temple and drove out all who were selling and buying in the temple,
and he overturned the tables of the money changers and the seats of those who sold doves.
He said to them, "It is written,
'My house shall be a house of prayer;'
but you are making it a den of robbers."

MATTHEW 21:12-13

PRAYER

O Christ who drove the moneychangers from the temple, drive from my heart all that keeps it from being a place of prayer. Lead me from the paths of greed, pride, and self-sufficiency. May my every breath be a prayer of trust in you. Be gracious and hear my prayer.

December 4

EXPECTATION

PSALM

How long, O Lord? Will you forget me forever?
How long will you hide your face from me?
How long must I bear pain in my soul,
and have sorrow in my heart all day long?
How long shall my enemy be exalted over me?

PSALM 13:1-2

MEDITATION

We *will*, that preachers and people, cultivate a spirit of mutual forbearance; pray more and dispute less; and while they behold the signs of the times, look up, and confidently expect that redemption draweth nigh.

The Last Will and Testament of the Springfield Presbytery (1804)

SCRIPTURE

But, in accordance with his promise, we wait for new heavens and a new earth,
where righteousness is at home.

2 PETER 3:13

PRAYER

Father, in the midst of pain, I cry, "Your kingdom come!" Lord Jesus, come quickly and bring the redemption of a new heaven and a new earth. How long, O Lord?

December 5

STRENGTH

PSALM

I love you, O Lord, my strength.
The Lord is my rock, my fortress, and my deliverer,
my God, my rock in whom I take refuge,
my shield, and the horn of my salvation, my stronghold.
I call upon the Lord, who is worthy to be praised,
so I shall be saved from my enemies.

PSALM 18:1-3

MEDITATION

Prayer is the means by which we receive the grace of God, and enjoy sweet communion with the Father and the Son. Enjoying this, we have communion one with another, and grow up into Christ our living head in all things.

BARTON W. STONE, *Christian Messenger* (1826), 236-237

SCRIPTURE

Now may our God and Father himself and our Lord Jesus direct our way to you. And may the Lord make you increase and abound in love for one another and for all, just as we abound in love for you. And may he so strengthen your hearts in holiness that you may be blameless before our God and Father at the coming of our Lord Jesus with all his saints.

1 THESSALONIANS 3:11-13

PRAYER

Father, strengthen my heart in holiness. Give me sweet communion with you and your precious Son, this day. I love you, O Lord, my strength.

December 6

PRAYER

PSALM

I call upon you, for you will answer me, O God;
incline your ear to me, hear my words.
Wondrously show your steadfast love, O savior of those who seek refuge
from their adversaries at your right hand.
Guard me as the apple of the eye;
hide me in the shadow of your wings
from the wicked who despoil me,
my deadly enemies who surround me.

PSALM 17:6-9

MEDITATION

God must be pleased when, in self-forgetfulness and humility, we do as he expected us to do when he made us—bring all our needs before him and expect him to supply them.

ASHLEY S. JOHNSON, *The Life of Trust*, 12-13

SCRIPTURE:

Now to him who is able to keep you from falling, and to make you stand without blemish in the presence of his glory with rejoicing, to the only God our Savior, through Jesus Christ our Lord, be glory, majesty, power, and authority, before all time and now and forever.

JUDE 24-25

PRAYER

God, my Savior, I long to stand in your presence. Keep me from falling, supply my every need, and guard me as the apple of your eye.

December 7

Being with the Lord

Psalm

The snares of death encompassed me;
the pangs of Sheol laid hold on me;
I suffered distress and anguish.
Then I called on the name of the Lord:
"O Lord, I pray, save my life!"

Psalm 116:3-4

Meditation

At the appointed time in the bright regions of eternal glory, we shall rejoin the loved and lost, where all sorrow shall be forgotten, all tears wiped away, all faithful love and fellowship restored, and where, amidst fullness of joy and spiritual blessedness, "we shall be forever with the Lord."

Robert Richardson, *Communings in the Sanctuary*, 113

Scripture

For the Lord himself, with a cry of command, with the archangel's call and with the sound of God's trumpet, will descend from heaven, and the dead in Christ will rise first. Then we who are alive, who are left, will be caught up in the clouds together with them to meet the Lord in the air; and so we will be with the Lord forever. Therefore encourage one another with these words.

1 Thessalonians 4:16-18

Prayer

God of life, I thank you that through the resurrection of Jesus, not even death can separate me from you or from those I love.

December 8

ADORATION

PSALM

Not to us, O Lord, not to us, but to your name give glory,
for the sake of your steadfast love and your faithfulness.

PSALM 115:1

MEDITATION

With what profound awe and reverence does the person of faith view all this! How exalted are the conceptions and emotions in view of the wonderful works of God; and how must one adore and admire the almighty hand that has lifted up and made one acquainted with the Father and with his Son, Jesus Christ our Lord—our only hope! Let us learn to reverence, adore, and praise him forever and ever.

BENJAMIN FRANKLIN, *The Gospel Preacher*, VOL. 2, 30-31

SCRIPTURE

To this end we always pray for you, asking that our God will make you worthy of his call and will fulfill by his power every good resolve and work of faith, so that the name of our Lord Jesus may be glorified in you, and you in him, according to the grace of our God and the Lord Jesus Christ.

2 THESSALONIANS 1:11-12

PRAYER

Glorious Father, Loving Lord, and Holy Spirit, may I glorify your name, not my own this day. I rejoice in your steadfast love and faithfulness. By your power, complete the good works I resolve to do.

December 9

COMING OF THE LORD

PSALM

But the Lord sits enthroned forever,
he has established his throne for judgment.
He judges the world with righteousness;
he judges the peoples with equity.
The Lord is a stronghold for the oppressed,
a stronghold in times of trouble.
And those who know your name put their trust in you,
for you, O Lord, have not forsaken those who seek you.

PSALM 9:7-10

MEDITATION

Every disciple of the Master is under the most solemn obligations to do what lies in his power to hasten the time when "all the kingdoms of this world shall become the Kingdom of our Lord and of his Christ."

J. H. GARRISON, *Alone With God*, 115

SCRIPTURE

To him who loves us and freed us from our sins by his blood, and made us to be a kingdom, priests serving his God and Father, to him be glory and dominion forever and ever. Amen. Look! He is coming with the clouds; every eye will see him, even those who pierced him; and on his account all the tribes of the earth will wail. So it is to be. Amen.

REVELATION 1:5-7

PRAYER

Father, I bow before your righteous throne. Give me faith to see your reign in the world today. Rule in my heart. May I know that you will never forsake me. Make me your priest to those I meet.

December 10

Communion with God

Psalm

I wash my hands in innocence,
and go around your altar, O Lord,
singing aloud a song of thanksgiving,
and telling all your wondrous deeds.
O Lord, I love the house in which you dwell,
and the place where your glory abides.

Psalm 26:6-8

Meditation

When a soul comes to itself, it at once begins to relish God's word, and to long for fellowship and communion with him. It will avail itself of private prayer and will not neglect the public worship of God. How sweet are the songs of Zion to a heart that thirsts for God!

J. H. Garrison, *Alone With God*, 29

Scripture

"Teacher, which commandment in the law is the greatest?" He said to him, "'You shall love the Lord your God with all your heart, and with all your soul, and with all your mind.' This is the greatest and first commandment. And a second is like it: 'You shall love your neighbor as yourself.' On these two commandments hang all the law and the prophets."

Matthew 22:36-40

Prayer

Loving God, my heart thirsts for your presence. May I long to live in your house and worship at your altar. Let my love for you, the love you have poured into my heart, overflow into love for my neighbor.

December 11

SUFFERING

PSALM

O Lord, all my longing is known to you;
my sighing is not hidden from you.
Those who seek my life lay their snares;
those who seek to hurt me speak of ruin,
and meditate treachery all day long.

PSALM 38:9, 12

MEDITATION

Had Jesus not assumed our nature, he could not have borne our griefs or carried our sorrows. He was, indeed, "crucified through weakness," yet it was at that moment of extremest weakness that he gained the victory.

ROBERT RICHARDSON, *Communings in the Sanctuary*, 84-85

SCRIPTURE

We must always give thanks to God for you, brothers and sisters, as is right, because your faith is growing abundantly, and the love of everyone of you for one another is increasing. Therefore we ourselves boast of you among the churches of God for your steadfastness and faith during all your persecutions and the afflictions that you are enduring.

2 THESSALONIANS 1:3-4

PRAYER

Dear Father, thank you for sending your Son in the flesh to share my weaknesses. Keep me steadfast and faithful in the face of suffering.

December 12

THE WEIGHTIER MATTERS

PSALM

Our steps are made firm by the Lord,
when he delights in our way;
though we stumble, we shall not fall headlong,
for the Lord holds us by the hand.
The mouths of the righteous utter wisdom,
and their tongues speak justice.
The law of their God is in their hearts;
their steps do not slip.

PSALM 37:23-24, 30-31

MEDITATION

Those who would interpret the oracles of God to the salvation of their souls, must approach this volume with the humility and docility of a child, and meditate upon it day and night. Like Mary, they must sit at the Master's feet and listen to the words that fall from his lips.

ALEXANDER CAMPBELL, *The Christian System*, 18

SCRIPTURE

"Woe to you, scribes and Pharisees, hypocrites! For you tithe mint, dill, and cummin, and have neglected the weightier matters of the law: justice and mercy and faith. It is these you ought to have practiced without neglecting the others. You blind guides! You strain out a gnat but swallow a camel!"

MATTHEW 23:23-24

PRAYER

Holy God, may your word be the constant meditation of my heart. May I practice the whole of your instruction, particularly justice, mercy, and faith. Do not allow my steps to falter this day.

December 13

DEPENDENCE ON GOD

PSALM

You are indeed my rock and my fortress;
for your name's sake lead me and guide me,
take me out of the net that is hidden for me, for you are my refuge.
Into your hand I commit my spirit;
you have redeemed me, O Lord, faithful God.

PSALM 31:3-5

MEDITATION

Prayer allays the passions, promotes the virtues, and harmonizes all the powers and faculties of the soul. It subdues the human will and makes the will of God the supreme law of the universe.

ROBERT MILLIGAN, *A Brief Treatise on Prayer*, 19-20

SCRIPTURE

But the Lord is faithful; he will strengthen you and guard you from the evil one.
And we have confidence in the Lord concerning you, that you are doing and will go on
doing the things that we command. May the Lord direct your hearts to the
love of God and to the steadfastness of Christ.

2 THESSALONIANS 3:3-5

PRAYER

Faithful Lord, my rock, fortress, and refuge, protect me from harm this day. Mold my will to yours. May I keep your commands this day, by the power of your Holy Spirit. Direct my heart to your love and steadfastness, through Christ.

December 14

KINGDOM

PSALM

O send out your light and your truth; let them lead me;
let them bring me to your holy hill and to your dwelling.
Then I will go to the altar of God, to God my exceeding joy;
and I will praise you with the harp, O God, my God.

PSALM 43:3-4

MEDITATION

We believe that all are bound to submit to the government and laws of Jesus, the Lord of all. Let Christians show by their peaceful, holy lives, that his laws are sufficient to govern the whole world in peace and love.

BARTON W. STONE, *Christian Messenger* (1843), 125-126

SCRIPTURE

And because of the increase of lawlessness, the love of many will grow cold. But the one who endures to the end will be saved. And this good news of the kingdom will be proclaimed throughout the world, as a testimony to all the nations; and then the end will come.

MATTHEW 24:12-14

PRAYER

Father, may your kingdom come! Even now may you alone reign in my heart. Do not let my love for you grow cold. I praise you, my God, at the altar where Jesus was sacrificed for me. Lord.Jesus, come quickly!

December 15

THE WORK OF CHRIST

PSALM

Bless the Lord, O my soul,
and do not forget all his benefits—
who forgives all your iniquity,
who heals all your diseases,
who redeems your life from the Pit,
who crowns you with steadfast love and mercy.

PSALM 103:2-4

MEDITATION

How perfect, then, in power, how complete in fullness is the work of Christ.
How far-reaching the consequences of his death, and how glorious the
salvation he accomplishes by his life. How precious the assurances of his mercy,
faithfulness, and truth. How blessed the hope of his return.

ROBERT RICHARDSON, *Communings in the Sanctuary*, 128

SCRIPTURE

But you have come to Mount Zion and to the city of the living God, the heavenly
Jerusalem, and to innumerable angels in festal gathering, and to the assembly of the
firstborn who are enrolled in heaven, and to God the judge of all, and to the spirits of the
righteous made perfect, and to Jesus, the mediator of a new covenant, and to the sprinkled
blood that speaks a better word than the blood of Abel.

HEBREWS 12:22-24

PRAYER

Living God, I bless you for the most precious gift of your Son. May I never
forget your love and mercy shown to me by Christ. Today, my Lord, forgive,
heal, and redeem me.

December 16

TRIALS

PSALM

Because of you we are being killed all day long,
and accounted as sheep for the slaughter.

PSALM 44:22

MEDITATION

How manifold and various are the tribulations that assail us here! What a
splendid philosophy is that which Christian faith lays hold of, by which all these
seeming calamities and adversities are transformed into so many kind providen-
tial agencies designed to promote our spiritual growth and development!

J.H. GARRISON, *Alone with God*, 108

SCRIPTURE

Because you have kept my word of patient endurance, I will keep you from the hour of trial
that is coming on the whole world to test the inhabitants of the earth. I am coming soon;
hold fast to what you have, so that no one may seize your crown. If you conquer, I will
make you a pillar in the temple of my God; you will never go out of it. I will write on you
the name of my God, and the name of the city of my God, the new Jerusalem that comes
down from my God out of heaven, and my own new name.

REVELATION 3:10-12

PRAYER

My God, give me endurance for the trials I face today. Give me courage to
suffer for your name. Give me faith to see my tribulations as a blessing.

December 17

VICTORY

PSALM

As we have heard, so have we seen
in the city of the Lord of hosts,
in the city of our God,
which God establishes forever.
We ponder your steadfast love, O God,
in the midst of your temple.
Your name, O God, like your praise,
reaches to the ends of the earth.
Your right hand is filled with victory.

PSALM 48:8-10

MEDITATION

Tyrants and imposters, priests and princes have ever enslaved the souls and bodies. But Christ has come to the rescue and will put down all at last.

WALTER SCOTT, *The Messiahship*, 119

SCRIPTURE

Listen! I am standing at the door, knocking; if you hear my voice and open the door,
I will come in to you and eat with you, and you with me. To the one who conquers
I will give a place with me on my throne, just as I myself conquered
and sat down with my Father on his throne.

REVELATION 3:20-21

PRAYER

Father, you are ruler of the universe; Christ, you are the conqueror of the world. Through your Holy Spirit, grant me victory over the world, the flesh, and the devil.

December 18

DELIGHT IN GOD'S WORD

PSALM

It is good for me that I was humbled,
so that I might learn your statutes.
The law of your mouth is better to me
than thousands of gold and silver pieces.

PSALM 119:71-72

MEDITATION

Take, then, the teaching, the divine and infallible teaching of Jesus and the apostles, read it, fill your memory with it, cherish it in your heart, meditate on it, delight in it, and love it, and follow it with all your whole mind and strength, and it will guide you peacefully, joyfully, and happily home to the haven of everlasting rest.

BENJAMIN FRANKLIN, *The Gospel Preacher*, VOL. 1, 203

SCRIPTURE

The beginning of the good news of Jesus Christ, the Son of God.
As it is written in the prophet Isaiah,
"See, I am sending my messenger ahead of you, who will prepare your way;
the voice of one crying out in the wilderness:
'Prepare the way of the Lord, make his paths straight.'"

MARK 1:1-3

PRAYER

This day, O Lord, may your word be in my heart, on my lips, and in my hands. May the good news of Jesus fill my life today. Humble me, O God, before your glorious throne.

December 19

THE HOLY SPIRIT

PSALM
Our soul waits for the Lord;
he is our help and shield.
Our heart is glad in him,
because we trust in his holy name.
Let your steadfast love, O Lord, be upon us,
even as we hope in you.

PSALM 33:20-22

MEDITATION

The Holy Spirit is, then, the author of all our holiness; and in the struggle for victory over sin and temptation, "he helps our infirmities," and comforts us by seasonably bringing to our remembrance the promises of Christ, and "strengthens us with all might, in the new or inner person." Christians are, therefore, clearly and unequivocally temples of the Holy Spirit; and they are quickened, animated, encouraged, and sanctified by the power of the Spirit of God, working in them through the truth.

ALEXANDER CAMPBELL, *The Christian System*, 66

SCRIPTURE

"I baptize you with water for repentance, but one who is more powerful than I is coming after me; I am not worthy to carry his sandals. He will baptize you with the Holy Spirit and fire."

MATTHEW 3:11

PRAYER

Father God, strengthen me inwardly today through your Holy Spirit. May I patiently wait and trust in your steadfast love. Make me holy as you are holy.

December 20

PRAISE

PSALM

I have not hidden your saving help within my heart,
I have spoken of your faithfulness and your salvation;
I have not concealed your steadfast love and your faithfulness
from the great congregation.

PSALM 40:10

MEDITATION

And, hence, the most pious have always been the most regular and constant in their family devotions. Indeed, we have never seen any very strong indications of vital piety where family worship has been neglected.

ROBERT MILLIGAN, *A Brief Treatise on Prayer*, 35

SCRIPTURE

When he had taken the scroll, the four living creatures and the twenty-four elders fell
before the Lamb, each holding a harp and golden bowls full of incense,
which are the prayers of the saints. They sing a new song:
"You are worthy to take the scroll and to open its seals, for you were slaughtered and by
your blood you ransomed for God saints from every tribe and language and people and
nation; you have made them to be a kingdom and priests serving our God,
and they will reign on earth."

REVELATION 5:8-10

PRAYER

Awesome God, may I praise you this day at home, at work, and in the great congregation of the saints present, past, and future. Christ, you are worthy!

December 21

BEING KNOWN BY GOD

PSALM

O Lord, you have searched me and known me.
You know when I sit down and when I rise up;
you discern my thoughts from far away.
You search out my path and my lying down,
and are acquainted with all my ways.

PSALM 139:1-3

MEDITATION

Christian reader, do you want to grow in grace? Do you want to make rapid progress in the divine life? Then retire to your closet at least three times every day; and let the burden of your prayer be, "Search me, O God, and know my heart; try me and know my thoughts; and see if there is any wicked way in me: and lead me in the way everlasting."

ROBERT MILLIGAN, *A Brief Treatise on Prayer*, 77

SCRIPTURE

But you, beloved, build yourselves up on your most holy faith; pray in the Holy Spirit;
keep yourselves in the love of God; look forward to the mercy of our
Lord Jesus Christ that leads to eternal life.

JUDE 20-21

PRAYER

Father, you know me better than I know myself. Keep me from self-deception. Keep me in your love, grace, and mercy. In your Holy Spirit, I pray that you will lead me to life eternal.

December 22

Seeing God

Psalm

Who shall ascend the hill of the Lord?
And who shall stand in his holy place?
Those who have clean hands and pure hearts,
who do not lift up their souls to what is false,
and do not swear deceitfully.
They will receive blessing from the Lord,
and vindication from the God of their salvation.

Psalm 24:3-5

Meditation

Then we shall see him as he is, face to face, and not through the veil of mortal flesh. The word "to see" frequently means to enjoy. In this sense the pure in heart enjoy their God on earth, through faith, and are as happy as mortality can bear.

Barton W. Stone, *Christian Messenger* (1843), 232

Scripture

For God so loved the world that he gave his only Son, so that everyone who believes in him may not perish but may have eternal life. But those who do what is true come to the light, so that it may be clearly seen that their deeds have been done in God.

John 3:16, 21

Prayer

Father, thank you for giving me clean hands and a pure heart through the gift of your Son. May this amazing blessing light my path today.

December 23

HEARING GOD

PSALM

Once God has spoken;
twice have I heard this:
that power belongs to God,
and steadfast love belongs to you, O Lord.
For you repay to all
according to their work.

PSALM 62:11-12

MEDITATION

Amidst the din of all arguments from the flesh, the world, and Satan, a person is so deaf that one cannot hear the still small voice of God's philanthropy. But, receding from pride, covetousness, and false ambition; from the love of the world; and in coming within that circle, the circumference of which is unfeigned humility, and the center of which is God himself—the voice of God is distinctly heard and clearly understood.

ALEXANDER CAMPBELL, *The Christian System*, 18

SCRIPTURE

And the Father who sent me has himself testified on my behalf. You have never heard his voice or seen his form, and you do not have his word abiding in you, because you do not believe him whom he has sent.

JOHN 5:37-38

PRAYER

O God, I wait for you in silence. I wait in faith and humility. May I hear your voice, today, through your Son and my Savior, Jesus.

December 24

THE BIRTH OF CHRIST

PSALM

Praise the Lord, all you nations!
Extol him, all you peoples!
For great is his steadfast love toward us,
and the faithfulness of the Lord endures forever.

PSALM 117

MEDITATION

In taking part of flesh and blood, Jesus partook of our infirmities, and bore our weaknesses, as, in his own body, he bore our sins. It is not in his maturer years merely that we are to behold the man Jesus Christ. It is rather in the feeble infant in its unrocked cradle, the helpless Christ-child, nurtured upon a mother's bosom.

ROBERT RICHARDSON, *Communings in the Sanctuary*, 84-85

SCRIPTURE

The angel said to her, "Do not be afraid, Mary, for you have found favor with God. And now, you will conceive in your womb and bear a son, and you will name him Jesus. He will be great, and will be called the Son of the Most High, and the Lord God will give to him the throne of his ancestor David. He will reign over the house of Jacob forever, and of his kingdom there will be no end."

LUKE 1:30-33

PRAYER

I praise you, Father, for sending your Son to be born of Mary to show your steadfast love.

December 25

GOD WITH US

PSALM
I will tell of the decree of the Lord:
He said to me, "You are my son;
today I have begotten you.
Ask of me, and I will make the nations your heritage,
and the ends of the earth your possession."

PSALM 2:7-8

MEDITATION
As Immanuel, he has brought God near to us; as the express image of the Father, he has truly revealed him; as God manifested in the flesh, he is love impersonated.

ROBERT RICHARDSON, *Communings in the Sanctuary*, 13

SCRIPTURE
But you, O Bethlehem of Ephrathah,
who are one of the little clans of Judah,
from you shall come forth for me one who is to rule in Israel,
whose origin is from of old, from ancient days.
And he shall stand and feed his flock in the strength of the Lord,
in the majesty of the name of the Lord his God.

MICAH 5:2, 4

PRAYER
Father God, I thank you for coming in the flesh, in the person of your Son, Jesus. Turn my heart to that child in the manger who is in reality the ruler of the world.

December 26

GOOD NEWS TO THE POOR

PSALM

Who is like the Lord our God,
who is seated on high,
who looks far down
on the heavens and the earth?
He raises the poor from the dust,
and lifts the needy from the ash heap,
to make them sit with princes,
with the princes of his people.
He gives the barren woman a home,
making her the joyous mother of children.
Praise the Lord!

PSALM 113:5-9

MEDITATION

Be an example in charity, or love, not in word or in tongue, but in deed and truth, by administering of your goods to the poor and needy. The salvation of their souls is equal to the kings of the earth.

BARTON W. STONE, *Christian Messenger* (1843), 259

SCRIPTURE

He has brought down the powerful from their thrones, and lifted up the lowly; he has filled the hungry with good things, and sent the rich away empty.

LUKE 1:52-53

PRAYER

Lord Jesus, you came to earth to feed the hungry, lift the lowly, and exalt the poor. Work in me this day to bring good news to those in need. Feed the hungry. House the homeless. Heal the sick. Raise the dead.

December 27

The New Jerusalem

Psalm

Praise the Lord!
How good it is to sing praises to our God;
for he is gracious, and a song of praise is fitting.
The Lord builds up Jerusalem;
he gathers the outcasts of Israel.
He heals the brokenhearted,
and binds up their wounds.

Psalm 147:1-3

Meditation

And whether the righteous remain forever in the New Jerusalem, on the newly renovated earth, or wing their way as messengers of love and mercy to worlds unknown, the same gracious hand that conducted them through their earthly pilgrimage will ever lead them to fountains of living waters, and wipe away all tears from their eyes.

Robert Milligan, *Scheme of Redemption*, 577

Scripture

I saw no temple in the city, for its temple is the Lord God the Almighty and the Lamb.
And the city has no need of sun or moon to shine on it, for the glory of God is its light,
and its lamp is the Lamb. The nations will walk by its light, and the
kings of the earth will bring their glory into it.

Revelation 21:22-24

Prayer

Father, this day bind my wounds, heal my broken heart, light my way, and gather me into your presence. Lord Jesus, come quickly and bring the New Jerusalem.

December 28

CHRIST THE KING

PSALM

The Lord is king, he is robed in majesty;
the Lord is robed, he is girded with strength.
He has established the world;
it shall never be moved;
your throne is established from of old;
you are from everlasting.

PSALM 93:1-2

MEDITATION

Reader, it is not the epic of Christianity or its drama chiefly that we are called to contemplate with affection and reverence, but its hero—the Lord Messiah. He is the diadem of revelation, its miter and its crown, and the basis of Messianic worship is laid down by the Most High when he installed him in the great mission of Redemption—"My Son."

WALTER SCOTT, *The Messiahship*, 242

SCRIPTURE

But there the Lord in majesty will be for us a place of broad rivers and streams,
where no galley with oars can go, nor stately ship can pass.
For the Lord is our judge, the Lord is our ruler, the Lord is our king; he will save us.

ISAIAH 33:21-22

PRAYER

Lord Jesus, I crown you king of my life today. Reign over all my desires and actions. You are the everlasting king, the Almighty who saves.

December 29

REDEMPTION

PSALM

Rouse yourself! Why do you sleep, O Lord?
Awake, do not cast us off forever!
Why do you hide your face?
Why do you forget our affliction and oppression?
For we sink down to the dust;
our bodies cling to the ground.
Rise up, come to our help.
Redeem us for the sake of your steadfast love.

PSALM 44:23-26

MEDITATION

The mysteries of God were revealed; the way of salvation was made known; the love of God to humanity was manifested; the fountain of grace burst forth from his lips; the world of glory—the heaven of eternal life and immortality was discovered; and the resurrection from the dead plainly revealed.

BARTON W. STONE, *Christian Messenger* (1843), 110

SCRIPTURE

Blessed be the Lord God of Israel, for he has looked favorably on his people and redeemed them. He has raised up a mighty savior for us in the house of his servant David, as he spoke through the mouth of his holy prophets from of old, that we would be saved from our enemies and from the hand of all who hate us.

LUKE 1:68-71

PRAYER

Gracious God, I thank you and praise you for the gift of your Son, Jesus. May I experience the redemption, life, and glory that comes through him.

December 30

HOLINESS

PSALM

Your decrees are very sure;
holiness befits your house, O Lord, forevermore.

PSALM 93:5

MEDITATION

Persons whose love, mercy, and benevolence have been excited and strengthened by the devotions of the prayer closet are savors of life wherever they go. They are living illustrations of the power of the gospel on the soul, and must always have an attractive as well as a transforming influence on the minds and hearts of others.

ROBERT MILLIGAN, *A Brief Treatise on Prayer*, 26

SCRIPTURE

The Lord has proclaimed to the end of the earth:
Say to daughter Zion, "See, your salvation comes;
his reward is with him, and his recompense before him."
They shall be called, "The Holy People, The Redeemed of the Lord";
and you shall be called, "Sought Out, A City Not Forsaken."

ISAIAH 62:11-12

PRAYER

I praise you, O Lord, my shield and protection from evil. Pour faith, love, and hope into my heart this day, so that I may be a light and blessing to others in your Name.

December 31

PRAYER

PSALM

In my distress I called upon the Lord;
to my God I cried for help.
From his temple he heard my voice,
and my cry to him reached his ears.

PSALM 18:6

MEDITATION

There are some who seem to think that prayer is good for the Christian as a kind of spiritual gymnastics; that it helps the Christian but does not move the Creator. This is the rankest of error. All the voices of nature, providence, redemption, and I may add, human experience, point in one mighty and triumphant declaration that our God is not too great, or too far away, or too busy to hear us and heed us when we cry to him!

ASHLEY S. JOHNSON, *The Life of Trust*, 20

SCRIPTURE

"Let anyone who is thirsty come to me, and let the one who believes in me drink. As the scripture has said, 'Out of the believer's heart shall flow rivers of living water.'" Now he said this about the Spirit, which believers in him were to receive.

JOHN 7:37-39

PRAYER

Father, hear me when I call. Give me your Holy Spirit today so living water will flow from my heart to others.